Belief and Resistance

Belief and Resistance

Dynamics of Contemporary Intellectual Controversy

Barbara Herrnstein Smith

HARVARD UNIVERSITY PRESS
Cambridge, Massachusetts
London, England
1997

Library of Congress Cataloging-in-Publication Data

Smith, Barbara Herrnstein.
   Belief and resistance : dynamics of contemporary intellectual
controversy / Barbara Herrnstein Smith.
      p.   cm.
   Includes bibliographical references (p.   ) and index.
   ISBN 0-674-06491-7 (cloth : alk. paper)
   ISBN 0-674-06492-5 (pbk. : alk. paper)
   1. Knowledge, Theory of.   2. Skepticism.   3. Cognition.
   4. Thought and thinking.   5. Constructivism (Philosophy)
   6. Philosophy, Modern—20th century.   I. Title.
   BD161.S56   1997
   121—dc21   96-44612

For Irwin & Fenja
Julia & Ed
Deirdre & Beth

Acknowledgments

Parts of this book were researched or written at the National Center for the Humanities, the Shelby Cullom Davis Center for Historical Studies at Princeton University, and the Rockefeller Foundation Study and Conference Center at Bellagio. I am grateful to the foundations and personnel involved, and especially to Natalie Zemon Davis. Reflection on these questions was lightened and sharpened by discussion with various colleagues and students at Duke University. They are too numerous to thank here individually, but I am conscious of their significant contributions to my thinking. I am particularly indebted to Julie Tetel Andresen, David Austin, Katharine T. Bartlett, Todd Davis, Allan Megill, Joseph Valente, and Joan Williams for valuable readings of early versions of individual chapters. Stanley Fish, Claudia Koonz, Richard C. Lewontin, John McGowan, David C. Moore, Susan Oyama, Richard Rorty, David Rubin, David Sanford, Judith Shapiro, Talbot J. Taylor, and Lindsay Waters offered useful tips and significant resistances. Alex Martin and Aisha Karim assisted ably in the editing. A number of key ideas here were shaped in correspondence with Andrew Pickering, who also provided welcome commentary on several chapters. I am especially grateful to Stephen Barber for his attentive and reassuringly responsive reading of the entire manuscript, and to Arkady Plotnitsky for many bracing and instructive conversations on matters theoretical and philosophical. Eve Kosofsky Sedgwick has been inspirational, intellectually and otherwise. And, for whatever skill in argumentation may be exhibited in these pages, much credit must go to Tom Cohen, who has been, all along, my keenest sparring partner.

The discussion of cognitive dissonance in the preface draws on my article, "The Complex Agony of Injustice," *Cardozo Law Review*

13 (1991): 101–104. Earlier versions of Chapters 1–3, each rewritten and expanded for this book, and Chapter 5, slightly revised here, were previously published as indicated below. I am grateful to the publishers for permission to reprint.

"The Unquiet Judge: Activism without Objectivism in Law and Politics," *Annals of Scholarship* 9 (1992): 111–133 [reprinted in *Rethinking Objectivity*, ed. Alan Megill (Durham, N.C.: Duke University Press, 1994), pp. 289–312].

"Making (Up) the Truth: Constructivist Contributions," *University of Toronto Quarterly*, 61 (1992): 422–429.

"Belief and Resistance: A Symmetrical Account," *Critical Inquiry* 18 (1991): 125–139 [reprinted in *Questions of Evidence: Proof, Practice, and Persuasion across the Disciplines*, ed. James Chandler, Arnold I. Davidson, and Harry Haratoonian (Chicago: University of Chicago Press, 1994), pp. 139–153].

"Unloading the Self-Refutation Charge," *Common Knowledge* 2 (1993): 81–95.

Contents

Preface

This book is about the play of conviction and skepticism, questioning and the resistance to questioning, in contemporary intellectual debate. The focus of interest here is not the substance or logical structure, in the usual sense, of individual arguments (though these are also considered), but the more general array of forces—cognitive, rhetorical, psychological, and to some extent social and institutional—that energize, shape, and sustain their opposition as such. What configuration of forces, for example, cements the familiar, perhaps eternal, adversarial embrace of skeptic and believer? Or again, what is happening when exchanges between proponents of rival views lead recurrently to deadlock and impasse? "You can't argue with these people," says one. "They don't play by the rules; they challenge every word you say." "It's like talking to a brick wall," says the other. "They don't hear a word you say; they keep repeating the same arguments." Part of what interests me here is what makes those "rules" work (or seem to) when they do and, conversely (if it is in fact converse), what holds the bricks in those walls together.

These questions are evoked especially by current debates over a cluster of ideas—*truth, knowledge, meaning, reason, objectivity,* and *justification* among them—central to Western thought and, in the view of many people (but not all), to the conduct of intellectual life as such. On the one side are arguments by scholars in various fields (academic philosophers, historians and sociologists of science, literary, cultural, and social critics, and theorists across a range of scientific disciplines) to the effect that traditional understandings and invocations of such ideas are conceptually problematic (for example, ambiguous, strained, unstable, based on empirically dubious assumptions, overly rigid, or fundamentally arbitrary) and that their pragmatic operations, so understood and invoked, are confining, unreliable, and at best ambivalent. On the other side are arguments to the effect that these challenges to, and related revisions of, traditional thought are descriptively inadequate (for example, unable to account for the explanatory, predictive, and technological successes of science), logically fallacious (for example, self-refuting), and otherwise conceptually counterproductive (for example, destructive of crucial concepts or well-established distinctions). These more or less philosophical objections to the contemporary critiques are joined by the objections of social critics and political activists, who charge that rejections of classical ideas of *truth, reason, objectivity,* and so forth are rhetorically or psychologically debilitating, undermining the claims and convictions necessary for social criticism or effective political opposition and supporting by default the status quo. And, to round out the array of arguments and players here, the latter set of charges is doubled or paralleled by those of cultural commentators, legal and moral theorists, and other academic and journalistic writers who see the rejections and revisions in question as ethically and socially irresponsible, making principled objections to evil and injustice impossible, inviting the toleration of manifestly intolerable practices, and opening the door to fraud, superstition, and civil chaos.

As some of these examples suggest, the charges and anxieties involved in these controversies often resonate with those familiar in more overtly social and political conflicts. For this reason and others to be mentioned below, the debates discussed in this book have an interest not confined to the scholarly arenas in which, for the most part, they are conducted. That interest is attested, in part, by the more than usual attention these (largely) epistemological controversies attract not only from the broader intellectual community but also from popular journalists, religious leaders, and sometimes even candidates for public office.

The exchanged charges of misunderstanding and incomprehensibility recurrent in these debates are not, I believe, incidental. Nor, it appears, can such charges—or the related sense of moral outrage or intellectual scandal often experienced by partisans and participants—be readily eliminated by further elaboration of points, due clarification of motives, or even lengthy and painstaking rearticulation of definitions, claims, positions, and implications. It appears, rather, that the sense, common among revisionists, of being misread and misrepresented by their traditionalist critics, and the corresponding impression, common among defenders of traditional convictions, of both the absurdity of the skeptics' denials and the opacity and irresponsibility of their alternative formulations, are intrinsic to the debates themselves: products not only of the specific assumptions and explicit claims that define the diverging positions as such but of the very nature of the divergences that sustain their conflicting relation.

The perplexities just mentioned seem also, however, to reflect more general cognitive and rhetorical dynamics, common not only to both or all (there are often and, in a sense, always more than two) sides of these debates, but to all intellectual controversy as such, including what we call "internal" controversy: that is, self-struggle, *psychomachia*, or what can be seen as the ongoing processes of stabilization, destabilization, restabilization, and transformation that constitute the general dynamics of belief. Accordingly, this book is also about the play of belief and resistance in a second, somewhat different sense, namely, as the general operations of *cognition*. In particular, I am concerned here to explore the broader theoretical implications of the development, in fields such as theoretical biology, neuroscience, and the history and sociology of knowledge, of significant new descriptions and understandings of cognitive process, both at the level of individual cognition and as reflected in the dynamics of intellectual history, including the history of science. Moreover, because human cognitive process, at both these levels, is seen here as profoundly intertwined with the operations of language, I also outline alternatives to standard but problematic views of verbal behavior and human communication. As will be clear, these two aspects of belief and resistance—that is, the dynamics of intellectual controversy and the nature of cognitive process—bear a reflexive or reciprocal relation to each other, mutually illustrating and, in a sense, mutually constituting.

Reflexivity and *reciprocality* themselves are recurrent themes in this book. One of the most striking features of the debates examined here, and centrally implicated in the kinds of difficulty they exemplify (mutual frustrations, recurrent charges, apparent dead-locks, and so forth), is the divergence of views among participants regarding the character and status of the very terms and moves through which the debates are conducted. For example, there are crucial differences between traditional and revisionist conceptions of the significance of *logic* and *evidence* in determining belief or knowledge. Or, to put this another (itself significantly different) way, they differ more or less sharply not only on how to understand the relevant force of the *terms* "logic" and "evidence," but also on how to understand the nature and operations of *concepts* more generally, and, as it always turns out, the nature and operations of *language* more generally. Similarly, disputes arise not only over which, or what kinds of, *criteria* are proper for assessing the claims and accounts being debated, but also over how any *propriety* of that kind is determined, and, sooner or later, over how any *determination* of that kind becomes established. The repeated eruption of these dizzying regresses and related quandaries of conceptualization and argumentation are what I refer to in the book as the "microdynamics of incommensurability." As I emphasize throughout, however, cognitive transformations and intellectual reconfigurations are no less inevitable than misconnections, collisions, and impasses, even if not so apparent as the latter and even if "resolutions" along classically supposed lines are not available.

The dynamics explored here reflect, at many points, the familiar but by no means simple phenomenon of *cognitive dissonance*. The experience itself is common: an impression of inescapable noise or acute disorder, a rush of adrenalin, sensations of alarm, a sense of unbalance or chaos, residual feelings of nausea and anxiety. These are the forms of bodily distress that occur when one's ingrained, taken-for-granted sense of how certain things are—and thus pre-sumably will be and in some sense *should* be—is suddenly or insis-tently confronted by something very much at odds with it. Percep-tually, it is the wave of vertigo one may experience at the unexpected sight of human disfigurement (a person with one arm, for example, or a badly scarred face), or the distinct discomfort felt at "clashing" colors or dissonant tones. As well as sensory or aesthetic, the per-cepts that elicit cognitive dissonance can be more or less intellectual and, in fact, textual. Thus a sense of intolerable wrongness in some journalist's description or fellow academic's analysis can set the mind's teeth on edge and produce a frenzy of corrective intellectual and textual activity: letters to the editor, exposures, rebuttals, and sometimes tomes and treatises. The corrective, restorative, "righting" impulse, here as elsewhere, is likely to be especially energetic when one experiences the wrongness as one's responsibility: not, that is, as one's fault but as bearing on one's personal safety, dignity, or even identity (social, professional, and so forth), so that a response seems summoned and obligatory.

In all these cases, the tendency, understandably, is to end the pain, to get things to be, feel, or look right (or "normal") again. Thus one turns away one's head, or removes or covers the disturbing thing, or strives to fix, adjust, or normalize it. Or, of course, the discordant percept may be incorporated (literally enough, that is, bodily) into one's sense of how things generally are (and thus will be and should be), so that what the previously ab-normal element must conform *to* or be consonant *with*—in effect, one's individual cognitive norm with respect to that sort of thing—is itself transformed. How one responds to cognitive dissonance on any particular occasion will depend, of course, on various features of the situation itself as well as on one's own relevant dispositions. While there is no single or simple predictor of such reactions, it does seem that individuals and entire communities or cultures have characteristic styles of responding to perceived anomaly, or what anthropologist Michael Thompson calls styles of "monster-handling." (See Michael Thompson, *Rubbish Theory: The Creation and Destruction of Value* [Oxford: Oxford University Press, 1979], p. 90.) For example, some people and communities seem characteristically to lock their gates to exclude monsters, others attempt to convert them, yet others are prepared to enlarge or re-arrange their houses to absorb them, and, of course, some people and communities regularly go forth to slay them. This last point reminds us, not altogether irrelevantly here, of the violence—from domestic abuse and vigilante justice to official inquisitions and international crusades—that may attend the attempted righting of what is perceived as violently wrong. Indeed, the pursuit of normative rightness—truth, health, morality, reason, or justice—may have its own corporeally violent motivations and expressions, the sometimes dubious justification of which is a perennial problem for moral theory.

If what I believe is true, then how is the other fellow's skepticism or different belief possible? The stability of every contested belief depends on a stable explanation for the resistance to that belief and, with it, a more or less coherent account of how beliefs generally are formed and validated, that is, an epistemology (though not necessarily a formal one). The two favored solutions to the puzzle just posed seem to be demonology and, so to speak, dementology: that is, the comforting and sometimes automatic conclusion that the other fellow (skeptic, atheist, heretic, pagan, and so forth) is either a devil or a fool—or, in more (officially) enlightened terms, that he or she suffers from defects or deficiencies of character and/or intellect: ignorance, innate incapacity, delusion, poor training, captivity to false doctrine, and so on. Both solutions reflect a more general tendency of some significance here, namely, "epistemic self-privileging" or "epistemic asymmetry": that is, our inclination to believe that we believe the true and sensible things we do because they are true and sensible, while other people believe the foolish and outrageous things they do because there is something the matter with those people. (I discuss this self-standardizing, other-pathologizing tendency elsewhere with particular regard to aesthetic judgments: see *Contingencies of Value: Alternative Perspectives for Critical Theory* [Cambridge, Mass.: Harvard University Press, 1988], pp. 36–42.)

One of the most interesting aspects and key issues of current epistemological controversy is, accordingly, the programmatic effort by certain revisionist theorists—notably, constructivist sociologists and historians of science—to maintain "symmetry" in their analyses and accounts of scientific and other beliefs, those beliefs currently seen as absurd or wrong as well as those now generally accepted as true. Contrary to widespread misunderstanding, this commitment to methodological symmetry is not equivalent to maintaining that all *beliefs* are equally *valid* (objectively? subjectively?). Such a claim would have to be, from a constructivist perspective, either vacuous (constructivism, by definition, rejects classic ideas of *objective* validity) or tautologous (to say all beliefs are equally *subjectively* valid is just to say that people really believe what they believe). That commitment *is* equivalent, however, to maintaining that the *credibility* of all beliefs, including those currently regarded as true, reasonable, self-evident, and so forth, is equally *contingent*: equally the product, in other words, of conditions (experiential, contextual, institutional, and so forth) that are fundamentally variable and always to some extent unpredictable and uncontrollable. So understood, epistemic symmetry, whether as an idea or a method, constitutes a strong challenge to familiar Whiggish history of science, to the normative project of rationalist philosophy of science, and to rationalist epistemology more generally.

Respect for the principle of epistemic symmetry in the analyses pursued in this book leads to an important and perhaps surprising observation, namely that some of the most notable, recurrent, and, from a skeptical perspective, problematic features of classic formulations and arguments (for example, their essentializing reifications and self-affirming circularities) seem to reflect cognitive tendencies that are, in certain respects, valuable or indeed indispensable. Thus, the question-begging or circularity of traditionalist defenses that can be so frustrating for the revisionists disputing them is seen here as an inevitable feature of all theory-construction and, indeed, as a fundamental aspect of the dynamics of cognition. Similarly and relatedly, while *cognitive conservatism,* the tendency of our prior beliefs to persist in the face of contrary-seeming (to other people) empirical evidence and credible-seeming (to other people) logical refutation, can certainly lead to stultification, it, too, is seen here as an ineradicable and, in some respects, distinctly positive tendency: crucial to our day-to-day operations as creatures who survive by learning, central to our individual sense of intellectual coherence, and implicated also in that severe intellectual rigor often taken as the supreme virtue of academic philosophy, at least by academic philosophers.

The *ambivalence* (or double-valuedness) just noted in the operations of logical circularity and cognitive conservatism emerges in the book as a more general principle, reflected in the logical dilemmas, rhetorical equivocations, and theoretical/pragmatic tradeoffs recurrent in the controversies examined here. Attention to the ambivalent operations of otherwise simply valorized, or simply rejected, possibilities is linked to another important principle or conceptual operator here, namely "more-or-less," meaning (in different contexts) contingent variability, conditionally adequate approximation, or gradient difference. Both principles (ambivalence and more-or-less) figure in my efforts here to suggest or indicate positive and viable alternatives to traditional absolutes, paralyzing dilemmas, and supposed mutually exclusive possibilities. (For the recent development of related concepts and conceptual operators in logic and mathematical set theory—sliding scales, variable approximations, intersecting and overlapping classes, continua, spectra, gradient versus digital quantification, matters of degree versus either/or distinctions, and so on—see Daniel McNeil and Paul Freiberger, *Fuzzy Logic* [New York: Simon and Schuster, 1993], pp. 12, 51–54. McNeil and Freiberger also offer a lively account and useful analyses of the resistance to such developments in the relevant philosophical, scientific, and engineering communities. See especially pp. 44–64, 73–77, 176–181, and 269–70).

The positive alternatives just mentioned are themselves different from the best-of-both syntheses, between-extremes middle ways, or beyond-X-and-Y transcendences frequently proposed as resolutions of current conflicts. Most (not all) of the formulations offered in such terms are, in my view, problematic: the syntheses tend to be superficial, the supposed middle ways commonly display a distinct rightward or backward tilt, and the "beyonds" similarly tend to fall earthward toward more familiar, established positions. And, in fact, most of these turn out to be highly unstable *as* resolutions, typically rejected by partisans of the more unorthodox side of the relevant controversy, often by those on both sides. This is not to say, however, that intellectual conflicts are immutable. On the contrary, new alliances, alignments, mergings, and mutual transformations of views (none of these the same as "resolutions") are altogether to be expected. Though their importance is not always announced, or even recognized as such by the agents involved, such events are of considerable significance in intellectual history. Indeed, one could say that, along with the playing out of controversy itself, they are just what makes up intellectual history.

As will be evident throughout the book, my own intellectual sympathies in the debates examined here are, for the most part, with the skeptics and revisionists rather than with the defenders and rehabilitators of traditional beliefs—"for the most part" because the array of positions on these issues is extensive and diverse, and one could no more readily embrace all revisionist ("antifoundationalist," "constructivist," "postmodern," and so forth) formulations than reject all traditional ones. It is nevertheless significant that the analyses in this book reflect a particular set of intellectual tastes and, in some cases, a participant's interest in the shape and outcome of the debates discussed. The question may arise, of course, as to whether my role as observer and analyst is not thereby compromised. At the least, it may be supposed, I cannot describe or represent the positions with which I disagree as well as those I endorse. I am sure that I cannot; nor, I think, could anyone. Indeed, this cognitive and rhetorical asymmetry seems to be an inevitable feature and perhaps inescapable condition of all theoretical debate: for, of course, the moment the skeptic understood the believer's position exactly as the believer did, or vice versa, then the difference—and dispute—between them would dissolve. It might seem, then, that explorations of theoretical controversies are best left to future intellectual historians, who can compare and assess them after all the feathers have settled and there are no longer any live issues, or that they should be undertaken only by contemporary observers with no intellectual investments in any of the positions. I doubt, however, that either of these conditions of presumed neutrality could be attained. Any intellectual controversy that remains interesting to later generations is likely to be connectable, along some lines, to current issues and positions; anyone well enough informed about a contemporary controversy to have something of interest to say about it is, by the same token, likely also to have a particular more or less partisan perspective on it. There is an alternative, however, to sheer polemics or blithely self-privileging asymmetry, though it is not, to my mind, either transcendentally guaranteed objectivity or a self-conscious (and, I think, inevitably strained) effort at rigorously symmetrical representation. It is, rather, something more familiar and mundane (though perhaps sublime enough in its way), namely, respect for the general principles and practices of intellectual fairness that are acknowledged *in* principle, if not always in practice, in the academic, journalistic, and broader intellectual communities to which this book is addressed: at the minimum, accurate citation, representative quotation, nontendentious summary, and forbearance from name-calling and motive-mongering. I cannot lay claim to all these virtues all the time in what follows, but I believe the descriptions and arguments offered here will be found no more wanting in those respects than those currently offered by the most strenuous contemporary affirmers of (classic conceptions of) *truth, reason,* and *objectivity.*

By way of introduction to the individual chapters, I might say a word about the widening focus reflected in their sequence. The first two chapters (also the earliest written) were provoked by what I saw as clear misunderstandings of certain revisionist views and by related charges (sometimes breath-taking) regarding their supposed moral implications and political or social consequences. In response to what I have come to see as a recurrent complex of misreadings, systematic non sequiturs, and self-fueling anxieties, I attempt in these two chapters ("The Unquiet Judge: Activism without Objectivism in Law and Politics" and "Making [Up] the Truth: Constructivist Contributions"), first, to clarify the specific aims, claims, and implications of the relevant critiques and projects; second, to indicate accordingly the unimpaired moral and political capacities of those who pursue them; and, finally, to suggest the more general pragmatic (including ethical and political) value of, respectively, "non-objectivist" conceptions of advocacy, justification, and justice, and "constructivist" conceptions of truth and knowledge. (The labels just mentioned and others in play in all these debates are, of course, extremely volatile, representing divergent perspectives *on* the positions in question as well as historically shifting and otherwise variable configurations of claims and ideas. Readers with personal experience of these controversies may consult their own pulses with regard to the label "relativism," which, though hardly new, is currently undergoing a considerable expansion of rhetorical function, invoked not only to identify or dismiss certain challenges to traditional epistemology but also to explain or denounce a wide range of complexly determined—and, in some cases, arguably positive—developments, from the rising rate of teenage pregnancy and recurrent denials of the Holocaust to ongoing revisions of the standard humanities curriculum in the nation's schools and universities.)

While striving, with notably mixed success, to untangle increasingly predictable misunderstandings and to answer what became, in time, absolutely predictable charges, I continued to puzzle over the conditions responsible for the generation, duplication, and persistence of both. It was clear, of course, that intellectual antagonisms were being inflamed, here as elsewhere and perhaps always, by various unedifying forces (ignorance, arrogance, resentment, opportunism, and so forth), and that the debates were in part themselves political: that is, their energies reflected more general institutional (for example, disciplinary) antagonisms as well as specific intellectual differences, and their outcomes could be expected to have significant effects on the distribution of intellectual authority and related forms of power and prestige, public and social as well as academic. It was also clear, however, that the motives exhibited in these debates were not altogether dishonorable nor, on either side, simply political, and that there were aspects of even the most frustrating of such exchanges that gave them a more general theoretical interest. That interest crystallized in due course as the set of questions posed at the beginning of this preface and, with them, the idea of a book outlining, reflexively enough, a (controversial) account of knowledge, language, and cognition as illustrated by contemporary controversies over knowledge, language, and cognition.

Chapter 3, "Belief and Resistance: A Symmetrical Account," is pivotal. My point of departure here is the current and to some extent chronic conflict between two conceptions of the relation between belief and evidence. One is the realist or positivist idea that our (objectively) mistaken beliefs are duly corrected by our encounters with an autonomously resistant reality, at least when all is well, as in (good) science. The other is the more controversial idea—familiar, in one form, as the hermeneutic circle—that our perceptions and descriptions of the things we encounter cannot be independent either of our prior beliefs about those things or of our more general assumptions and verbal/conceptual practices. In line with the latter idea, the chapter goes on to develop a constructivist-interactionist account of belief, first in regard to the formation, transformation, and stabilization of belief (or "knowledge") in intellectual history, including the history of science, and, second, in regard to the corresponding *micro*dynamics of individual cognition. This general account of belief, elaborated further in subsequent chapters, is "symmetrical" in that it seeks (with due irony) to exemplify the contructivist idea and ideal of epistemic symmetry described above, and also in that it sets into play a number of mirror themes, including reflexivity and reciprocality, that become increasingly important here. (Throughout the book, including its title, the operations of *belief* and *resistance* are understood and represented as themselves reciprocal: the maintenance of any belief involves resistance to other beliefs; any skepticism, in the sense of resistance to other beliefs, is itself a configuration of beliefs.) Theories of reciprocal organism/environment interaction currently emerging from evolutionary and developmental biology figure significantly in Chapter 3, as elsewhere in the book. As I indicate, however, the non-realist, non-teleological conceptions of individual cognition and intellectual history outlined here collide directly with the strenuously realist assumptions and progressivist/adaptationist models of most so-called evolutionary epistemology.

Chapter 4, "Doing without Meaning," explores a set of issues in contemporary language theory that bear significantly on controversies examined elsewhere in the book. Central to the chapter is an account of communication as a system (or circuit) of reciprocally effective social interactions that I call "the language loop." The formulations developed here intersect with as well as complement the ideas of *cognitive* circularity and reciprocality set forth in Chapter 3, the key point in this respect being the continuous interlooping of our verbal and social interactions with our individual perceptions and other behavior in the formation and stabilization of knowledge. The operations of the language loop also suggest ways to understand the emergence and operation of linguistic (and, more generally, social) norms, understandings that serve later (in Chapters 6 and 7) as alternatives to the ideas of communicative and moral normativity associated with contemporary Frankfurt School "discourse ethics."

The next two chapters, like the first two, consider recurrent charges directed at anti-foundationalism or epistemological skepticism. Here, however, the relevant charges are those put forward on logical rather than moral or political grounds. Chapter 5, "Unloading the Self-Refutation Charge," considers the most ancient and probably still most common of such logicist arguments, namely that the truth-denier, in affirming the truth of her own denial, refutes herself. The idea that a rejection of realist/objectivitist conceptions of *truth* or *validity* is necessarily self-refuting is often the lone item in a traditionalist's logical toolbox. It comes, however, with a venerable warrant, being commonly regarded as all that Socrates needed to refute Protagoras's epistemological "relativism" and all that anyone will ever need to refute all subsequent relativisms.

The charge can be seen as itself logically defective in several respects, but more interesting here is its rhetorical power, both as displayed against Protagoras (or his ghost) in Plato's *Theaetetus* and as evident in current arguments against "postmodern" skepticism. That power is clearly considerable but more complexly determined, I suggest, than is usually assumed.

Chapter 6, "The Skeptic's Turn: A Performance of Contradiction," examines the most sophisticated contemporary version of the self-refutation charge, namely, the idea of "performative contradiction," especially as developed by Jürgen Habermas. The focus of the analysis here is a series of moves executed in the course of a hypothetical debate that Habermas stages (in a recent book) between a neo-Kantian moral theorist and a resistant skeptic. The debate is explicitly designed to demonstrate how the skeptic's self-contradiction not only refutes his skepticism but also validates the specific norms of discourse ethics. As I attempt to indicate, the demonstration falters, but its conduct illustrates, along with other issues of interest here, the tenacity of essentialist conceptions of language and the immense resourcefulness of foundationalist logic. Also, since the skeptic whom Habermas creates and ventriloquizes in this debate is at a considerable argumentative disadvantage, he (or she) is given his (or her) turn to speak, from time to time, propria persona.

Chapter 7, "Arguing with Reason," considers certain recurrent and evidently quite general perplexities in rationalist philosophy, as exemplified by Habermas's efforts to rehabilitate currently challenged Enlightenment claims and concepts. Of particular interest here are, first, the awkward alliance between rationalism and (quasi-)empirical science, and, second, the evidently reciprocal relation between practical (including political) responsiveness and theoretical rigor. Ultimately, I suggest, that reciprocality (or trade-off) may be a feature of all intellectual life, reflecting the irreducibly ambivalent operation of the processes of cognition themselves. The chapter concludes, accordingly, with some genial speculations on the reciprocal relation between belief and skepticism, represented here by orthodox rationalism (or, as it is sometimes seen, philosophy proper) and a variety of heterodox (or, accordingly, improper) philosophies.

The concluding chapter, "Microdynamics of Incommensurability: Philosophy of Science Meets Science Studies," considers the recent effort by Philip Kitcher, a philosopher of science, to defend and rehabilitate rationalist/realist understandings of scientific truth and progress in the face of rival accounts from the sociology and history of science. Kitcher's perplexed responses to certain key constructivist formulations (notably those of Bruno Latour) and his asymmetrical explanations of the due acceptance or, in his view, cognitively dysfunctional rejection of various scientific revelations prove instructive, especially in relation to the ever-hovering issue of in/commensurability. At the end, this issue and several other themes central to this book (including symmetry, circularity, reciprocality, and ambivalence) are put into play in relation both to each other and to the general question of the dynamics of controversy.

A concluding prefatory word. The sorts of controversies examined here are commonly represented as occurring between parties or sets of parties ("the skeptic" versus "the rationalist," "foundationalists" versus "anti-foundationalists," and so on) who occupy opposed but otherwise unsituated and severely abstracted positions. This way of representing intellectual disagreement is ancient and perhaps ubiquitous, but always oversimplified and often, for a number of reasons, significantly so. First, adversarial intellectual exchanges may involve a variety of configurations of participants: literal-enough duels between just two persons, hostile encounters between one person and a group of others, simultaneous and serial battles among innumerable pairs and sets of antagonists, and so forth. Intellectual controversies, moreover, like other more or less adversarial social interactions (for example, military battle, sports matches, trade wars, legal disputes, or family quarrels), always involve parties other than the obvious participants: specifically, those who have interests of one kind or another in formal or substantive aspects of the contest or stakes in its outcome. In the discussions that follow I indicate a number of these possibilities where they are relevant, and, in Chapter 5, examine one in some detail, namely, the triangular configuration of good teacher, bad teacher, and student (plus interlocutor and audience) that recurs in philosophical dramas of exposure and refutation.

Second, intellectual controversies occur under a variety of specific social and circumstantial conditions that may themselves be determinative. For example, the respective institutional positions and related resources of the parties to a debate (parents and children, employers and workers, senior and junior faculty members of a particular department of philosophy, and so forth) could hardly be thought irrelevant to its dynamics or outcome; nor could the particular arena in which the debate is conducted (courtroom, neighborhood backyard, provincial classroom, columns of a professional journal, and so forth). Controversies may also occur over significantly different periods of time: from the one-shot exchange between featured visiting lecturer and anonymous local audience-member to the lifelong dispute between village priest and village atheist, or, to stress another point, the ongoing contest between believer and skeptic that makes up much of our individual psychic lives and that constitutes perhaps the most significant—certainly inescapable—intellectual controversy in which any of us is likely to participate.

Finally, I would suggest that intellectual *polarization* itself—that is, the tendency for an array of multiple, variously differing, more or less shifting, configurations of belief to move toward and become stabilized as contradistinctive and mutually antagonistic positions—is not only a significant component of the dynamics examined in this book but also an intriguing phenomenon in its own right. The conditions under which such polarizations tend generally to occur and the particular forces involved in the historical occurrence of various otherwise interesting ones remain, I think, important questions for social theory and the history of science and philosophy—especially because, in this respect as in others, and for better or worse, the dynamics of intellectual controversy seem to shadow, model, and predict so closely those of other types of human conflict.

Belief and Resistance

1

The Unquiet Judge:
Activism without
Objectivism in Law
and Politics

A major project of classical ethics and epistemology has been to
ground—justify and underwrite—the claims of some judgments to
objective validity. *Objective,* in this tradition, is understood to mean
independent of particular historical, cultural, or circumstantial conditions, and independent, also, of the perspectives of particular
persons. Throughout the past century and increasingly in the past
decades, this project—"foundationalism" or "axiology" as it is
sometimes called—has been subjected to strenuous criticism and
significant reformulation or outright rejection.[1] The defense of objectivist claims (moral, cognitive, aesthetic, and other), however, has
hardly been abandoned. On the contrary, the efforts of axiological
skeptics ("anti-foundationalists," "postmodernists," and so on) have
themselves been subjected to strenuous criticism and, as well, to a
certain amount of demonization—commonly via the classic charge
of "relativism," but, more recently, and perhaps especially from critics on the political left, the charge of "quietism."

In its historical and general usage, "quietism" suggests a personal
withdrawal from worldly pursuits (by mystics, for example) or a
principled refusal to participate in armed conflict. In the debates
just mentioned, however, the term is commonly meant to evoke the
supposed politically disabling consequences of a rejection of objec-

tivism: the supposed refusal to make value judgments, the supposed disinclination to take sides on ethical and political issues, and, accordingly, the supposed passive support of—or, in the current phrase, "complicity" with—all or any present regimes.[2] Significantly, what counts as a "refusal to make value judgments" is, often enough, just a disinclination to maintain that the judgments one makes are objectively correct. Similarly, what counts as a "refusal to take sides" is often just a disinclination to maintain that the sides one takes are transcendentally mandated. "Quietism," in other words, the supposed political distemper of non-objectivist theory, seems, often enough, to be nothing more or other than a disinclination to conceive—and, accordingly, to characterize—one's judgments, choices, and acts in objectivist terms.

The identification of non-objectivist conceptions of judgment and action with political passivity follows, it appears, from the logic and psychology of objectivist thought itself. It is currently argued, for example, that unless we "believe in" and can "appeal to" objective validity and related concepts, then we cannot expose falsehood, struggle against injustice, or claim rights for ourselves or other people. Thus, Thomas L. Haskell worries whether there can be "any intellectually respectable justification for the claim 'I have a right' " in an age such as our own, racked as it is, in his view, by Nietzschean relativism and lacking "the objective (or at least intersubjective) moral order implied by words such as 'ought' and 'duty.' "[3] But there is no reason—other than the compliments that objectivist thought pays to itself—to think that all usage of the terms "ought" and "rights" presupposes specifically objectivist conceptions of moral obligation and political legitimacy. Consequently, there is no reason to fear that all intellectually respectable justification for political claims would vanish if classic objectivism disappeared—unless, of course, one *defines* intellectual respectability as conformity to the canons of classic objectivist thought.

Experience indicates that pointing out the circularity of such arguments does not allay fears of political paralysis or quash charges of quietism. On the contrary, although self-affirming arguments may be indicted as logically defective, they remain compelling for people who make the crucial assumptions—which, in the case of a traditional view like classic objectivism, will be a good many of those debating these issues. Moreover, the assumptions themselves are not dented by objections raised to their self-affirming use in specific debates. Indeed, when those debates involve what are seen as high political stakes and evoke, vividly and passionately, what all present would agree are manifest oppressions and injustices, then objections to logical trespasses, even to utter logical hollowness, may appear callous as well as irrelevant. Logical cruxes, however, cannot be easily bypassed in arenas of political debate, for they are often an index of political cruxes as well.

Those schooled in classical moral theory and persuaded, accordingly, of the political necessity of objectivism, commonly cannot imagine themselves—or, by extension, anyone else—making judgments, taking sides, or working actively for political causes without objectivist convictions and justifications. Consequently they resist—indeed, cannot grasp—the idea that the reason other people reject objectivism is not only that its claims seem, to them, conceptually ("theoretically") problematic, but that such claims are, for them, otherwise ("practically" or "politically") unnecessary. Contrary to the charge of quietism, non-objectivists need not and characteristically do not refuse to *judge*. Nor, also contrary to that charge, must they or do they characteristically refuse to *act*. Nor must they be, or are they characteristically, incapable of acting *effectively*. Nor are they incapable of *justifying*—in the sense of successfully explaining, defending, and promoting—their judgments and actions to other people. Moreover, contrary to the current and classic charge of self-contradiction, when non-objectivists *do* judge, act, and justify their actions, they do not stop being non-objectivists.

The Rhetoric of Political Justification

The quietism that supposedly attends non-objectivist thought is often seen as a more or less literal *muteness*—that is, a condition of politically disabling verbal privation or constriction. To those who reason via classic dualisms such as "objective reasons" versus "mere subjective preferences," "universal interests" versus "merely partisan desires," and "intrinsic value" versus "mere utility," judgments that do not claim objective status can be presumed to express only idiosyncratic personal tastes and to reflect only narrow "special interests" and/or considerations of crude and immediate expedience.

The viability and necessity of those classic oppositions are, however, questionable, and the rhetorical alternatives they seem to imply are not (and never were) the only choices available.

People who are (formally or de facto) non-objectivist in their conceptual commitments can and do argue, credibly and persuasively, that their judgments and proposals (political critiques, judicial rulings, legislative programs, and so on) reflect not merely their individual or partisan preferences but the interests and values of larger relevant groups, including, sometimes, the entire relevant community. Moreover, such people can and do argue the superiority of their judgments on similarly compelling, though not classically objective, grounds: the fact, for example, that those judgments reflect more extensive, more current, or more pertinent information than rival or prevailing judgments, or that they take into account a wider range of significant factors or subtler and longer-range implications. It is not necessary to argue that one's judgments are objectively right or universally valid in order to make them forceful for, and acceptable to, the relevant audiences. Nor is it necessary to claim that they are grounded on "human nature" or the unchanging features of "the human predicament"[4] in order to argue their superiority to rival or prevailing judgments.

There is, perhaps, a certain grandeur to the rhetoric of objectivist justification (though not, as it happens, to my ears). What is sacrificed to obtain that grandeur, however—namely, acknowledgment of both human variability and the mutability of the conditions of human existence—is likely to be paid, sooner or later, in political coin. It is no accident that groups and movements whose ideologies center on absolutist, universalist claims commonly respond to emergent conditions (and unpredicted human predicaments) with self-defeating dogmatism, or that they commonly respond to divergent perspectives (and deviant human "natures") with suppression and self-destroying schism, purge, or defection. The cause that wins the day by objectivist rhetoric seems to risk losing itself in the long run.

To be sure, political rhetoric, like any other kind, must be sensitive to the contexts of its intended reception, including the linguistic habits of its intended audiences. It by no means follows, however, that objectivist rhetoric is the only kind that can be used effectively. Like the idioms of any other discourse, those of political discourse evolve continuously in response to the pressures of changing usage, as do also the meanings of individual terms—"obliga-tion," "rights," "legitimacy," and so on.[5] Political positions framed in non-objectivist terms—as those who actually produce them can testify—can be rhetorically compelling to *any* contemporary au-dience, no matter how philosophically (or "theoretically") unso-phisticated and no matter how caught up in particular battles. Moreover, political positions framed in non-objectivist terms—and accepted in those terms—have the considerable long-range *political* advantage of flexibility and responsiveness. The cause or movement that acknowledges the contingency of its own analyses, judgments, and justifications is less liable to fall apart in face of differing per-spectives or to become paralyzed when new conditions emerge.

Historically, the rhetoric of objectivism—the invocation of self-evident truth and objective fact, of intrinsic value and absolute right, of that which is universal, total, and transcendent—has had enor-mous power. It is the power we call inspirational when produced by those we follow or admire, demagoguery when produced by those we have reason to fear or despise. Either way, however, it is a perilous power. In view of the politically and ethically ambiguous successes of objectivist rhetoric in the past, I do not think the failure of that rhetoric is what we have most to fear in the future.

Political Distinctions, Normative Asymmetries

To make some of these points more concrete and also to indicate the specific sorts of debates from which they emerge, I turn now to an article by the feminist legal scholar, Robin West.[6] West main-tains that, in the field of law, the questioning of objectivist justifi-cations is both unnecessary and undesirable. It is unnecessary there, she argues, because the legal community is already thoroughly dom-inated by what she calls "economic relativism;" and it is undesirable because that domination is, in her view, just what is wrong with law as currently practiced. West's arguments could be queried along several lines, including the accuracy of her depiction of the ethos of the present judicial community. Of particular interest here, how-ever, are her efforts to redeem objectivist claims on a politically selective basis and, in that connection, to establish a quasi-logical link between non-objectivist theory and legal and political conser-vatism—or, in her terms, between "relativism" and "quietism."

West's defense of objectivism proceeds in two parts. In the first, she contends that, while objectivist claims may be oppressively authoritarian under some conditions, they need not be so and, under other conditions, will not be so. In the second part, she contends that, in the specific context of legal adjudication, it is only through "objectivist evaluative reasoning" that judges can avoid endorsing the sociopolitical status quo and, as she puts it, "sacrificing justice for efficiency" (1500). The first of these contentions may appear reasonable enough, but it harbors a significant misunderstanding crucial to West's larger argument and, more generally, to all politically selective defenses of objectivist claims.

West seems to concede much of the force of current critiques of traditional objectivism, citing with approval, for example, the relevant discussions in my book, *Contingencies of Value*.[7] "There is no doubt that objectivist forms of evaluative reasoning in a wide range of disciplines are authoritarian in precisely the way that Smith describes" (1479). The crucial turn on this endorsement occurs four pages later, where she writes: "It is not clear, however, whether authoritarianism is a necessary consequence or an inevitable component of objective evaluative reasoning" (1483). In her endorsements as well as in her objections, however, West misses the central point of the critique of objectivist claims. For the argument is not, as she repeatedly and erroneously frames it, that "objective evaluative reasoning" is always "authoritarian," but that such reasoning *never occurs*.

To prevent other misunderstandings: this is not to say that the characterization of some judgment as (relatively) objective is meaningless or that all judges are culpably biased. The perspectives reflected in some judgments are certainly more widely shared, stable, and/or recurrent than those reflected in others; some judgments are certainly more responsive than others to a broader range of relevant considerations and/or reflect greater than usual effort to identify and control the operation of irrelevant factors; and people sometimes, perhaps quite often, indicate such matters of degree by praising such judgments as (more) "objective." It is to say, however, that no judgment is or could be objective in the classic sense of justifiable on totally context-transcendent and subject-independent grounds. Claims of objectivity in this latter sense may be (relatively) benign—at least for the moment and for those most obviously concerned—and uncontested. Nevertheless, such claims are always empirically dubious or logically hollow, depending either on questionable appeals to supposed self-evident facts, undeniable intuitions, or human universals, or on prior taken-for-granted but contestable and thus question-begging norms. For these reasons, objectivist claims may operate in quite negative ways under certain conditions for certain members of the community and, for the reasons suggested above, reliance on such claims are perilous in the long run both for any particular cause and for the community at large.

Objectivist claims, as West is eager to acknowledge, are often put forward to justify the historically and otherwise contingent judgments of the dominant members of a community (men, let us say). What she does not acknowledge, however, is that, even if those claims are put forward to justify the equally historically and otherwise contingent judgments made on behalf of a community's subordinated members (women, let us say), they will *still* be dubious and perilous in the ways just mentioned. It is possible, of course, to defend and promote judgments made on behalf of subordinated people with effective *non-objectivist* arguments. But that is just the possibility that West, like many other politically concerned defenders of objectivism, fails to grasp.

The crucial argument against claims of noncontingent objectivity is not that they are authoritarian (though they often are that) but that they are empty and obscurantist—which means empty and obscurantist *no matter who is making them*. West does not recognize the significance of the symmetry here emphasized. On the contrary, her defense of a politically selective objectivism depends, as such defenses commonly do, on a presumption of prior normative and/ or epistemic privilege, which is to say, asymmetry. This questionable asymmetry consists not simply in preferring your own judgments or beliefs to those of other people (a self-privileging that is not, in itself, theoretically problematic—or otherwise corrigible), but in maintaining that you and the members of your group prefer your judgments or beliefs because they are objectively correct (the products of enlightened rationality, infallible intuition, rigorous deduction, the hermeneutic method, the scientific method, total disinterestedness, and so on) while other people prefer their differing judgments or beliefs because those people are benighted or otherwise deficient. Correspondingly, the alternative presumption, normative and/or epistemic symmetry, is not the idea that all judgments or beliefs are "equally good" or "equally valid,"[8] but the idea that all judgments and beliefs, including one's own, are produced and operate equally contingently, that is, are formed in response to more or less particular and variable conditions (experiential, historical, cultural, discursive, circumstantial, and so on) and operate with greater or less validity (in the sense of applicability, force, or adequacy) in relation to such conditions.

West wants to argue that objectivism is wrong when practiced by the wrong people for the wrong reasons, but right when practiced by the right people for the right reasons. Specifically, she contends that objectivist arguments are culpably "authoritarian" when they issue from powerful agents attempting to justify their own self-interested actions, but laudably "critical" when they issue from disinterested agents exposing the unjust acts of powerful people against subordinated people. Such distinctions, however, appear impossible to maintain either theoretically or practically.

For one thing, it seems impossible to eliminate, as the objectivist claim requires, the crucial factor of perspective. West writes:

> [T]he danger that objectivist claims are being made in a manner that reifies and thus reinforces dominant interests is far more *pronounced*, more *obvious*, and perhaps even more often realized when objectivism is used by the actor himself, rather than the critic . . . If objectivism does indeed bolster and strengthen the interests and power of the dominant . . ., then it will do so much more *visibly* when it is used to justify the actions of the strong than when it is used to criticize those acts. (1490, emphasis added)

But to whom will those dangers be "obvious" and "pronounced"? For whom will those motives be "visibl[e]"? And if it is not everyone, then how would West handle the people for whom they are not obvious, pronounced, or visible? Would she ignore them, or discount their views, or take their blindness as evidence of their "false consciousness"? And if properly critical objectivists can dismiss the differing perspectives of other people so readily, then how do their arguments differ from the arguments of culpably authoritarian objectivists? Are they not both equally arrogant embellishments of the epistemically self-privileging claim itself—that is, "we are objectively right, they are objectively wrong"?

Also, as an example will help to make clear, West's distinctions are practically unworkable. In 1988, Lynne V. Cheney, then head of the National Endowment for the Humanities, and William Bennett, then Secretary of Education, issued statements condemning Stanford University and other educational institutions for revising their humanities curricula to secure more classroom attention to works by authors other than white, male, and European. In criticizing those acts, Cheney and Bennett appealed to objective standards of literary greatness which, they claimed, transcended such considerations as time, place, gender, and race.[9]

Is this an example of powerful agents using objectivist arguments in an authoritarian way to justify the interests of the dominant? Or is it an example of morally responsible agents using objectivist arguments to oppose the acts of the dominant? It is possible to decide the matter, of course (and West and I would probably decide it the same way), but not by using West's criteria and not, in any case, *objectively*. For, although Cheney and Bennett were defending traditional practices, they were not making objectivist claims in order to justify their *own* acts. On the contrary, they made those claims in just the way that West speaks of as "*critical* discourse."[10] Moreover, although Cheney and Bennett themselves occupied high governmental offices, they claimed to speak on behalf of the subordinated and marginalized. Thus they condemned university administrators for capitulating to the menacing tactics of militant students and to radical professors who, they maintained, now dominated the literary academy.

West argues that, in the case of the wrong kind of objectivism, "the consequences of the false reification of private interest into objective reality are made immediately apparent by the act itself" (1490). In the case of the defense of the traditional humanities curriculum, the connection between certain reifications and various private interests could, I think, be traced by a careful analysis, and the ethical and political implications of that connection may in time be widely acknowledged. Significantly enough, however, neither the connection nor its implications were "immediately apparent" to the many journalists, academics, and members of the public who immediately applauded and endorsed the Cheney-Bennett critiques. Indeed, the connection and its implications continue to elude quite a few of these people, even after some determined efforts at exposure and demonstration.[11]

The supposedly clear—and objective—distinction between politically desirable and politically undesirable objectivist claims breaks down or becomes murky, it appears, at every point; or the distinction can be drawn readily enough, but only in relation to prior, politically defined, and manifestly contestable—and thus also manifestly non-objective—criteria. For the committed objectivist, this means one must strive even harder to locate truly objective criteria.[12] For the non-objectivist, it means that classic objectivist claims cannot be redeemed on a politically selective basis any more than on any other basis and, since they are not politically necessary or ultimately politically desirable, should be abandoned.[13]

Pragmatic Tests and Political/Ethical Dilemmas

Other pragmatic and political implications of the disputes and asymmetries discussed above are illustrated vividly enough by certain questions raised, and related dilemmas posed, in West's article. By way of testing—*"pragmatically,"* she stresses—the "quietism" of the "version of relativism" represented in my account of value, West seeks to determine whether, in the articulation of that account, "the desires and preferences upon which value is contingent [are ever] themselves put into question" (1492, 1493). This means, it turns out, seeing whether I declare at some point that some desires are objectively false and some preferences objectively wrong. West observes, correctly, that I do not, which is hardly surprising since what my account does put into question is the substance and logical coherence of such declarations.

As an example of a definitively *un*quietistic putting-into-question—and by way of contrast to my own telling refusal to endorse the "crucial" concept of "false consciousness" (1493)—West cites the work of the feminist legal scholar Catharine MacKinnon: "Professor MacKinnon's exposure of the expropriation of women's sexuality in patriarchal society crucially depends upon the critical claim that women's felt desires or preferences for heterosexuality, and their felt experience of those desires as on occasion non-coerced, are false" (1494). For West, it appears, "quietism" consists of being less than eager to operate with such traditionally certified but otherwise dubious ideas as objectively false desires, objectively wrong preferences, and the objective truths of human (or female) nature. If this is so, however, then the issue, here as elsewhere, is not the non-objectivist's alleged quietism—for which, in its current sense of political/ethical complacency or passivity, West produces no evidence—but the activist-objectivist's conviction of the political necessity of just such ideas.

Contrary to the latter conviction, politically significant differences of belief and preference can be handled quite effectively, in practice as well as theoretically, without appealing to traditional objectivist contrasts (e.g., between "genuine knowledge" and "false consciousness"). Moreover, under some and perhaps quite a few conditions, political interventions pursued in accord with non-objectivist conceptions of belief and preference can be more generally desirable—because more ethical (as generally accounted)—as well as more effective than those pursued in accord with such traditional contrasts.

An illustration of this last point is provided by West's uneasy treatment of what she sees as the dilemma of the ethically responsible political—here, feminist—agent. The uneasiness is signaled by the ambiguous or shifting population denoted by the first-person plurals ("we," "us," "our") in the following passage, which follows her discussion of MacKinnon's work: "The preferences and desires of *all of us*, but particularly *those of us* who . . . are relatively disempowered, cannot be the basis of *our* evaluative practices. Those preferences and desires are themselves the product of social structures of which *we* must be critical" (1495–1496, my emphasis). Is West is saying here that we (women) must *all*, in our evaluative practices, be self-critical regarding our *own* preferences and desires—or, quite differently, that *some* of us (women) must, in our evaluative and related practices, be critical of the preferences and desires of *some other* of us (women)?

The ambiguity or perplexity is also reflected in what West frames explicitly as a dilemma:

> The political actor, as well as the critic worried about social hierarchy, finds herself on the horns of a dilemma which is profoundly ethical and practical, not just logical: She can *either* legislate in such a way that quietistically rests on the authority and givenness of presently constituted preferences . . . or she can legislate in such a way that aggressively attacks the social structures that create those preferences—running the risk of authoritatively and oppressively running roughshod over the experiences and felt

interests of the very subordinated whom she is trying to help. (1495)

The risk to which West refers here is faced, I would say, not only by every activist legislator but by every teacher, parent, missionary, and would-be benevolent leader: that is, by all those who have enough institutional power to enforce changes that *they* think are proper and beneficial, even though other people, notably those in subordinate positions, do not agree. And, to make clearer the severity of that risk or the sharpness of that second horn, I would add that what could be run over roughshod in the enforcement of those changes are not only the "experiences and felt interests" of the very people one is trying to help but, sometimes, their bodies and lives as well.

It is the "apparent strategy of the . . . relativist," West remarks, "simply [to deny] the existence of one of the horns of the dilemma" (1495). This is quite inaccurate. On the contrary, precisely because "the relativist" is not locked into the objectivist's gratuitous oppositions, he or she has a broader range of responsive actions. Indeed, what West sees as a practical/ethical dilemma can be recast in a non-objectivist form that acknowledges the difficulties that concern her, but—not being, in this form, a dilemma at all—also permits a range of practical solutions that she would probably agree are also ethical. The point can be approached thus:

All of us (people, women, etc.)[14] are more or less "critical" of the structures (practices, institutions, laws, etc.) of our various communities in the sense that we are more or less inclined to evaluate those structures, feel more or less dissatisfied with some (perhaps a great many) of them, and think that some of them should be changed in certain (perhaps quite radical) ways. *Some* of us, commonly by virtue of our professions and offices and in accord with our temperaments, personal histories, and/or subject-positions, are especially inclined or obliged to examine those structures very closely, are especially disturbed by what we see as their undesirable operations and effects, and, accordingly, develop what we think are good proposals for how to change them for the better. We find, however, that the adequacy of our analyses, the propriety of our objections, and the desirability of the changes we propose are not immediately evident to everybody concerned. Indeed, we find that they are not immediately evident even to certain subordinated people we are specifically trying to help, including, as may happen, people—such as our children, students, or native parishioners—who are subordinate to *us*. On the contrary, we find that our analyses, critiques, and projects are regarded by the various people concerned—commonly in accord with *their* professions, offices, temperaments, personal histories, and/or subject-positions—as intrusive, oppressive, dangerous, uninformed, self-interested, harebrained, prohibitively costly, unnecessary, or uninteresting. How shall we understand this and what, then, should we do?

I do not think that we should understand the differences of our views and their views as reflections of our enlightenment and their benightedness. Rather, as just described, I think we should understand those differences as products of our and their more or less different personal histories (familial, social, educational, and so on) and current positions in the relevant society. This means, among other things, that we would recognize that what *we* see as highly desirable change may not only *seem* but, indeed, *be* quite undesirable to some of them; for people usually want to retain what they experience as their current goods—advantages, privileges, satisfactions, and so on—unless they are persuaded that other goods would be secured by their yielding some of them. I also do not think that the chance of those other people coming to change their minds (and/or their practices) would be significantly increased if we argued the objective rightness of our critiques and projects and the objective falseness of their preferences and desires. Granted, however, that argument ("education," "persuasion") is an option at all, we might increase the chance of at least quite a few of them changing their minds, perhaps enough to effect the changes we see as desirable, if we indicated, as explicitly as necessary and as vividly as possible, the following:

1. the considerations that produced our own judgments (for example, evidence of the undesirable operation of present practices and descriptions of the probable outcomes of the proposed changes);
2. the relevance of our analyses to their experiences (for why should we think *their* experiences less pertinent than *ours* to the undesirable operation of those social structures?); and

3. the desirability of the proposed changes in relation to their interests and projects.

By indicating these matters, we might alter the meaning of many of those people's experiences for them and introduce a new set of desires into their desires. We might, in other words, change their "felt experiences and desires" in a direction that we think is preferable; and we will have done so without having "run roughshod" over those experiences, desires, or people in the process. Moreover, precisely because we do not posit the objective truth of our knowledge and the objective falseness of their consciousness, we might, in the same process, discover something about *their* experiences and desires that made us change *our* analyses and proposals.

This way of understanding and affecting people's politically significant beliefs and preferences is, I think, both pragmatic and ethical, and thus escapes West's dilemma. It is, however, a method for handling differences of belief only where, as in the case of West's perplexed feminist legislator, one already has substantial authority and argument is an option. Under other conditions, other approaches would be required. When, for example, a child's safety or health is at stake but efforts at verbal persuasion are ineffective (or, as with very young children, not an option), one might very well act contrary to the other party's apparent preferences or attempt to change his or her practices by direct, even coercive, intervention. The question for ethically responsible actors in these and comparable situations of asymmetrical power relations but (presumably) benevolent intent (for example, doctors dealing with patients, or well-educated, socially established feminists dealing with other relatively uneducated, socially subordinated women) is whether it is *quite clear* that the other party is incapable of appropriate judgment on his or her own behalf.

Other sets of conditions, often vividly evoked in these debates, involve individuals or groups suffering peril or injustice that is nevertheless sanctioned, legally or otherwise, by some part of the local community: for example, the practice of cliteridectomy or the criminalization of homosexual acts. The idea is that, under such conditions, only an appeal to a *higher* normative authority, and thus, it is claimed, a transcendentally objective authority, can effectively thwart the peril or end the injustice—and, therefore, that the anti-foundationalist or non-objectivist is, in such cases, either useless or a positive impediment. There are several arguments to be made here. First, there is no reason other than objectivist presumption to translate "higher" or trans-local into transcendentally objective: appeals to more general goods and/or to the norms of broader relevant communities would meet that criterion just as well. Second, past and recent history indicates that the political/pragmatic effectiveness of specifically transcendental appeals can hardly be counted on. Third, nothing in a non-objectivist's intellectual commitments obliges her to contemplate such conditions of peril or injustice passively. To be sure, what she will *do* about them—in default of issuing resounding condemnations on putatively objective grounds— cannot be described in general terms. That is because her specific actions will depend on the specific conditions that obtain: the nature and extent of her relation to the individuals or groups involved (whether, for example, they are members of her immediate community or relatively remote), the opportunities for effective response presented by her own circumstances and resources (whether, for example, she already has normative authority in the relevant community or must first acquire it), and so forth. In all these respects, however, the non-objectivist is like any other social-political agent, including her objectivist critic.

Although the non-objectivist's skepticism regarding ideas such as objectively false (or objectively authentic) desires and beliefs may distinguish some of the strategies she pursues, they do not distinguish her general *motives* for social action or, in relation to particular political/ethical issues, the particular *stances* she takes. If, for example, a danger or wrong appears substantial to her, then the non-objectivist might seek, alone or in concert with other people, to limit the other fellow's ability to act on his desires and preferences: perhaps by having him fined or imprisoned, perhaps by voting him out of office, perhaps by taking up arms against him. These last options indicate the ways in which a non-objectivist, like anyone else *and* altogether self-consistently, could operate politically against, say, rapists or Nazis. For, of course, one need not find someone else's desires and beliefs objectively false in order to find them—or the actions in which they issue—decisively undesirable.[15]

The Un/Quiet Judge

I turn now to the specifically legal implications of the current controversy over objectivism. According to West, when non-objectivist views are put into practice in law, they necessarily yield quietistic judges. Given her tests for "quietism" and how she implicitly defines the term—that is, as a rejection of objectivist dualisms and a consequent disinclination (or, in West's view, inability) to invoke objectivist justifications for one's actions and judgments—this may very well be true. But then the question is whether we, or the members of any community, would really want any *other* kind of judge.

We may note, first, certain significant characteristics of non-objectivist judges per se. One is that because, by definition, they believe that every evaluation is a judgment call "all the way down," such judges must take individual responsibility for their rulings. That is, they must be accountable for the particular contexts, perspectives, and considerations in relation to which their rulings are made.[16] This does not mean that all such considerations must be (or, in fact, could be) explicitly described. What it does mean is that, for the non-objectivist judge, a challenge to any of these cannot be complacently deflected by the claim that his or her ruling was generated by pure deduction from objective principles grounded in nature, history, scientific fact, scripture, or revelation. Non-objectivist judges cannot insist that their own perspectives, as shaped by their experiences, assumptions, values, and goals, had nothing to do with their rulings. Nor can they insist that the particular contexts—venues, societies, cultures, historical moments, and so forth—in which their rulings were framed had no effect on those rulings. Non-objectivist judges need not and, if they are self-consistent, will not deny the operation and possibly significant effect of all these factors in shaping the rulings they issue. Objectivist judges, however, do deny them: indeed, it is precisely the denial of the operation of such contingent factors, precisely the claim of that transcendence, that defines a judge—or judgment, or justification—as objectivist.

As indicated in the earlier discussion of rhetoric, non-objectivist judges have extensive and effective explanatory and justifactory resources at their disposal. Contrary to the common charge or fear, then, neither the authority nor the persuasiveness of a non-objectivist judge's rulings would be hobbled by the fact that, in justifying them, she did not invoke any "objective grounds" but only indicated the various conditional considerations that went into their making: what she figured, for example, as the relevant stakes, possible alternatives, and probable outcomes; or how she weighed and weighted such matters in the light of historical evidence and judicial precedent (as she interprets them), broader communal interests and communal goals, and her own general values, beliefs, and prior experiences. Indeed, just such figurings, weighings, and weightings of relevant considerations are, I think, just what people usually mean by "having good reasons" for a judgment—unless, of course, they have been persuaded that the only reasons that count as "good" ones are those that are certifiably deduced by pure reason from universally valid, transcendentally necessary principles. In the latter case, however, one must wonder whether those so persuaded have ever actually *heard* a "good reason" for a judgment—and, conversely, whether the major effect of the insistence on such criteria has not been simply to sustain the conviction of the necessity of a certain objectivist *rhetoric*.

None of this is to say that the rulings made by non-objectivist judges will always be the best ones possible—or even good ones—from the perspective of all concerned. There is, moreover, no way to guarantee either that such a judge will always estimate the relevant stakes or outcomes accurately or that the judicial consequences of his or her particular interpretations, general values, or prior experiences will turn out to be beneficent, in the long run, for the community at large. But these uncertainties apply equally well to the rulings of a judge making objectivist claims, rulings that, however much he or she would deny it, are as contingent in their production and operations as those of any other judge.

There is, I believe, no method that can automatically generate good legal judgments. There is also none, I believe, that can guarantee the wisdom and responsiveness of judges and legislators. We—those of us who care about such matters—can only attempt to enhance the conditions that make it more likely that our judges and legislators will be informed and responsive, and that the laws and rulings they produce will be good for us and for the community at large. And we can do that only by continually monitoring and evaluating the effectiveness of the relevant institutional structures, processes, and practices—that is, traditions of legal training, routes of professional certification, laws governing law-making, and the discourses that sustain all these, from canonical judicial opinions to prevailing philosophical theories of judgment and justification—and by striving to modify them accordingly. It is important, I think, to recognize the *political* significance of such everyday critical (precisely) practices in the legal profession—and of corresponding forms of criticism and activism in other professions, disciplines, and institutional domains.

We may, then, take a final look at West's effort to link non-objectivism with legal quietism and de facto political conservatism. Toward the end of her article, West invokes another supposed dilemma—what she describes as the "difficult bind" of non-objectivist judges when faced with "hard cases," that is, cases where the law is ambiguous. Since, she argues, such judges by definition cannot appeal to an "objective moral reality," then the justification for their decisions can rest only on the evident interests and preferences of the parties or communities involved.[17] And, she concludes, in basing his decisions on what is "present" or "given," the non-objectivist judge is "by necessity" culpably quietistic. Two key passages in this argument read as follows:

> The interests, preferences, and "economies" of the interested parties *must* be taken as given if they are to be authoritative. Thus, for relativism to fulfill its function—to be of "use" to the non-objectivist adjudicator—it *must* be quietistic . . . (1499)
>
> The judge has some measure of power, which presumably ought to be put toward the end of justice. Satisfaction of the present interests, preferences, and projects of the relevant communities may indeed provide the best measure of justice, but they may very well not. Where they do not, the judge who abdicates to "interest" . . . is sacrificing justice for efficiency. (1500)

As I think is clear, important issues are obscured here by tendentious language. For what West calls "justice," and opposes to "economies," "interest," and "efficiency," could also be described as different social and political arrangements that some, but evidently not all, members of the community desire. Accordingly, it could be said that what West would apparently prefer to the present judicial ethos is one in which justice would be sacrificed to the promotion of particular, partisan ends. This is, of course, exactly the charge made by conservatives against what West would presumably regard as properly activist, progressive judicial rulings. Indeed, some political activists and perhaps West herself, thinking only of the social changes that feminist and other progressive judges might wish to promote, might defend the latter sacrifice as a desirable tradeoff: a matter, they might argue, of certain (merely bourgeois, perhaps) ideas of justice given up in exchange for the objectively desirable empowerment of certain social groups. The only trouble—but it is, I think, a decisive one—is that there is no way to define that sacrifice or tradeoff so as to restrict its performance to *only* properly progressive judges and the service of *only* properly progressive changes. Once again, the recognition or denial of symmetry seems to be a key issue, and its significance here can hardly be overestimated.

My intention, as I trust is clear, is not to endorse a conservative perspective on judicial activism but to highlight one of the most venerable and celebrated principles of natural law, symmetry, and, perhaps, social justice, namely, *what's sauce for the goose is sauce for the gander.* For there are, of course, judges who are firmly persuaded, on what they sincerely believe to be objective moral grounds, that the personal preferences, felt desires, and given interests of gay men, lesbian mothers, and women contemplating abortion are objectively false, generated and fostered (such judges might say) by the objectively immoral beliefs and practices of a secular, permissive society. Moreover, a number of those objectivist judges seem prepared to use their "measure of power" accordingly—and as aggressively as the current judicial ethos allows.

According to West, if a judge believes that the felt desires and preferences, and given interests, of the parties (or communities) involved in a case were generated by objectively wrong social structures, then it is an abdication of office for that judge not to . . . *do what?* She does not say. That is, West gives no indication of the appropriate *specific* conduct of an unquietistic judge, either when confronting hard cases or otherwise. I can think of three possibilities. First, such a judge could just rule contrary to the professed desires and preferences of the parties involved. Second, he could rule in accord with those desires and preferences but express his views of their social pathology in his formal opinion. Third, he could rule in accord with those preferences and desires but otherwise work actively to change the social structures he believed engendered them.

The first possibility, being the most aggressive, is presumably the least quietistic. But, as a feminist, West could hardly argue that its pursuit would always be desirable. In a custody battle between a lesbian mother and her former husband, for example, such judicial activism could be exemplified by a judge who, appealing to "an objective moral reality," overrode the felt desire of the child to live with her mother and the woman's felt preference for a lesbian relationship.[18] Of course, West may have had in mind other sorts of cases. She could have been thinking, for example, of *EEOC v. Sears,* where the charge was sexual discrimination in employment practices and where the defense argued that women generally, and thus presumptively those applying for jobs at Sears, preferred less demanding (though also lower-paying) positions.[19] If so, West might see this as a case where the judge should have recognized the objective falseness of the felt preferences of one of the parties (here, the women applicants) and ruled accordingly (here, against Sears). That, however, is not the only option and, in my view, not the best option from a feminist or progressive perspective.[20] For, in cases like *EEOC v. Sears,* legal briefs and judicial rulings can appeal to such strictly non-objectivist points and arguments as (a) that people's preferences are usually a function of, among other things, their perception of the range of their available choices, and (b) that the nature of individual preferences cannot be securely predicted on the basis of gender identity alone and therefore should not be routinely presumed on that basis.[21] To the extent that lawyers and judges appeal to these and similar non-objectivist arguments, they reinforce the power of such arguments to operate as judicial principles in the future and simultaneously discourage the sort of objectivist claims and arrogant—and, in my view, unjust—rulings illustrated by the child-custody case.

As for the other two possibilities for unquietistic judging (that is, either registering social criticism in judicial opinions or working for social change through other political channels), both of them seem to be realized recurrently, for better and for worse ("social change" can also be regressive), in the activities of numerous judges in the present legal community—a community, we recall, that West characterizes as thoroughly and necessarily quietistic. There are certainly reasons to think that socially progressive views should be found more widely than they now are among lawyers, judges, and legal scholars. There is, however, no reason to think that the legal community's traditional and continuing political conservatism is a product of the quietism allegedly entailed by its alleged relativism or, conversely, that its politics would be one whit more progressive were its epistemology or moral theory more objectivist.

Projects and Praxis

Is this conclusion pessimistic? I do not think so. To be sure, the preceding account of non-objectivist judicial and political agency does not map any grand avenues to political reform and social justice; nor does it end with a call for or promise of their ultimate achievement. I would say, however, that such mappings, calls, and promises are not, in any case, what is wanted.

West's own conclusion is pertinent here. Turning from specific political concerns to the need, in the legal community, for a general *ethical* project, she writes:

> [W]e need to focus more attention on . . . [the] question: How should we act? Within the legal context, this means that we need a conception of virtue that can guide legislative, judicial, and adversarial *action* . . . If it is possible to meet the challenge—to adjudicate . . . fairly . . .—it is possible because particular individuals possess and exhibit the requisite strengths of character. Thus, it is virtue, not legal process, and not moral philosophy, . . . that makes possible good judging. It is of what that virtue might consist, and what those strengths of character might be, which constitutes the unaddressed agenda of this post-realist and post-critical era in legal scholarship. (1501–1502, my emphasis)

Having begun by calling for a form of "objectivist evaluative reasoning" that she evidently hoped would yield only progressive *judgments*, West ends by calling for a catalogue of personal virtues that she evidently hopes will yield only progressive *judges*.

The ethicist turn here, however, moves West no closer to her own apparent goals. On the contrary, the new agenda only perpetuates, in a different sphere, the classic difficulties of all such axiological projects: that is, the suppression of crucial but contingent variables, the tacit privileging of particular, contestable perspectives, and the circular operation of prior, unacknowledged norms. These difficulties are exhibited in West's wrap-up list of the characteristic virtues of the "ideal judge," a series that includes "a commitment to justice and the social good" and "a heightened sensitivity to the plight of others, particularly the silenced, the outsider, and the subordinate" (1502).[22] Such a commitment is no doubt a fundamental desideratum in any judge, and I would agree that such a heightened sensitivity (or should we not say *bias?*) would be a desirable quality in at least a good many judges. The possession of such virtues, however, would still leave indeterminate how a judge would decide, in particular cases, *what* "the social good" was and, often enough, which parties *were* the "subordinate" ones. That is, West's list, even if many more virtues were added, would still leave the specific determination of justice contingent and contestable—as, I have suggested here, *any* general judicial principle must.

Like many other legal and moral theorists and also like the classic axiologists, West seeks a principle that would guarantee the production and identification of only good judgments: that is, of only those judgments that she (and some set of other) people believe(s) are good or, as she (and they) might put it, only objectively good ones. That goal, the discovery of such a general principle, though classic, is, I believe, chimerical. It is chimerical because the idea of objectively good judgments, as distinct from judgments that are good under certain (perhaps quite broad ranges of) conditions and from the perspectives of certain (perhaps highly relevant sets of) people, appears fundamentally untenable. It follows that, no matter what principles we erect or invoke, whether epistemological, ethical, or procedural, "the best judgments" will still always be contingent in their production and operation, and also only contingently and contestably identifiable as "the best." As I have sought to argue, however, the alternative to the dream of objective judgment is not pessimism, cynicism, or torpor but attentiveness, responsiveness, and activity, both intellectual and pragmatic. Since no axiom can generate our judgments and no principle can secure their objective goodness, we must continuously figure and work them out ourselves, making them as good and justifying them as well—all things considered—as we can.

2

Making (Up) the Truth: Constructivist Contributions

There is, it appears, the appearance of truth—"verisimilitude"—and, over and against that, the reality of truth, truth itself. Or so it appears, but perhaps it is not true, or not any longer. Certainly, the certification of truth and knowledge in their classic senses—as, for example, the accurate affirmation or faithful representation of an altogether autonomous reality—has proved elusive. Meanwhile, alternative conceptions of truth and knowledge—as, for example, the relatively coherent, relatively reliable, and relatively stable products of various social, discursive, and institutional practices—have been proposed in recent years, and have proved relatively coherent, reliable, and stable. These alternative conceptions have emerged from a number of fields: philosophy, of course, especially along lines marked by Nietzsche and Wittgenstein, but also other fields, such as biology and psychology, which have yielded important redescriptions of the interactive mechanisms of language, perception, and cognition, and, of particular interest here, the history and sociology of science, which, during the past two decades, have developed a pragmatist/rhetoricist approach to these questions often referred to as "constructivism".[1]

I shall not attempt to describe here the work of individual constructivists, nor will I be discussing in any detail their characteristic investigations, analyses, and arguments. I would note at the outset, however, the strong affinities and, in fact, extensive intellectual connections between the latter—that is, the analyses and arguments of constructivist theorists, if not the historical and sociological investigations themselves—and the critiques of traditional epistemology and language theory associated with deconstruction and poststructuralism. Indeed, it is often difficult to tell exactly which of these is intended by such descriptively vague though clearly adversarial terms as "postmodernism," "extreme relativism," and "fashionable irrationalism."[2] Adversarial matters shall be of further interest, below. First, however, we may consider the broader topic at hand.

Truth in Fiction

The paradoxical theme—"truth in fiction"—that occasions these reflections[3] evokes a number of related paradoxes of the literary and critical tradition: the "truer truth" that is told only, or best, in fiction; the poetry that, in being "the most feigning," is also the truest; the poet who, in not telling—or not offering to tell—the truth, cannot lie; and so forth. These puzzles are signs and reminders of the conceptual and verbal instabilities that attend—and, it seems, have always attended—the familiar distinctions on which they play: truth and fiction, being and pretending, telling and fabricating. They are also signs, I think, of the more fundamental instabilities and incoherences of the classic accounts of truth, knowledge, and language that generate such distinctions: the idea, for example, that certain discourses—notably those of history and, as we would say now, science—offer (at least ideally) direct, objective, and thus properly credible representations of an autonomous reality, or the corollary idea that such discourses are (at least ideally) quite distinct from such manifestly rhetorical and presumptively *non*-credible discourses as poetry and fiction. But, of course, the classic ideas (and ideals) of objective description and unmediated representation have become increasingly problematic, as have, with them, the corollary distinctions between rhetorical and non-rhetorical uses of language.[4]

I do not mean to rehearse here the history of twentieth-century thought or contemporary commonplaces on these topics. Indeed, the focus of my concern, below, will be certain practical, political, and what could be called "public-relations" problems that these developments seem to entail. Of considerable interest in relation to those problems, however, are recent constructivist studies of how the sense of truth is produced—that is, how verisimilitude and credibility are achieved and secured—in fields such as medicine, microbiology, and physics.[5] For example, in their engaging and illuminating study, *Leviathan and the Air-Pump*, Steven Shapin and Simon Schaffer describe the beginnings of modern empirical science and the related development of what they call "the technology of virtual witnessing." What they mean by this is an array of textual techniques—largely verbal but also iconographic, such as painstaking descriptions of experimental procedure or minutely detailed illustrations of experimental equipment, charts, diagrams, figures, and so on—aimed at "producing in a *reader's* mind ... such an image of an experimental scene as obviates the necessity for either direct witness or replication."[6] As Shapin and Schaffer observe, this textual technology, as developed and championed by Robert Boyle, endorsed by the "experimental philosophers" of the Royal Society, and institutionalized in the conventions of Western science-writing, has become one of the most powerful means for constituting scientific facts, all the more powerful because, by now, so thoroughly taken for granted. Other historians and sociologists of science have described the development and institutional transmission of related truth-making techniques, such as the precise reporting of precise measurements, the extensive certification of the authority of the authorities cited, the eradication of all signs of the investigator's personal characteristics, individual perspective, specifically professional interests, and so forth.[7] As this list suggests, the scientific truth-teller produced and simultaneously effaced by such textual technologies is cousin to the "reliable narrator" of prose fiction: that is, the self-effacing witness whose fictive "telling" is ideally experienced by the reader as a transparent "showing."[8]

The rhetorical techniques through which modern disciplinary science constitutes facts and stabilizes knowledge are not, of course, altogether the same as those by which the truth is forged (in both senses—or maybe it's only one sense) in literary fictions. Nor do their shared techniques serve altogether the same ends. Science-writing, for example, characteristically strives to eliminate or obscure not only all flagrantly subjective features but also any features that would foreground what is called, in literary studies, the "materiality" of the text (e.g., homonyms, rhyme, assonance, alliteration, and so forth). Conversely, verisimilitude in literary fiction is characteristically incidental to the production of other effects, such as imaginative interest, emotional excitement, moral inspiration, and psychological insight. Nevertheless, the overlap between the two is substantial and reminds us that, while it is not true that all truth-making is *simply* truth-making-up, it is true that the conditions that make truth-effects possible are also the conditions of possibility for fiction and lying.

Any act that can be performed at all—done, we might say, straightforwardly and sincerely—can also be "performed" fictively: mimetically, for example, or duplicitously or in jest. Any motive that can be expressed at all can also be "expressively" simulated or dissimulated. And any verbal sign, no matter what the conditions under which it is normatively ("conventionally," "properly," "truth-fully") produced, can be produced under virtually any conditions. Indeed, common conceptions of linguistic sincerity and propriety, whether these are seen as normal and ordinary or as ideal but necessarily presupposed, have been revealed by contemporary analyses of language as deeply problematic.[9] It is clear, in any case, that the techniques of truth-making documented by historians and sociologists of science are also available to—and, for better or worse, characteristically honed and cultivated by—novelists, playwrights, publicists, propagandists, salesmen, lawyers, and candidates for public office. Plato could suggest barring poets from a well-ordered state, but, as he no doubt recognized, one could not bar the possibility of their *emergence* without also barring law, government, science, philosophy, and, indeed, all discourse.

Truth in Question

I turn now to the adversarial issues mentioned above. The achievements of the constructivist project in the history and sociology of science have proved exceptionally interesting and relatively widely appropriable. But the very interest and appeal of its accounts of knowledge-production and the very force of its critiques of classic conceptions of truth—along with those developed in related critical projects, including deconstruction—have seemed to entail certain alarming practical and political consequences: *seemed* to, but perhaps have not truly done so.

The sense of alarm here is registered across—or certainly at both ends of—the political spectrum. On the right, for example, neo-conservative historian Gertrude Himmelfarb sees in these developments an irresponsible abandonment of traditional ideas and ideals of historical fact and evidence, and, thereby, a threat not only to the established practices of historiography but to "society and the polity" more generally.[10] Himmelfarb's book is dedicated, she writes, "to the proposition that there are such things as truth and reality and that there is a connection between them."[11] On the left, Marxist critics Terry Eagleton and Christopher Norris, among others, see these accounts and critiques (or, again, "abandonments") as contributing to the entrenchment of established political authority. Thus Eagleton writes of "the postmodern or poststructuralist concern to place the skids under truth" as "complicit[ous] with certain of the less palatable realities of late bourgeois society" and warns that "those who have developed the nervous tic of placing . . . 'truth' and 'fact' in fastidiously distancing scare quotes should be careful to avoid a certain collusion between their own high-toned theoretical gestures and the . . . strategies of the capitalist power-structure."[12] Norris, in a similar vein, laments: "There are few things more depressing on the current intellectual scene than this collapse of moral and political nerve brought about—or at any rate deeply influenced—by various forms of postmodern-pragmatist thought. For the result of such ideas is firstly to undermine any sense of the epistemological distinction between truth and falsehood, and secondly to place ethical issues beyond reach of argued responsible debate."[13]

The problem for a political and academic conservative such as Himmelfarb is that contemporary reconceptions of classic ideas of truth and knowledge effectively challenge the authority of traditional explanations of and justifications for existing social and political arrangements as well as traditional notions of proper historiographic method.[14] The problem for academics and critics on the left is that it cuts both ways: that is, the analyses in question create difficulties for *all* claims of absolute or objective epistemic authority, including those traditionally and currently mounted from the left. This perplexity, which recalls the problems of epistemic symmetry and asymmetry examined in Chapter 1, is reflected not only in the passages from Eagleton and Norris quoted above but also in controversies among intellectuals on the left that have been repeated, during the past ten or fifteen years, in virtually the same terms in virtually every quarter of the academic world. On the one hand, analyses of the social and political operations of claims to truth and knowledge are welcomed as politically significant developments, valuable in destabilizing the authority of established (imperialist, patriarchal, etc.) narratives and justifications. As becomes evident, however, many of the left's own established narratives and justifications cannot be protected from a certain amount of disturbing destabilization along the same lines. Thus, analyses such as Foucault's that were once (or in some quarters of the academy) celebrated as politically revolutionary are now (or in other quarters) denounced as politically complicitous; or conceptually strained efforts are made to appropriate the *politically* radical ("critical") force of those analyses while their more general *intellectually* radical implications are rejected, ignored, or equivocated.[15]

There is an alternative, of course, to denunciation and politically selective appropriation, namely, the development of different, and different *kinds* of, narratives and justifications, including less Manichaean accounts of Left and Right and more conceptually subtle and historically responsive analyses of political dynamics more generally. Efforts along such lines are currently pursued by (some) feminist scholars and other evidently progressive-minded social and political theorists, who, however, are not always thanked for their pains (their task is not, of course, an easy one).[16] On the contrary, precisely to the extent that the formulations they develop are genuinely different, that is, do not seek to obliterate or finesse the conceptual problems of classic ideas of *truth, knowledge, objectivity, reason,* or *reality* and, for that very reason, cannot be readily incorporated or translated back into standard scripts and stories, they are likely to be regarded as, at best, politically irrelevant ("too theoretical") or, once again, as "complicitous."

The charges of moral irresponsibility or political collusion in the passages by Himmelfarb, Eagleton, and Norris quoted above are, to my mind, clearly tendentious, but they draw on general anxieties that have considerable currency in the academic community. These anxieties were voiced with special edge in the early 1990s in connection with a rash of advertisements in college newspapers in the

United States declaring the Nazi Holocaust a hoax. Don't such events, it was asked, embarrass constructivist (or, as it was commonly put, "postmodernist" or "relativist") accounts of truth? And, conversely, it was (and continues to be) said, doesn't the very possibility of such events indicate the need to affirm traditional distinctions between objective science and mere propaganda, historical facts and mere ideology, and, accordingly, the need to defend orthodox epistemology?

I am sympathetic to the anxieties that produce such questions (some of them, anyway), but my answer to the questions themselves would be negative: no, these events do not cause such embarrassment; no, these possibilities do not indicate such necessity. This is not to deny the political and ethical significance of official public deceptions or obsessive—and sometimes eagerly accepted—denials of historical crimes. That significance, however, does not eradicate the conceptual instabilities of the traditional distinctions, or the practical problems of the rhetorical limits of objectivist truth-claims, or the ethical problems of *their* ambiguous moral, social, and political operations. Indeed, it is precisely because of the fundamental nature of those instabilities and the intractability of just those problems—practical and ethical, it must always be stressed, as well as conceptual—that critiques of traditional epistemologies have recurrently been pressed and that *alternative* accounts of truth and knowledge have been developed and, where they seemed more conceptually, practically, and ethically workable, appropriated.

Clearly, I think, a rehabilitation of orthodox epistemology *per se* would not erase the possibility of government deceptions, media distortions, or declarations that the Holocaust never happened. Nor, though the point is evidently not as clear, would such a rehabilitation dissolve the credibility of those deceptions, distortions, and declarations for some members of their public audiences. For, contrary to now commonplace allegations, it was not the questioning or rejection of classical epistemology or the development of constructivist accounts of truth and knowledge that made those deceptions and distortions credible in the first place—or any of the other deceptions, distortions, and false declarations that have gushed forth from on high and down low in previous decades, centuries, and millennia, and that were evidently found credible enough at the time without the assistance of "postmodernism." The resounding reaffirmation of an absolute distinction between truth and rhetoric, fact and fiction, science and superstition, will not in itself do the crucial substantive, technical, and often arduous *work* of effectively differentiating among specific competing, conflicting, claims of truth or between mutual charges of falsehood. Nor will a general affirmation of the inestimable value, irrefutable possibility, and transcendent ideality of genuine objectivity identify where, in any particular instance, objectivity lies—or (the pun is apt enough) "lies." Indeed, since it remains the case, even under the regime of traditional epistemologies, that any act can be performed deceptively, any motive dissimulated, and any verbal sign produced under virtually any conditions, the strenuous *claim* of truth can always be enlisted to serve thoroughly ideological and otherwise dubious purposes—as, of course, it has been often enough in the past.

Among the contemporary theorists censured by Norris in the terms indicated above is Jean-François Lyotard, who, in his book, *The Differend*, analyzes the grotesque argument by French historian, Robert Faurrison, that, since he could not locate any eye-witnesses to the gas-chambers among Jews, the Holocaust must not have occurred.[17] Acknowledging ("to be fair") Lyotard's identification of a difficult ("sensitive") case, but failing to grasp the point of his analysis, Norris rehearses his usual charges: "But his position makes it difficult for Lyotard to denounce this imposture as a downright lie, a massive falsification of the truth whose political motives are evident enough, and which could only win credence by playing upon the ignorance, stupidity or malice of a like-minded readership."[18] It would be more accurate to say, however, that Lyotard's analysis of the *conditions* of both that massive falsification and its credibility for that readership (to whom those political motives were evidently not "evident enough," or were perfectly acceptable as such) might make it difficult for *anyone* to imagine that a denunciation of that "downright" kind would, under those circumstances, be worth much of itself.

One of Lyotard's points, developed throughout his book, is that, in addition to the profound injuries and injustices suffered currently and historically by persons and groups such as Jews, slaves, political dissidents, and colonial subjects, they suffer(ed) the further injustice of being deprived of effective speech in the relevant tribunals, either because they are or were literally silenced or because the authority of their testimony is or was discounted and the legitimacy of their protests denied. This particular type of injustice, Lyotard argues, is made possible by the inevitable but often invisible social-political operations of all language, which, accordingly, it is the responsibility of contemporary (one could say post-Holocaust and post-colonial) theory to delineate.

It is with reference to these arguments, among others, that Norris charges postmodernism with "undermin[ing] any sense of the epistemological distinction between truth and falsehood, and . . . plac[ing] ethical issues beyond reach of argued responsible debate."[19] Here as elsewhere, Norris casts contemporary theory as the morally culpable *agent* of the conceptual, ethical, and practical perplexities that it seeks (often enough, as in Lyotard's book, in response to an evident sense of moral summons) to *expose* and *illuminate*.[20] The sort of discursive breakdown that concerns Lyotard is illustrated well enough by Norris's own failed engagement with just that point. According to Norris, Lyotard's claims regarding the limited force and scope of logical and discursive norms (or, in Norris's terms, of "argued responsible debate") follow only "if we accept Lyotard's major premise, namely that the various speech-act 'genres' . . . are so radically heterogeneous that their truth-claims exist in a state of perpetual conflict." He continues: "What [Lyotard] thus fails to recognize—for reasons bound up with his doctrinaire postmodernist stance—is the fact that in the great majority of cases there is no such conflict between truth-telling motives . . . on the one hand and issues of ethical accountability on the other."[21] Perhaps in most cases the conflicts—or differences[22]—of genres, idioms, motives, assumptions, and so on are not especially significant for any of the parties involved. Lyotard, however, is concerned with just those cases where they *are*. If, as Norris claims, it is Lyotard's "doctrinaire postmodernist stance" that keeps him from recognizing the many cases where breakdown does *not* occur, then what is it that keeps Norris from recognizing (or acknowledging) the significance of the cases where it *does*?[23]

Constructing Knowledge

Contrary to recurrent misapprehension and a certain amount of determined misrepresentation, constructivist accounts of the production and stabilization of belief do not maintain or imply that truth is the prize of political power or just what's handy for someone to believe. Nor do they conflate historiography, science, and philosophy with fiction. Nor do they reduce reality to language or equate knowledge with majority opinion. These supposed positions or implications are familiar. As I have sought to suggest, however, they are generated not by constructivist (or pragmatist or anti-foundationalist) accounts themselves but by the failure of critics leveling such charges to engage those ideas and accounts accurately or adequately—a failure fairly guaranteed, it seems, by those critics' prior and continued conviction of the undeniability, transparency, necessity, and unique propriety of the classical ideas at issue. Thus, indications of complex relationships are seen as erasures of otherwise clear distinctions; questionings of familiar conceptualizations are seen as abandonments of autonomous entities; efforts to illuminate difficulties are seen as creating them; and acknowledgments of the existence and operation of differences that are otherwise forgotten, suppressed, or denied are seen as celebrations of discord or delight in chaos.[24] I have examined the self-affirming logic and self-scandalizing effects of these recurrent charges elsewhere and return to them in other chapters of this book.[25] What I wish to stress here, however, is that, contrary to the suppositions and anxieties noted earlier, constructivist accounts of truth and knowledge are neither discredited by, nor *useless* with respect to, determined official deceptions or challenges to the authority of established historical fact—and, indeed, that such accounts indicate which ways are likely to be most effective in responding to such events and possibilities.

Indicate which ways are likely to be most effective, not provide failsafe shields or infallible weapons. An important consequence of current critiques of traditional epistemology is the understanding that no general, all-purpose epistemic methods are available: no touchstones of truth, no automatic refutations of error, no ready-made exposures of deception. By the same token, however, the idea of the contingency of truth, in the sense of its irreducible *conditionality,* reminds us of what all professional publicists know, namely, that the kinds of response that will be most effective in any particular instance will depend on, precisely, the particular *conditions* that obtain, including the rhetorical platforms involved, the prior assumptions, interests, and investments of the relevant audiences, and the credibility of the contending parties; that is, the epistemic authority of the agents of the deception (or distortion) and, not to be forgotten, that of the would-be refuters themselves.

In the case of denials of the Holocaust, it is clear that the vigorous assignment of labels (or their simple mirror-reversal)—"*this* genuine history versus *that* mere propaganda," "no, *these* objective facts versus *those* barefaced lies"—would not in itself cancel the credibility of those denials for certain audiences. It is also clear, I think, that staunch reaffirmations of the reality of Reality in the pages of *The Journal of Metaphysics, The New York Review of Books,* or *PMLA* would not prevent such denials from being issued, or cancel their credibility for *some* audiences. (To be sure, as Norris proclaims, denials such as Faurrison's "only win credence by playing upon the ignorance, stupidity or malice of a like-minded readership." The "downright lie" denunciation he urges as the proper response, however, does not in itself remedy that ignorance or stupidity, or neutralize that malice.) To the surprise and distress of many American college professors, those gullible audiences included a number of their own students, some of whom had evidently not come to know, either through family remembrance, formal schooling, or otherwise, what no one, of course, was ever born knowing, but who had, perhaps, been only too well-schooled, through more diffuse channels and informal instruction, in a quite different "common knowledge."[26]

What *can* counter the credibility of denials of the Holocaust for those students (and the credibility for other audiences of other floutings of what we know or believe to be historical or scientific fact) are other sorts of responses. These responses, like strenuous insistences on the factuality of the facts or passionate denunciations of the falsehood of the lies, are also "rhetorical," but less *simply* enunciatory and rather more arduous. I speak here of such counteractivities as the gathering, analysis, labeling, and public exhibition of original documents and photographs, the development and public dissemination of vivid narratives incorporating exact descriptions of circumstantial details, and the identification, citation, and credentialing of survivors and other participants: the production, in effect, of a sense of "virtual witnessing," the *construction,* in short, of *knowledge* . . . to which must be added, as the inevitable and necessary other side of this process, the deconstruction of *other* presumed knowledge.

For reasons already indicated here, such efforts are not guaranteed to turn the trick in all instances, that is, expose the deception decisively or dissolve the credibility of the denial for all audiences: certainly not where an audience is deeply instructed and strongly invested in contrary beliefs, and sometimes not within the time or with the sorts of technical and other resources immediately available. (These are, of course, just the sorts of circumstances examined by Lyotard. Nothing that is said here or, I believe, anywhere else can eliminate the *possibility* of the difficulties he delineates. Nor do I see any wisdom or virtue in either denying that possibility or minimizing those difficulties.) If, however, one's goal *is* constructing knowledge and not just registering publicly the strength of one's own convictions, then such efforts—including, as required, the pursuit of further resources—are necessary. They are necessary not because postmodern theorists put *truth, fact,* and *history* in quotation marks or because sophomoric egalitarians announce that all opinions are equally valid, but because the affirmation of and appeal to truth, fact, and history cannot and never did, *in themselves,* turn that kind of trick.[27]

Another point must be stressed here. It sometimes happens that the sorts of knowledge-constructing or belief-securing efforts just described are ineffective because, after further investigation, it turns out that the historical documents, experimental findings, and certified authorities are less substantial, more ambiguous, or more compromised than we had previously supposed. To assert that symmetrical possibility, however, is only to acknowledge that "we"—whoever we are (and who *are* we here?)—are not necessarily always already in the right. Moreover, on other occasions, the *ineffectiveness* of just such efforts to shore up credibility may be just what we are counting on. For, of course, it is sometimes *we ourselves* who are in the position of denying prevailing belief or of challenging (alleged) "historical truth" or (supposed) "scientific fact." We cannot always—or on principle, so to speak—want *all* such denials or challenges to fail.

This possibility of "critical" challenge or protest is, of course, just what constructivism has allegedly put at risk. Challenge and protest, however, are no less likely or less effective when pursued under the regime of "postmodern" thought than under that of traditional epistemology. To be sure, there can be, from a constructivist perspective, no prior presumption of epistemic privilege on the part of any particular set of challengers: no assumption of inherent truth- or lie-detecting powers (or dependable truth- or lie-declaring inclinations) on the part of any persons or groups by virtue of their personal or professional identity cards; no equation of truth with credibility, nor of sincere educational motives with adequate rhetorical means. Rather, it is understood that everyone—war protester as well as warmonger, ideology critic as well as propagandist, feminist as well as male supremacist, and, yes, Holocaust-documenter as well as Holocaust-denier—is obliged to *produce,* for each audience, the credibility of his or her challenge, the truth of his or her counter-claim. This seems, however, always to have been the case, under every epistemological regime.

Constructive Reflection

Experience indicates that a reflexive gesture is called for here.[28] Among the other projects implied by constructivist conceptions of science as truth-*making* and of knowledge as truth-*made* is the rhetorical project of its own self-credentialing or, as it might be seen, self-"verification." Consistent with their own arguments and analyses, constructivists cannot seek to accomplish this by citing brute facts, appealing to universal intuitions, or declaring the manifest illogicality of classic conceptualizations. The alternative conceptualizations (or, in the classic idiom, truths) of constructivism are not, by its own lights, ontologically prior, that is, already constituted (or, in that sense, already "made up"), waiting only to be discovered by the duly alert and acknowledged by the duly astute. Rather, like all other conceptualizations or truths, those of constructivism must themselves be constructed. Consistent with its own arguments and analyses, then, the strengthening of the credibility, stability, and epistemic authority of constructivism can be accomplished only through the sorts of rhetorical, pragmatic, social, technical, and institutional labors indicated above. What that would mean, in its own case, is extending constructivist analyses of knowledge to broader domains of pragmatic operation, forging conceptual links between constructivist accounts of truth-making and related accounts in other fields, and disseminating constructivist ideas and arguments to practitioners and theorists in other intellectual communities. These, among other things, are tasks I have undertaken in this chapter and more generally in this book. Accordingly, although my arguments here cannot and do not claim truth in a classic sense, they may and do seek to have epistemic value, otherwise measured.

3

Belief and Resistance: A Symmetrical Account

Queen: Alas, how is't with you,
That you do bend your eye on vacancy,
And with the'incorporal air do hold discourse?
. . . Whereon do you look?
Hamlet: On him, on him! Look you how pale he glares!
. . . Do you see nothing there?
Queen: Nothing at all; yet all that is I see.

Hamlet, Act III, scene iv

Questions of evidence—including the idea, still central to what could be called informal epistemology, that our beliefs and claims may be duly corrected by our encounters with autonomously resistant objects (for example, bricks, rocks, facts, and texts themselves)—are inevitably caught up in more general views of how beliefs are produced, maintained, and transformed.[1] In recent years, substantially new accounts of these cognitive dynamics—and, with them, more or less novel conceptions of what we might mean by "beliefs"—have been emerging from various non-philosophical fields (for example, theoretical biology, cognitive and developmental psychology, neuroscience, and the sociology of knowledge) as well as from disciplinary epistemology. Because of the distinctly reflexive nature of all these developments—that is, revised beliefs about belief, new conceptions of concepts, invocations of evidence in defense of particular ideas of evidence, and so forth—the framing of positions and deployment of arguments become especially difficult here, as does even the description of the relevant events in intellectual history. Indeed, since virtually every major term in these debates is potentially implicated in the general problematic itself, virtually any statement or move is open to questioning at the most

37

radical level. My aim in the present chapter is twofold: first, to
frame an account of belief that indicates the more general interest
and significance, beyond the fields in which they are being developed, of these emerging reconceptions of cognitive dynamics; and,
second, to suggest how such an account may illuminate these epistemological disputes themselves. Also, since such an account cannot
escape the logical/rhetorical difficulties just mentioned, part of my
procedure here will be to foreground them in the framing itself.

Beliefs in Collision

In the confrontation between belief and evidence, belief is no push-
over. And yet beliefs do change—evidently in response to, among
other things, evidence. Taken together, these two observations are
not controversial. The urging of one in opposition to the other,
however, together with different ways of explaining each, marks a
perennial debate pursued in our era as constructivist-interactionist
accounts of knowledge, scientific and other, versus more or less
traditional (rationalist/realist) epistemologies. The former stress
the apparent *participation* of prior belief in the perception of present
evidence, a phenomenon familiar in literary studies as the hermeneutic circle. The latter insist on the possibility of a *correction* of
prior belief by present evidence—or, one could say, of a rupture of
the hermeneutic circle by autonomous, observer-independent reality—and the normative occurrence of just such correction in (genuine) science.[2]
    The divergences here are not just matters of emphasis: the two
views, at least in the terms just outlined, appear mutually incompatible. Efforts at mediation have, however, been made: attempts
to narrow and bridge the differences, to modulate what are seen as
extreme formulations, or to combine what is seen as the best of
each side.[3] Two points central to both the present account and the
more general argument of this book may, accordingly, be stressed
here. One is that the intellectual success of any such mediating
position is no less liable to diverse assessment than the conflicting
positions themselves: that is, there is no obvious way to adjudicate
objectively (in the classic sense) among them, no evidence that
would demonstrate conclusively the correctness of just one of them,
no logical analysis that would expose, once and for all, the flaws,

failures, or fallacies at the heart of each of the others. It does not follow, however, that these efforts are futile or that the conflicting sides must remain forever constituted and divided exactly as before. For—and this is the second point to be noted—at the level of both individual cognitive activity and general intellectual history, the mutual abrasions of mutually resistant beliefs, in interaction with other events and contingently emergent conditions, may yield significant and relatively stable modifications of each and, thereby, significant and relatively stable *new* cognitive configurations and intellectual alignments. This recurrent possibility implies, among other things, that we may speak of conflicting and apparently incommensurable beliefs (theories, accounts, interpretations, and so on) as crucially and (from some perspectives) profitably *affecting* each other without having to maintain that one (and only one) of them must or could be, in the classic sense, correct.

Symmetrical Reflection

The preceding discussion is relatively even-handed, but my views on these issues are not neutral. On the whole, I find revisionist accounts of belief, along the lines indicated in this chapter, more conceptually congenial and otherwise serviceable than those offered in traditional realist/rationalist epistemologies. At the same time, however, and with no apparent undermining of my own relative cognitive stability, I believe that I believe those revisionist accounts (in the sense of "belief" outlined below) for the same general sorts of reasons and by way of the same general cognitive dynamics as anyone, including the believer in traditional epistemology, believes anything.[4]

Macrodynamics of Belief

The dynamics of belief may be described at two major levels of analysis. One is with respect to the formation, stabilization, destabilization, and transformation of the beliefs of individuals during their personal lifetimes, as commonly examined and theorized in cognitive psychology, disciplinary epistemology, and philosophy of mind. The other is with respect to the beliefs of populations of subjects over more extended periods of time, as described and analyzed in intellectual history and the history, philosophy, and sociology of science. I will begin here by considering the latter macrodynamics of belief, illustrating the points with changing beliefs *about* belief.

It appears that classic beliefs (in the sense of prevailing theories) about belief (in the sense of cognitive processes and products) are changing in the ways and for the reasons that most beliefs (scientific or philosophical, formal or informal, practical or political, and so on) change. Specifically, relatively novel beliefs, experienced as more conceptually congenial, pragmatically reliable, and otherwise serviceable than the ones they are replacing, are being articulated by and appropriated and disseminated among various groups of people. These relatively new beliefs are experienced as more conceptually congenial in relation to other relevant beliefs, both prior and recently emerging but, in the latter case, already relatively stable and reliable: for example, beliefs (or, as we sometimes say when they *are* relatively stable and reliable, "knowledge") about the structure and functions of the nervous system, the relations between cognition and language, and the historical and social operations of scientific practices. They are experienced as more practically reliable and otherwise serviceable in relation to a broad array of projects, both technical and conceptual: for example, efforts to diagnose perceptual/behavioral disorders in stroke patients, to construct working robots, and to understand how scientific controversies are settled. Among the people involved in these developments are some with considerable intellectual authority in the relevant domains and disciplines: for example, prize-winning theoretical biologists, esteemed neurophysiologists, accomplished computer engineers, and established historians and philosophers of science. It appears that these processes of articulation, dissemination, and appropriation are at a point where various sets of relatively new beliefs about belief have become fairly stable among substantial portions of the populations just mentioned and figure more and more extensively in their various projects.[5]

Of course, beliefs about belief are not changing everywhere or among all groups of people. There are numerous places where constructivist reconceptions of belief (cognition, thought, consciousness, memory, and so on), along with the conceptions they seek to replace, have little interest or significance. And there are certainly groups of people who experience these reconceptions as distinctly uncongenial and unserviceable: specifically, those who assess their conceptual coherence in relation to quite different arrays of prior beliefs (for example, patristic teachings on the freedom of the will, commonsense intuitions of personal agency, or formal philosophical analyses of the relation between reason and action), and those who assess their pragmatic serviceability in relation to quite different projects (for example, the furtherance of social justice for one or another group of people). My examples here are not random: they are intended to evoke some of the most strenuous or otherwise significant forms of resistance currently encountered by constructivist reconceptions of belief.[6] They are framed, however, so as to make it difficult to distinguish skeptics and believers, promoters and resisters—or the reasons for their respective reactions—as intellectually pathological versus wholesome, irresponsible versus responsible, or interested versus disinterested. At the same time, there is no suggestion here that all these positions or reasons are "equally valid." Indeed, given the present account of cognitive dynamics, it would be hard to imagine a perspective from which their validity, in the sense of epistemic value, could be assessed as equal, and, of course, impossible to imagine what epistemic value could mean independent of *any* perspective. Nevertheless, the various positions and reasons—pro and con, changing and resisting—are framed here as equally worthy of understanding and equally needful of explanation. They are framed, in short, symmetrically.

The preceding description of how and why beliefs about belief seem to be changing does not speak of enlightenment or progress. It evokes reasons (plural and heterogeneous), but not Reason, and, emphasizing *specific* disciplines and intellectual domains and the ongoing projects of *selected* academic (and other) populations, it does not speak of science or human knowledge in the abstract. It might be said that, in the absence of reference to reasoned choices, preferences for one belief over another are depicted here as ("merely") matters of taste. In a sense, that would be true. The "merely" would disappear, however, for tastes, understood as contingently shaped preferences, would not, in this account, be distinguished from and opposed to (the operation of) Reason(s) but would be, rather, a way of reconceptualizing the latter.[7]

Another symmetry becomes significant at this point. The reasons (as described above) why some people now prefer constructivist-interactionist conceptions of belief to more traditional conceptions are the same *general sorts* of reasons that people have had in the past for preferring conceptions, models, theories, or beliefs (about belief or anything else) that "turned out," as we say, to be *true*—or, at least, seem now to be conceptually stable, pragmatically reliable, and otherwise serviceable under a quite broad range of conditions. But they are also the same general sorts of reasons that people have had in the past for entertaining beliefs that turned out (some very quickly, others after some time) to be incompatible with other significant beliefs and/or inapplicable or unreliable under many important conditions—or, in that sense of the term, *false*. It might be thought that what makes the difference or breaks the symmetry here is, precisely, evidence: that is, the winnowing processes of "experimentation," "verification," "falsification," "trial and error," and so forth. And, in a way, that would be correct, or at least in accord with the present account. For all these can be seen as names for our *continuous more or less (in)formal or (un)controlled playing out of our beliefs under a variety of conditions and evaluating them accordingly.* There is an important difference, however, between those familiar conceptions of the adjudicative operations of evidence and the alternative account offered here. For what is displayed in that process of playing-out-and-evaluating is not, in this account, the truth or falseness that *was always there* in our beliefs (theories, models, etc.), but, rather, their truth/value under, and in relation to, those particular conditions, which is to say, their *contingent* truth/value. Since evolutionary models will be of interest later in this chapter and throughout this book, we might note that the distinctions here parallel those between popular and Darwinian understandings of biological "fitness." For a good many people, the fitness of an organism is understood as the intrinsic superiority of its traits as proved by its survival and flourishing over time. For most contemporary theoretical biologists, however, it is understood as the very fact—seen post hoc—of that organism's thriving, with whatever traits it happened to have, under the conditions that happened to occur.

It is instructive to recall here that the "we" who do the testing of "our" beliefs under new conditions will always be more or less different from the population(s) who developed and preferred those beliefs at some earlier time. That difference is most obvious in the case of socially and institutionally transmitted beliefs, such as those of established science, where the populations are spatially discrete as well as separated by considerable expanses of time.[8] It is not, however, restricted to such cases; for "we" are also different from *ourselves* over the course of our individual lifetimes, and each of us continues to play out and evaluate his or her beliefs under conditions other than those in or from which they first emerged. The implications of these differences—obscured by generalized allusions to "human progress" or "the advances of Western science"—are substantial. For they mean that not only will the *conditions* (technological, economic, institutional, and so on) under which "our" beliefs operate alter and be extended, but so also will the *considerations* (interests, values, projects, goals, and so on) in relation to which they are evaluated and preferred—or, to continue the Darwinian analogy, "selected." Moreover, *other* knowledge and skills (for example, new instruments, new analytic techniques, more highly elaborated theories, ideas in other disciplines) will be developed along the way in response both to those altered and extended conditions and also to those new explorations and evaluations themselves, all of which will yield significant investments (cognitive as well as material) that future generations (or versions) of "us" will have an interest in conserving. One may think here, for example, of how different are the material and intellectual conditions in which Copernican models of the solar system are now tested and routinely verified from those in which they were initially developed. Or, at the level of the individual believer, one may think of how a born-again Christian's embrace of his faith *itself* transforms the interests and projects in relation to which he tests and evaluates that faith.

The historical processes of testing and verifying beliefs (scientific and other) may be seen, then, not as the gradual shaping-up of our more or less errant but malleable beliefs by the autonomously resistant features of a fixed reality but, rather, as the continuous mutually shaping interactions between our more or less changing beliefs and the more or less changing worlds in which we operate with them.

Historical Reflection

In a recent narrative account, Stephen J. Gould remarks that "the central principle of all history [is]—*contingency*."[9] Gould is concerned here primarily with geological time and biological history, but also with human time and intellectual history. It may be surmised that Gould's strictly non-teleological conception of historical change seems right to him, given everything else he believes or believes he knows. And, on the same basis, he may be persuaded that this conception—as variously formulated and elaborated—will turn out to be conceptually congenial, practically reliable, and otherwise serviceable over a broad range of conditions for many other people who deal with such ideas. Neither Gould nor anyone else, however, can know in advance what specific conditions—or, for that matter, specific cognitive tastes—will actually turn up. Under his own account, then, the future history of the idea that "the central principle of all history is contingency" is itself contingent. That could be considered a liability, however, only by someone—unlike Gould, one supposes—who believed that a contingently good belief was not good enough.

Microdynamics of Belief

The beliefs of individuals are traditionally conceived as sets of either discrete, true/false mental *propositions* about the world or discrete, correct/incorrect interior *representations* of it. Beliefs may be reconceived, however, as *configurations of linked perceptual/behavioral tendencies* of various *degrees* of strength, continuously formed, transformed, and reconfigured through our ongoing interactions with our environments. That is, rather than sentences about, or pictures of, an *outside* world located *inside* the organism's mind, brain, or body and motivating its actions accordingly, what we call beliefs could be seen as the *entire* organism's complexly linked—and continuously shifting, growing, weakening, and recombining—tendencies to perceive and act in the world in certain ways. In such a reconception, the configurations of perceptual/behavioral tendencies that constitute our beliefs would be understood as only *relatively* stable and coherent for the individual. It would also be supposed, however, that certain of those configurations are, for one reason or another, especially available to self-observation and/or especially susceptible to verbal articulation; and these latter possibilities would be seen as producing and sustaining traditional conceptions of beliefs as sets of logically linked credos and/or as maps of an autonomous exterior reality.

The sense of having "thoughts about" and "images of" the world is common, strong, and sometimes taken as an undeniable fact of mental life. But this sense, like various other phenomena that make up what we call consciousness, can be seen as a response to our own responses, or a belief about our own beliefs, rather than an objectively introspected feature of our interior functioning. Similarly, the sense we may have of an autonomous reality, or of the simple out-thereness of "what's out there," can be seen not as an irreducible intuition of an ontological given but as a relatively stable product of complex processes of perceptual and behavioral coordination. These processes would include the production of relatively similar and stable patterns of response to relatively recurrent and stable environmental conditions, patterns of activity ("habits," "routines") that would be, accordingly, relatively predictable and reliable in their consequences. We may appreciate, then, the experiential sources of classic ideas of true beliefs corresponding to reality and of false ones being corrected by independent evidence without endorsing those ideas in their classic forms or presupposing any isomorphism or relation of symbolic representation between the structure of mind (or thought, knowledge, or belief) and the structure of nature (or reality).

Various features of this reconception of belief are relevant to current epistemological controversies. Not all of them can be spelled out here, but a few especially significant ones may be indicated.

1. Beliefs are *modified* in the same ways, through the same general mechanisms, as they are *maintained*. Specifically, our individual tendencies to respond in certain ways to certain perceived cues are strengthened, weakened, or reconfigured by the *differential consequences* of the responses we actually make. That is, depending on the consequences (harmful or beneficial, as predicted or contrary to prediction, and so on) of the actions we perform by virtue of the beliefs that we have, certain of our beliefs (tendencies to perceive and behave in certain ways) will be strengthened, others will be weakened, and various sets of them will be reconfigured. I alluded, above, to the idea of theories being "winnowed" by experience, experiment, trial and error, and so on. That quasi-adjudicative process would be seen here (as above, but now in relation to the individual's

lifetime) not as a separating-out of beliefs in accord with their putatively objective truth or falseness, but as a continuous process of
strengthening, weakening, and reconfiguring of beliefs (perceptual/
behavioral tendencies) in response to the variable consequences of
their being acted on under the particular contingent conditions encountered.[10]

It is often charged that constructivist or hermeneutic accounts of
knowledge make it impossible to explain how individual beliefs
change.[11] Given the *general* cognitive dynamics described here,
however, no *special* account of how individual beliefs change is required; for there would be no reason to think they would *not* be
changing more or less continuously. To explain why any particular
set of beliefs—practical, philosophical, religious, political, and so
on—was maintained or modified by some individual, what would
be required is a specification of the *particular* conditions operating
in his or her history. For example, to understand why, in cases where
all other general (historical, cultural, intellectual, and so on) conditions appear more or less the same, some of us remain traditional
epistemologists and others become skeptics or constructivists, we
would have to examine quite subtle specific details of our individual
life-histories (educational, social, professional, and so on) as played
out in relation to our more or less diverse cognitive temperaments.

2. The second feature concerns the limits of human knowledge
or of cognition more generally. Our interactions with our environments are a function of our individual structures *and* how they
operate. Both points are significant. It is not merely that our structures define what we can *detect* about the world, but that the world
we *occupy*—the world we can act *on* and can be acted on *by*—is a
particular perceptual and behavioral niche. Thus, what we speak of
as "*the* environment" of some creature, whether bat, paramecium,
or human being, is unique to that creature insofar as its own structure and functioning are unique. The classic epistemological question is whether it is possible for any creature, and specifically a
human being, to cognize *the* universe around the corner, so to speak,
of the niche that it occupies, and also whether creatures in different
niches can come to share the same—thus universal, thus objective—cognitions. The answer to both questions, so posed, would
be negative here. In terms of the present account, however, that is
not lamentable, since the negation does not abandon, destroy, or

prevent anything (for example, the possibility of communication, community, science, art, or duly justified law) that might be thought to depend on a positive answer.[12]

Our "natural environments" include, of course, our fellow creatures, our and their practices, and what we and they have produced—*culture*, in that sense—which, in the case of human beings, includes conceptual systems, verbal idioms, theories, texts, pieces of equipment, technical skills, routines of training, and the institutions that conserve and transmit all of these.[13] The reason that our beliefs cannot be formed or transformed *independent of* cultural practices and products (*pace* some strenuously positivist suppositions) is that they are continuously formed and transformed *in response* to them. Like dubious nature/culture dualisms, dubious mind/body (and related inside/outside) dualisms are deeply implicated not only in formal and informal epistemology but in virtually all explanatory discourses, including the idioms of empirical psychology and much cognitive science. It must be stressed, then, that our "environments" also include our own bodies, which are not themselves separable from our own beliefs in the sense of perceptual/behavioral tendencies. These continuities imply, among other things, that our *beliefs* are continuously formed and transformed by our (in one sense) lifelong interactions with our (in a somewhat different sense) *selves*, including our own other and prior beliefs.

3. The third and perhaps most significant feature of this reconception of belief follows from the two just described and returns us to the hermeneutic circle. The specific characteristics of a creature's global (organic) structure at any given time can be seen as the joint product of two histories: the evolutionary history of that creature's genetic makeup and its life-history in a particular environment. Neither our individual structures, however, nor the ways they will develop are fixed at birth. On the contrary, throughout our lives we interact with our environments in ways that continuously modify our structures *and* the ways they operate, and these structural and functional modifications affect our subsequent interactions with our environments, both in *what we perceive* and in *how we behave*. This continuous *mutual*—and, in that sense, "circular"—process of environmental interaction and organic modification is what we commonly refer to as "cognition" and "learning"—and sometimes as "development." The structural and behavioral modifications them-

selves, when relatively stable and available to both self-observation and verbal articulation, are what we commonly speak of as (acquired) "knowledge" or (changed) "beliefs"—and sometimes as "enlightenment."

The process just described may appear quite close to what informal epistemology describes as the *resistance* offered to our beliefs (scientific theories, historical accounts, literary interpretations, and so on) by facts, rocks, bricks, texts themselves, and those other (supposedly) intractable and manifestly out-there objects to which I alluded at the beginning of this chapter. In regard to the key issues, however, its operations are decisively different. For, given the *interactive* character of that process as traced here, we can never become pure spectators of the universe, observing, cognizing, and representing an altogether exterior, altogether autonomous, reality. Nor—commonly seen as the correlate of that denial—are we forever *locked out* of the universe, prisoners of our own beliefs and idioms. Rather, ourselves always changing, we are inextricably *interlocked with* our always changing worlds. Our relation to the universe is both dynamic and reciprocal: our interactions with it continuously change us and, thereby, the nature of our subsequent interactions with it. The hermeneutic circle does not permit access or escape to an uninterpreted reality; but we do not keep going around in the same path.[14]

Truth and Survival

What seems, minimally, to keep our beliefs going is that they allow us to continue to function as thus-believing creatures. It might be argued, then, that we cannot keep believing things that literally kill us. But we obviously *do* keep believing such things, and not merely because the killing is sometimes slow. It is, rather, because our beliefs are sustained by social/linguistic coordinations as well as by our more obviously physical interactions with our environments. The acquired beliefs of a cat whose beliefs kill her are unlikely to survive the cat, but those of a human creature very well may. Social/linguistic stabilization and cultural transmission introduce considerable complexity into the mechanism of the survival of beliefs and, along with other factors indicated below, confound Panglossian

appropriations of evolutionary theory to underwrite traditional realist epistemology.[15]

The fact that our species evolved and continues to survive in a
particular universe means that whatever specific, innate perceptual/
behavioral tendencies we have must permit our minimal individual
survival in such a universe. It does not mean, however, that our
"natural" or "immediate" perceptions must deliver objectively veridical representations of that universe. Suppositions along the latter
lines figure prominently in the arguments of so-called evolutionary
epistemology. Thus Robert J. Richards maintains, *contra* the idea
of the hermeneutic circle as he understands it, that genuine scientific theories "finally rest" on "harder, ultimately biologically based
beliefs . . . constituted by more immediate perceptions and reason,"
both of which have been tested and guaranteed valid "by that great
reality principle, natural selection"—a principle that Richards illustrates in the figure of a sabre-toothed tiger purging the species
of those individuals whose perceptions of reality are askew.[16] Aside
from the question this raises as to the epistemic status of the immediate perceptions of beetles, bats, and goldfish,[17] it misses a key
point—and indeed, as it can be seen, crucial epistemological implication—of evolutionary theory. For, while our individual perceptual and behavioral tendencies are certainly shaped by, among
other things, the history of the species' more or less effective interactions with its environment, the *reciprocal* of this *also* obtains.
That is, the features of the environment, sabre-toothed tigers included, with which we and past members of the species *could* (have)
interact(ed) have never been independent of our particular structures and how we were already operating as perceiving and behaving
organisms. In other words, the ways in which we have evolved have
depended at every point on what we already were, which means
also what we *believed,* as well as vice versa. Reciprocal determination
of this kind is a central mechanism in the dynamics of cognition as
described in this chapter and also a crucial (indeed, defining) feature
of the hermeneutic circle, which, it seems, the complex processes
of evolution neither shatter nor escape but, on the contrary, sustain
and reproduce.

Another word may be added on those supposedly naturally selective tigers. While the formation and operations of our beliefs do

depend on, among other things, our evolved perceptual/cognitive structures, no set of beliefs, including the most strenuously empirical, can be assumed veridical by reason of being "ultimately biologically based." For the shaping and survival of any belief, along with the shaping and survival of the individual creature or creatures who harbor it, depend on a variety of contingent circumstances, which, in the case of human beings, always include social conditions and cultural dynamics. Thus, while people who still see sabretoothed tigers after they are generally presumed extinct may be thought insane and, accordingly, socially ostracized and reproductively disabled, such people may also be honored by segments of their communities as visionaries and defenders of the old truths and old ways—and, accordingly, may live long, rich, culturally powerful and reproductively potent lives as poets, preachers, or full professors, successfully perpetuating, through both cultural *and* biological transmission, both their tiger-visions and their visionary powers.

The Ambivalent Operations of Belief: A Symmetrical Conclusion

Recent studies in the fields of decision science and social psychology suggest that certain cognitive dispositions and related biases—from the miscalculation of particular forms of probability to the systematic forgetting of disconfirming evidence—are endemic, that is, species-wide.[18] Human fallibility is no news, of course, but of special interest here is the further suggestion that, although such tendencies are clearly disadvantageous under many conditions, they may nevertheless have (had) advantages for the species as a whole or for the individual under a wide range of conditions, or they may be by-products of structures and mechanisms that have (had) such advantages. Among these double-valued (some times or ways advantageous, some times or ways not) dispositions is a complex of tendencies I refer to as "cognitive conservatism," which could also be described as *the resistance of belief to resistance.*[19] Plasticity of belief is obviously advantageous and indeed necessary for any creature that survives, as human beings do, by learning. It does not follow, however, that the more plastic our beliefs, the better off we are. On the contrary, the countertendency—that is, mechanisms that foster the *stability and persistence* of beliefs—would, under a broad range of conditions, *also* be necessary and advantageous. We are, it seems, congenitally both docile and stubborn.

Human history indicates that people will maintain their beliefs not only in the face of apparently contrary evidence but even when those beliefs have severely disagreeable and disadvantageous consequences for them—not to mention for many other people. Millenarianism survives each non-apocalyptic millennium; the dream of flight survives the fall, many times over, of Icarus. Moreover, as stressed above, while the specific (acquired) beliefs of a cat whose beliefs are fatal to her will (usually) die with the cat, those of a human being very often do not. For better and for worse, cultural transmission complicates the dynamics of cognition and amplifies the ambivalent operations of both its plasticity and its conservatism.[20]

Biology, like history, is one discourse—one institutional discipline, one conceptual idiom—among others: the evidences of each are subject to diverse interpretation, the interpretations of each to diverse appropriation. I have invoked biology (and also history) in this chapter as evidence for the constructivist-interactionist views proposed here. Like history, however, biology has been invoked by other theorists as evidence for the traditional epistemologies they would retain, and to help keep constructivism at bay. The arguments thereby generated are in my view exceedingly dubious, but their very existence suggests a final—aptly symmetrical—point.

Invocations of contemporary evolutionary theory in support of classic realist/rationalist epistemology illustrate the energy and resourcefulness of cognitive conservatism, which is not merely the tendency and ability to *hold fast* to one's beliefs but to *incorporate* into them whatever comes along and, often enough—to the amazement of skeptics and exasperation of adversaries—to turn what might otherwise be seen as evidence *against* one's beliefs into evidence *for* them. In operating this way, however, cognitive conservatism may also be, at both the micro (individual) and macro (sociohistorical) levels, a creative and productive mechanism. For, as human history (and biography) also indicates, the intense, obsessive effort to maintain coherence between present evidence and prior belief has generated some of our most innovative beliefs—and what have sometimes turned out to be our most radically transformative ones.[21]

4

Doing without Meaning

The term *meaning*, like a number of other all-too-interesting terms (*truth, reason,* and *reality,* among them), is something we cannot do without and, increasingly, can do little with. Idiomatically indispensable, theoretically intractable, *meaning*, again like those other terms, dominates all informal talk of human action and experience and frustrates all effort at formal definition and determination. The title of this chapter alludes, first, to this perplexity. Traditional conceptions of language, both commonsense ideas (as reflected in what is sometimes called folk linguistics) and also the formalization of those ideas in the academic discourses of language (logic, rhetoric, philology, hermeneutics, the philosophy of language, and so forth), have been subject throughout the century to strenuous critique. To the extent that such critique has involved the exposure of traditional ideas of meaning as profoundly problematic, we are doing without meaning, some of us better than others. But my title alludes also and no less pointedly to current sequels to critique and perplexity: specifically, to the development, in fields such as evolutionary biology, cognitive science, and neurophysiology as well as at the outposts of disciplinary linguistics itself, of alternative approaches to language—approaches that focus not, as traditionally, on verbal forms or the putative transfer of messages between more or less disembodied minds but, rather, on the interactive practices of distinctly corporeal agents and which, in this sense, can be said to place *doing* rather than meaning at the center of linguistic theory.[1]

These latter approaches, clearly rather pragmatist and naturalistic in flavor, are not altogether new. Revisionary proposals along such lines can be found in the works of, among others, Nietzsche, Wittgenstein, Volosinov, Austin, Skinner, and Goffman—not all of them systematically developed but all sufficiently against the conventional grain to have been consistently bracketed, denatured, or demonized.[2] That is, their more radical implications have been generally set aside, neutralized by interpreters, or left undeveloped by disciples; and their naturalistic, non- or anti-rationalist mode, especially in the cases of Goffman and Skinner, has been seen as cynical or sinister. The resistance to such approaches, now as before, is not insignificant and is itself a topic of some interest here (I return to it below). It appears, however, that especially strong (counter-resistant, we might say) versions of them are now emerging from the quarters just mentioned: strong because individually well-developed, mutually connectable, and capable of being articulated with the powerful reconceptualizations of language developed during the past quarter of a century by such continental theorists as Foucault, Derrida, Bourdieu, and Lyotard, a body of work still ignored, for the most part, in Anglo-American disciplinary linguistics and analytic philosophy of language.[3] The inter-articulation of these various approaches will take some doing, of course, but there is reason to believe that the century of the linguistic turn—during which the study of language emerged as an independent discipline and the problematics of language marked virtually every other discipline—will, by the end, have something more to show for it all than neo-Cartesian grammar, neo-Kantian communication theory, and the perpetual redemption of realist epistemology and rationalist philosophy of mind.[4]

In accord with the reconceptualizations of language mentioned above and related reconceptualizations of cognition indicated in Chapter 3, this chapter outlines the operations of what I call *the language loop:* that is, the dynamic system of social interactions through which, without either mental telegraphy or meaning in any classic sense, communication (or something like it) seems to occur. In pursuing the implications of this idea for the issues explored in this book, I focus on the question of linguistic normativity: that is, how we might explain, without appeals to determinate meanings or other so-called objective constraints, why readers, writers, speakers, and listeners ever do (or should) behave as law-abiding citizens of their verbal communities. As will be seen here and in later chapters, the exploration of that question engages—and perhaps illuminates—a number of recurrent and to some extent interrelated controversies in epistemology, language theory, and social theory.

The Language Loop

Communication may be seen as, among other things, a circuit or system of *reciprocal effectivity*, that is, a dynamic process that works—has appropriate effects, but not the same effects—for both those who *act* and those who *re-act*: speakers and listeners, or writers and readers (etc.), respectively. (The "etcetera" here embraces all forms of reciprocally interactive agents, whatever the mode or medium—oral, textual, gestural, pictorial, tactile, electronic, and so forth—through which their acts and reactions are produced or, in any instance, transmitted.) That circuit or system may be described as a set of more or less naturally occurring interlooping acts and reactions and their more or less appropriate consequences for the various parties involved: "naturally occurring" in the sense that those acts and reactions are continuous with other forms of human (and, in some respects, more broadly organic) action and reaction and, accordingly, require no special, unique mechanisms for their explanation.[5]

The following tour of the language loop exhibits the key features of its reciprocal dynamics:

1. As speakers or writers, members of a community of interacting agents tend, relatively recurrently, to produce (verbal) acts of more or less the same form in response to more or less similar heterogeneous conditions, or what we may speak of as circumstances, states of affairs, objects, events, ideas, memories, feelings, intentions, and so forth.[6]

2. As listeners or readers, members of such a community tend, relatively recurrently, to re-act to the traces of the (verbal) acts of their fellow creatures in certain ways that are, from the latter's perspective (that is, that of speakers and writers), more or less appropriate.

3. Because listeners and readers tend to re-act to particular (verbal) forms—that is, the traces of (verbal) acts—in certain relatively recurrent ways, speakers and writers learn that, by producing par-

ticular (verbal) forms, they can affect the beliefs and sentiments and thereby the *behavior* of their fellow creatures more or less predictably in more or less desirable ways.

4. Because speakers and writers tend, relatively recurrently, to produce particular (verbal) forms in response to particular sets of (what come to be discriminated as) relatively similar conditions, listeners and readers learn that, by attending to such forms, they may discover interesting (informative, amusing, comforting, inspirational, and so on) things about the conditions (circumstances, objects, ideas, feelings, intentions, and so on) in response to which their fellow creatures (that is, speakers and writers) produced them.

5. Because, sooner or later, listeners and readers will not attend or react or respond to verbal forms that are not, often enough, interesting to them, speakers and writers learn that, to secure the attention of their fellow creatures so as to be able to affect their beliefs and behavior in appropriate ways, they must produce forms that are, often enough, interesting (and so on) to their various listeners and readers.

6. Because, sooner or later, speakers and writers will not produce verbal forms that do not, often enough, elicit re-actions from their fellow creatures that are more or less appropriate (that is, in accord with their own—those speakers' and writers'—expectations, designs, and desires), readers and listeners learn that, to continue to have possibly interesting verbal forms produced, they must, often enough, respond to them in ways that are, from the perspective of those who address them, more or less appropriate.

The linked tendencies and consequences indicated here are, in this account, what makes the whole machine go around. Or, better, the whole machine (one could call it "language") just *is* that going around. Reciprocal effectivity—something (but not the same thing) for everyone, occurring through each one's action on, and re-action to the actions of, the other (but not through the making-common of anything between or among them all)—is what makes communication occur well enough, often enough, to keep itself, that very circuit or circle of reciprocal effectivity, going. The relatively *stable* going of that circuit is what makes our behavior as verbal agents seem rule-governed, and also what makes it seem that particular recurrent verbal forms (words, phrases, inscriptions, inflections, gestures, intonations, pauses, and so on) have particular os-

tensive, connective, effective, or evocative powers—"meanings"—
within or attached to them.

The two "seemings" just mentioned, that is, the impression we
may have that verbal agents *follow* autonomous rules and that verbal
forms have *inherent* signifying powers, are of particular interest here
and worth pausing over. Both impressions, I think, reflect certain
widespread, perhaps endemic, cognitive tendencies (similar in some
respects to other such tendencies discussed in Chapter 3): first, our
tendency to interpret the emergent effects of complex processes as
the product of simple, linear causes; second, our tendency to interpret our own experientially-shaped *responses to* events as the result
of autonomous forces located *within* those events; and third, our
tendency to experience our own cognitive constructions as prior,
independent entities. Thus, we reify the relatively regular patterns
of our verbal practices as rules and then treat those rules, which are
our own descriptions of our own verbal practices, as the underlying
directors of those practices. And thus also we project our own
experientially-shaped responses *to* particular words back into the
words themselves, and then treat those projections as inherent
properties of those words, exercising autonomous force over us. The
operation of these general cognitive tendencies in our general efforts
to make sense of the complex, elusive phenomena of language may
help explain the tremendous tenacity of many otherwise dubious
elements of so-called folk linguistics, even among some otherwise
quite sophisticated folks.

Verbal animism, or the tendency to confuse the contingent effects of verbal forms with forces inherent in the forms themselves,
is especially tenacious. There is no denying that verbal forms—
from the words of a marriage vow or a political slogan to the
scrawled letters "q.u.e.e.r" or "n.i.g.g.e.r"—can have powerful effects on audiences or readers, or that the relative predictability of
those effects can be successfully exploited for various purposes, good
or ill: to say this is simply to observe the rhetorical operations of
language. It remains the case, however, that those effects are not
dormant within or attached to the forms themselves. In themselves,
marks on a page or wall are quite flat, inert things; patterns of sound
waves are materially quite unimpressive and evanescent. If such
marks or sounds elicit specific responses in particular readers or
listeners—that is, suggest, evoke, or "mean" more or less specific

objects, events, situations, intentions, and so on for them—it is because of those particular listeners' or readers' prior histories with respect to such forms (how they were used, by what sorts of speakers or writers, with what otherwise evident sorts of intentions, emotions, actions, consequences, and so on) under various sets of conditions. In the absence of such relevant prior experiences (as might be the case with children or those unfamiliar with the language), the forms themselves would not have those effects; or, encountered by the same readers or listeners under other conditions, they would have more or less different effects. Indeed, as illustrated by in-group usage ("nigger"), bravado re-appropriation ("queer"), or satirical re-production (East European jokes about government slogans), any form can be divested (as we say) of what might otherwise *seem* to be its inherent (insulting, inspirational, ideological, or whatever) force and turned to different purposes with, again, more or less predictable effects. These are elementary points, which, so stated, few contemporary legal or literary scholars, linguists, or philosophers of language would, I think, dispute. What is of interest and significance here is that they are so often forgotten, or that their force is so readily over-ridden by other compelling claims, conceptions, or intuitions.[7]

If communication is conceived as reciprocal effectivity, then what is usually called a language can be seen as a slice of social life, that is, as a set of the ongoing activities of some group of interacting agents—but a highly selected set. So-called verbal communities cannot, of course, be readily indicated on maps. They are populations with only relatively stable demographic features, roughly locatable spatial boundaries, and roughly definable temporal or historical identities. Even more significantly, it is by no means clear where and when in the ongoing activities of individual agents the realm of the verbal itself begins and ends, or what exactly that realm includes and excludes (facial expressions? bodily gestures? clothing? material equipment? painting? architecture? any act whatsoever? any event whatsoever?).[8] The selection certainly could be, and has been, made differently: that is, the domain of the "verbal" and the "linguistic" has been conceived, by various language theorists, as variously thicker or thinner slices of our activities and interactions. Also, the *temporal* borders by which we usually mark the occurrence of a verbal or linguistic transaction could certainly be extended much further. It is not clear, for example, when a given reader's response to the present remarks will end. Nor is it clear when the present author's act of producing these remarks began: certainly much before the moment of her physically inscribing this text; perhaps many years ago and, no doubt, in some respects quite early in her childhood. What we call "language" is an extraordinarily complex set of phenomena and, surely, making sense of that set of phenomena is the goal of any specific "linguistic" theory. There seems, however, no good reason to suppose that the best place to look for sense or law-and-order—that is, either conceptual coherence or regulative force—is either in or under verbal *forms* per se. On the contrary, any theory of language that excludes the material bodies, experiential histories, and ongoing social interactions of verbal agents has, it seems, already begged the question of what "language" is.

The same applies, in my view, to any theory of "communication" that conceives the role of the listener or reader as altogether receptive, interior, or mental (as consisting, for example, only in the "receiving of information," or in the "understanding," "decoding," or "interpretation" of verbal "signs") or, indeed, as altogether linguistic (as restricted, for example, to the issuing of micro-entities from the mouth in exchange for such micro-entities entering the ears). Such conceptions beg the question of what, if anything, is communicated (made common or, in standard telegraphic versions, "conveyed") in communication and, no less significantly, obscure the crucially *re-active* role of listeners and readers. For listeners and readers, no less than speakers and writers, are verbal *agents* ("doers," in that sense), and their relevant actions can be seen to include the full range of responsive human actions. Indeed, what a listener or reader *does* in re-acting to someone's words, from passing an instrument ("Scalpel, please") to rescuing a swimmer ("Help!") to casting a ballot ("Citizens should remember that . . .") to firing a bullet ("Ready, aim, . . ."), is often quite overt and material, not in the usual sense "linguistic" at all, and, most significantly, distinctly consequential *for the speaker or writer*. To omit this last point, that speakers and writers typically want and expect—and often enough get—more than "understanding" from their audiences, is to miss a crucial element of the circle of reciprocal effectivity that makes language "do" anything at all.

I referred above to the sets of more or less similar conditions that elicit verbal acts of more or less the same form from the members of a verbal community. One may think here of the sorts of conditions under which people (Anglophone in my examples) tend to produce forms such as *hat, rain, clock, not now, probably, You'd better...*, *Oh damn—it's raining, I like that hat,* and *It can't be eleven o'clock already.* Three points may be stressed here. First, it would be very difficult to specify any physical or objective "referent" or "signified" for many of these forms. (What is the referent of *You'd better...*, the object, event, or state of affairs signified by *not now* or *probably?*) Second and relatedly, the conditions that elicit these forms are in every case heterogeneous, that is, by no means confined *either* to some bounded, external, or physical object or event, or to some internal, psychological, or mental idea or feeling. The eliciting conditions are, one could say, always *both* external and internal, physical and mental, objective and subjective. But, and this is the third point to be stressed, the conditions in question are conceived in the present account as *neither* "out there" in a presumed autonomous world nor "in here" in a presumed mental container. Indeed, all these always problematic dualisms become irrelevant here. To be sure, some of the conditions to which a speaker is responding—the rain, someone's hat, the numerals on a timepiece—will appear from an observer's point of view to be outside the speaker's body. As the speaker's own percepts and sensations, however, the hat, rain, and numerals are no less "inside" (or, better, *part of*) her body than any of the other so-called "mental" conditions that may also be involved in eliciting her words: for example, her *disappointment* at the rain, her *delight* in the hat, her *recollection* of an appointment at that hour, or her *intention* to make any of these conditions known to (or believed by)[9] her audience. What is significant here is that all these conditions (rain-sensations, hat-percepts, disappointment-feelings, appointment-recollections, intentions-to-inform, and so on), which are commonly dichotomized as either external *or* internal, objective *or* subjective, referential *or* expressive, and so forth, operate together in unbroken and inseparable unity as part of the speaker's or writer's global organic state as a living, responsive creature. That global state is, in effect, the only "state of affairs" out of which anyone ever responds in speaking or writing or, one could say, *to* which anyone ever "refers."

I stress these points, that is, the global and heterogeneous nature of the states of affairs to which we respond as verbal agents, in view of the persistence of Cartesian, realist, rationalist, and otherwise problematic formulations in contemporary language theory. Thus, one still hears of individual words or strings of words "denoting"—or, understood as a quasi-ostensive operation, "picking out"—certain presumably prior and autonomous objects which, in turn, are invoked as the "objective" conditions that "make our statements true or false."[10] In the conception of communication outlined here, however, the relation between our utterances (including apparently straightforward "naming" statements) and (the features of) our world is not only historically and causally complex but also cognitively reciprocal. That is, the specific features of the global sets of conditions to which we respond verbally are understood here as *specified*—discriminated, assembled, configured, and related to each other (or, as it is sometimes put, taking advantage of the pun on speech and segmentation, *articulated*)—by and through our prior and ongoing activities, which include our prior and ongoing verbal activities themselves. Thus one can say that there is, here, a *double* loop. The ongoing perceptual/behavioral reciprocality that we call "cognition" (which is to say, our coming to know the world, which is also to say our continuing to conduct our lives relatively effectively in our particular physical, social, and cultural environments) operates in human beings *through* the language loop, so that whatever objects, events, ideas, feelings, and so forth we respond (or "refer") to verbally (hats, clocks, rain, disappointment, desire, and so on) are distinguished as such—that is, perceived and interacted with as integral entities or sets of conditions with particular boundaries, salient features, and relations of sameness and difference to each other—at least partly through our coordinated social/perceptual/behavioral activities of verbal responding and responding-to-verbal-responding themselves.

A further point relating to familiar conceptualizations of *meaning* may be stressed here. What we (Anglophone, Western speakers) often speak of idiomatically as *the* meaning (*Bedeutung, signifié,* and so on) of a word seems to be some *part* or *aspect* of the set of conditions that, in our particular verbal communities, recurrently elicits the production of more or less that verbal form: usually the most concrete, visible, medium-sized, and clearly outlined part or aspect (if there is any; though, of course, there often isn't). That is one reason why, when the idea of linguistic meaning is being discussed, we hear so much about salt, rain, hats, and Morning Stars and so little about "Not now," "Yes Ma'am," "I don't know," and "You'd better..." The latter verbal forms are no less common than *hat, salt,* or *rain,* and their effective, appropriate usages ("meanings," in that idiomatic sense) seem to be grasped no less readily by children. Clearly, however, children do not and cannot find out about *not now* or *You'd better* by asking "What's *that?*" It is no accident that commonsense, referential conceptions of meaning become increasingly strained the further we move away from common experiences of naming concrete, visible, medium-size objects and events or providing the names of such objects and events to children and foreigners: no accident because those common experiences appear to be precisely what generate and sustain those commonsense referential (ostensive/naming) conceptions.[11] One solution to the problem—that is, how to handle the putative referents or denotations of such forms and, especially, how to explain their acquisition—is to create special semantic or non-semantic categories for them ("function words," "phatic expressions," "institutionally bounded utterances," "mere social formulae," and so on) and, as needed, special accounts of how they are learned or got hardwired. Another solution is to rethink the notion of the "semantic" altogether and to undertake the long-deferred project of investigating how verbal forms *generally* emerge and are stabilized in the behavioral repertoires of groups of interacting agents—which is pretty much where the present remarks began.

Linguistic Law and Order

Journalists and others who inveigh against the heresies of postmodern thought routinely equate critiques of traditional conceptions of meaning with the duly scandalizing claim that texts and utterances are, in the idiomatic sense, "meaningless." This is, of course, both naive and mistaken. No less mistaken, however, is the somewhat more sophisticated objection to the effect that a rejection of the idea of objectively determinate meaning implies that anything goes in the domain of verbal practices: that we can say whatever comes into our heads; that all literary interpretations are equally valid; that lawyers can put whatever construction they please on contracts; and so forth. The charge or fear of "anything goes" here—that is, the conviction that doing without (determinate) meaning amounts to producing or endorsing linguistic anarchy—gains force from familiar oppositions between rigorous necessity and total arbitrariness or objective determination and personal whim. These oppositions, however, are themselves dubious. Indeed, the idea of reciprocal effectivity suggests why, although perhaps anything always *could* go in principle, not everything ever *does* go in fact, either in language or in any other domain of social practice. This is not to say that verbal and social lawlessness never occur: it is to say, however, that no verbal or social behavior, even that which is most destructive, perverse, or irrational as commonly accounted, can occur independent of a shaping history and a set of shaping conditions.

What are commonly posited as the laws, rules, maxims, principles, or innate hardwirings that constrain, or are presupposed by, verbal practices can be alternatively seen as reifications (that is, hypostatized abstractions) of the *relatively stable patterns* of those practices themselves: that is, the patterns of coordinated verbal action and re-action that emerge from the ongoing practices of interacting speakers and listeners and are stabilized by their differential consequences for them as verbal agents.[12] In other words, what keeps us more or less in line as verbal citizens is neither any abstract regulative force *nor* any biologically inscribed internal necessity, but the fact that producing and responding to verbal forms in certain ways rather than other ways works out for us, on the whole, better rather than worse.[13] To be sure, people's verbal productions and responses may also be more or less in accord or with whatever rules, instructions, and corrections they have received from various normative authorities: parents, schoolteachers, helpful associates, imperious superiors, academies for the preservation of the purity of the national tongue, and so forth. In the present account, however, these conformities of verbal practice to explicit prior or current rules are not crucial to the emergence and stabilization of linguistic norms. What is crucial is that agents (both speakers and listeners) learn, from the specific and different ways their verbal interactions take place (whether frustratingly or enablingly, whether disappointingly or as expected, whether agreeably or—sometimes literally—

punishingly), that using and responding to verbal forms in one way rather another way—and thus not just "any" way—is, under particular sets of conditions, the better way to go.

To say that specific verbal tendencies are *learned* is not to say that they are explicitly *taught*. It is to say, rather, that they are formed and stabilized in the course of our life histories.[14] Contrary to the argument of some language theorists, the informality of most language acquisition is not evidence that our tendencies to engage in specific verbal practices are innate. "Specific" is the crucial term: to say *learned* is also not to say inscribed on a *tabula rasa*.[15] Nothing said here contradicts the idea that there are evolved species-wide structures or tendencies relating to the verbal behavior of human beings. It appears, for example, that we have evolved in such a way as to be able and inclined to attend to quite subtle features of the conditions under which other people produce verbal forms and also to pick up quite subtle cues as to the effectiveness of our own behavior in the course of all social interactions. Recent studies in neurophysiology suggest that other such tendencies, perhaps more specific than these, are the product of endemic structures and mechanisms.[16] The idea of evolved language-related structures, mechanisms, and tendencies should be distinguished, however, from the idea—which has considerable currency among generative linguists, artificial-intelligence engineers, and rationalist philosophers of language—that human beings are born with highly *specific* and *identical* grammatical and/or semantic computers already hardwired into their minds or neurons.[17]

The emergent norms of verbal practice may be registered and formalized, of course, as the contents of grammars and dictionaries, and, for listeners or readers, as specifications of proper interpretive procedure. Grammars, dictionaries, and hermeneutic manuals, however, are always incomplete, more or less obsolete, and relatively crude. There are always more individual instances of a general verbal practice, with more regional, historical, contextual, and personal variation than any committee of lexicographers or grammarians could encounter in their collective lifetimes or definitively assemble, or than any hermeneutics could anticipate or control.[18] Moreover, because verbal practices are never completely stable, the empirical norms that reflect their stability—that is, what may be observed as their relative frequency and reliability—are always themselves shifting. Thus, by the time a particular norm is registered in a dictionary, it is likely to be in some respect, in some place or domain, already different, already out of date. The norms of verbal practice registered in dictionaries and grammars are also inevitably crude: inevitably so because, in order to serve their primary functions as formalizations, they must confine the variability, arrest the fluidity, and abstract from the more or less subtle responsiveness of ongoing verbal practices themselves. What is thereby omitted or abstracted, however, may turn out to be of particular interest in certain circumstances. For example, as philosophers often remark, dictionary definitions of terms such as *truth, knowledge,* and *reality*—and, we could add here, *meaning*—do not begin to reflect the subtlety or complexity of their meanings: that is (in the terms of the present account), the heterogeneous and sometimes quite subtly variable conditions to which people are responsive when, as verbal agents, they actually produce and react to such terms. The "clarification of concepts" offered by analytic philosophers could be seen, then, as a kind of supplementary or perhaps higher lexicography: that is, as the discrimination and specification of especially elusive features of the conditions under which certain broadly interesting but problematic abstract terms (*truth, belief, meaning,* and so on) are recurrently used in the relevant community and which, accordingly, those terms are recurrently taken, by members of that community, to imply. It must be added, however, that this supplementary dictionary-work is not what "conceptual analysis" usually claims to be, which is something more philosophically interesting than that, and certainly more epistemically ambitious.[19] I return to this point in Chapter 6.

The term "constraints," recurrent in discussions of linguistic normativity, is itself troublesome, for it commonly evokes notions of external forces—comparable to ropes, chains, fences, and policemen—that compel us to behave verbally in certain ways over and against our personal inclinations. Verbal behavior is, of course, subject to institutionally enforced coercion and restraint and, at times, to literal enough ropes, chains, fences, and policemen.[20] Constraints of those kinds are not required, however, to sustain reciprocally effective verbal interactions or to produce verbal regularities and norms. On the contrary, the major locus of linguistic normativity in the operations of the language loop is precisely *in* our individual, experientially shaped inclinations as verbal agents. Part of the crux here may be the force of traditional conceptions, both ethical/theological and political, of personal inclinations as randomly eruptive, inherently irrational, or culpably individualistic whims.[21] Hence the familiar conviction that, lacking strong external constraints, "anything" could and would "go." As conceived here, however, people's personal inclinations (with respect to, among other things, specific verbal production or response) are their individual global (organic) tendencies to act and re-act one way rather than another as shaped by the differential consequences of their prior and ongoing actions and interactions. There are, accordingly, no conditions under which *anything* would have an equal probability of *going*. But, of course, that does not mean that the only things that go are, as commonly measured, good things, or good for everyone.[22]

Loop Ethics and Pidgin Talk

The present account of linguistic norms is not itself normative. It does not *require* that individual verbal agents be trusting, cooperative, or morally responsible, nor does it claim to have demonstrated why they *should* be. Indeed, the present account indicates that, under some conditions, speakers and writers will find it effective and personally advantageous to deceive their audiences, and that listeners and readers will often find it prudent to mistrust speakers and to disappoint the evident expectations, or ignore the evident intentions, of those who address them. It also suggests that, under some conditions, we will find it amusing or profitable to talk or write nonsense or to make nonsense out of other people's speech or writing. But, of course, not even the most normatively exacting theories of communicative normativity, such as Frankfurt School discourse ethics, can obviate these unruly possibilities.

The language loop does not *require* moral agents for its operation: but its dynamics *predict* that, as long as the members of a community interact with one another verbally in ways that are, often enough, more or less effective on all sides, then more or less congruent patterns of verbal production and uptake will continue to emerge and become more or less stable. It follows, of course, that *unless* the members of a community interact with one another verbally in ways that are, often enough, more or less effective on all sides, then more or less congruent patterns of verbal production and uptake will *not* continue to emerge and become more or less stable, and the system of reciprocal effectivity that is thereby constituted will cease to exist. And, one could add (somewhat tautologically), it would seem to be in the general interest of all those who, on the whole, benefited from the operations of such a system that it continue to exist.

The quasi-ethical cast of this last point may be acknowledged, but its limits in that respect should also be noted. Thus, although it could certainly be said that all members of a community of interacting agents benefit on the whole from whatever system (or systems) of reciprocal effectivity emerge from their interactions, it remains the case that not all members benefit equally all the time. Indeed, by virtue of existing inequalities of social power and relevant resources (access to audiences and information, institutional authority, verbal skills, and so on), some members of a verbal community enter (most) verbal interactions with significant advantages over other members. Moreover, since the dynamics of the language loop permit (even if they do not require) deception and manipulation, the latter practices—in the absence of specific communally instituted regulations such as copyrights, libel laws, speech codes, or mandated freedom of the press—can operate to entrench the power of the powerful and multiply the resources of the resourceful.

The ethical and political implications of these ambivalent possibilities are themselves ambivalent. Where there is concern to prevent or reduce what are otherwise determined to be unacceptable inequalities of power and resources, the members of a community may subject the operations of the system in question to institutional regulations directed to those ends. (Regulations can also be instituted, of course, to *secure* the power of the powerful.) But the determination of inequalities of that kind *as* "unacceptable" cannot be established on the basis of the system's operations per se . . . or vice versa. That is, the general functionality of a social system does not itself establish the objective or moral desirability of any of its specific operations, or, in short, it is not the case that whatever is, is right.[23] The ethical and, with it, political burden of the language loop, then, remains *indeterminate*. Though, like other self-organizing, self-maintaining social systems, it may recall the "invisible hand" of classic economics, nothing in the operations of the system per se (or in their description) obliges anyone to respond to it in the classic ways, for example, as requiring non-intervention or as a justification for ruthlessness.[24]

As already noted, the account of linguistic normativity outlined here differs significantly from Frankfurt School discourse ethics and related neo-Kantian philosophy of language. In the latter, linguistic norms are conceived as rules, maxims, or principles that are pre-supposed by all language use and that operate only by virtue of extensive commonalities and mutualities among the interacting parties: for example, their joint orientation toward achieving mutual understanding or their shared claims or assumptions of truthfulness and sincerity.[25] In contrast, such norms are conceived here as rela-tively stable patterns of behavior observed to emerge recurrently from verbal interactions among agents who have more or less dif-ferent verbal histories, different verbal expectations, and different tendencies to respond, as well as more or less different sets of mo-tives and interests with respect to any particular interaction. "More or less different" is equivalent, of course, to "more or less similar." What is crucial for reciprocality, however, is not the degree of *iden-tity* of the participating elements but the extent of their *congruence* or, it could be said, mutual "fit." Pidgin languages—the sorts of dialects that emerge from repeated transactions between commer-cial traders speaking different languages or between colonists and native workers—provide a good model and vivid example of how linguistic norms can emerge through ad hoc pragmatic coordination among parties who are otherwise different, unequal, and perhaps mutually competitive or bitterly antagonistic. Odd or chilling though it may seem, the fact that language can operate as an in-strument of personal or political oppression does not negate the possibility of mutually congruent linguistic norms emerging from the recurrent interactions of the parties involved.[26]

The issue of difference versus commonality joins current contro-versies in linguistic theory with those in epistemology. Pursuing the points just made, we could say that, in the case of *conceptual* idioms, as of linguistic ones, there is none that is fundamentally proper. There are, of course, idioms, both conceptual and linguistic, that become standardized, that is, acquire normative force because em-ployed by most of the members of a verbal or epistemic community or by its otherwise dominant members. There is, however, no way to establish a claim to the effect that one idiom, conceptual or linguistic, permits a better grasp of the world than all others, or is a better instrument of communication. Each idiom, if it is operating at all, is operating well enough for some community of people; each, if it is being used at all, is being used by some people to interact effectively enough with others who employ more or less the same idiom.[27]

The analogy here is instructive in both directions. Effective verbal communication does not presuppose identical pronunciation, shared lexicons, or mutually benevolent motives any more than effective intellectual exchange presupposes shared cognitions, common interests, or identical orientations. Similarly, the non-identity of our verbal productions and interpretations does not doom us to verbal chaos, solipsistic speech, or the breakdown of the social collectivity any more than the non-identity of our cognitions dooms us to conceptual chaos, solipsistic belief, or the breakdown of intellectual life. Of course, we get along less well—*linguistically,* anyway, though not necessarily otherwise—with those whose idioms are very different from our own. Even in the most widely divergent cases, however, if "getting along" is desirable for both parties or enforceable by one of them, there will emerge a pidgin dialect. As noted above, pidgins (or, as they are also called, "contact languages") seem to arise most commonly under conditions of recurrent commercial transactions or political conquest or domination. They could also be said to emerge, however, wherever there is some advantage to (or pressure for) pragmatic coordination between or among people with more or less divergent "native idioms"[28]—in which case it could also be said that all verbal transactions, including those between intimate companions speaking nominally the same language, are conducted, in effect, in pidgin.

Normative Theories and Cognitive Tastes

We may return now to the two general accounts of linguistic normativity cited above: the normative, moral-theoretical account represented by Frankfurt School communication theory and the non-normative, more or less naturalistic one represented by the present outline of the language loop.[29] There are, of course, points of contact between both and intertranslations between the two could no doubt be produced.[30] Whether they would be accepted as adequate by all the interested parties is, however, another matter. For example, it could be observed that both sides are agreed on the inevitability of certain reciprocal norms of verbal interaction, in the one case as empirical/phenomenal emergence, in the other as a priori inescapability. Just that difference, however, is crucial: for although, in the present account, the dynamics of those reciprocalities are conceived as *general* (extending, by definition, to all members of the relevant community of interacting agents), the norms that emerge from them are not conceived as universally or otherwise noncontingently binding.[31] Nor would it be a negligible matter to the transcendental moral philosopher that everything in the present account is framed as "more or less," "good enough," or "relatively recurrent," and that nothing in it is posited as *even ideally* identical, absolute, universally shared, totally predictable, or inescapably necessary. A hopeful mediator might venture that both accounts acknowledge the fundamentally reciprocal and thus fundamentally ethical nature of communication since, even in the language loop, verbal exchanges are represented as finely tuned, mutually responsive, and mutually modifying interactions, and their effectiveness is seen to depend on each party's assumptions (or at least instructed expectations) concerning the other's likely behavior. Something, however, must be added here as well. For if verbal communication can be described as fundamentally ethical on that basis, then a very wide range of other reciprocally effective interactive practices would *also* have to be granted that status, including commercial transactions, competitive sports, and sexual flirtations.

What these failed moves toward reconciliation suggest is that the differences between the accounts in question are to some extent matters of conceptual idiom and cognitive taste. Differences of that kind do make theoretical inter-articulation difficult and, of course, put in doubt traditional ideas of the ultimate convergence or underlying unity either of science or of "thought." They do not imply, however, that diverging idioms or tastes cannot interact (via intellectual pidgin languages, for example) or cannot affect each other. As will be seen, Habermas's recent work is energized largely in reaction to alternative ("postmodern") ideas of normativity,[32] and, reciprocally, many features of the present account have been shaped by its author's engagement with Habermas's elaborations and defenses of discourse ethics.

Differences of cognitive taste appear to structure many theoretical controversies over language or communication, including some commonly posed or seen as matters of ideology. For example, political objections to neo-Kantian (Gricean and Frankfurt School) theories of linguistic normativity have been raised by feminist and other leftist critics, who charge—correctly, from the present perspective—that idealizing descriptions of the extensive commonalities and cooperative mutualities supposedly presupposed by human communication obscure the significance of common-enough inequalities of relevant resources among verbal agents, and also obscure the significant operation of our commonly asymmetrical social relations with our interlocutors: for example, as workers talking or listening to bosses, as students talking or listening to teachers, or as women talking or listening to men.[33] At the same time, however, alternative naturalistic or poststructuralist accounts of communication (such as the present one) in terms of our irreducibly differing histories and distinctly sublunary motives as verbal agents, risk being charged by traditional moral theorists with cynicism *and* by Marxist critics with "pessimism." The reason for the charge in each case seems to be pretty much the same, namely the failure of such accounts to endorse a redemptive script—either religious, moral, or political—of underlying human unity and ultimate human transcendence.[34] Although, as I stress above, the specifically *political* implications of naturalistic theories of communication can be seen as ambivalent or indeterminate, charges of these kinds certainly indicate their more general intellectual, social, and sometimes personal implications, implications that follow from, among other things, connections between people's cognitive tastes and their other intellectual and institutional investments. Indeed, differences and connections of those kinds, that is, among cognitive tastes, conceptual idioms, and institutional investments (though not necessarily the same ones in each case), appear to shape the issues and sustain the energies of virtually all the controversies noted in this chapter: debates over classical versus poststructuralist understandings of language, referential versus nonreferential theories of meaning, rationalist versus pragmatist conceptions of normativity, or innatist versus empiricist accounts of the formation and stabilization of human language abilities and practices.[35]

A final set of (duly ambivalent) implications may, accordingly, be worth stressing. I have suggested here that what we call linguistic rules, laws of language, and presuppositions of communication can be seen as hypostatized descriptions of relatively stable patterns of verbal practice. It is significant, of course, that our verbal practices *are* at least relatively stable: that is what makes them relatively predictable and reliable for other people and more or less effective all around. But the other side of this coin, ignored or treated with some disdain in Frankfurt School communication theory, is no less significant: that is, what secures the stability of our verbal practices is precisely their effectiveness for us as individual agents, including their effectiveness in connection with our individual interests (immediate or long-range) and projects (mean or noble).[36] Moreover, while (as just stressed) our verbal practices must be *at least* relatively stable to be effective, they can never be more than that, either. The conditions that elicit particular verbal forms are never exactly the same from one occasion to the next; the forms we produce are not themselves exactly the same from one occasion of production to the next; and, of course, our individual prior experiences with particular verbal forms and conditions are never exactly the same as anyone else's experiences. It is clear, however, that exact sameness all the time is not necessary here: same enough, often enough, is good enough—that is, the relatively frequent recurrence of relatively effective interactions among agents using what they experience as relatively similar forms and responding in what appear to others as relatively similar ways is good enough to keep the circuit of reciprocal effectivity going for all of them. Nor, I believe, is exact sameness, all the time, *wanted* here. Instability and difference in our verbal histories, practices, assumptions, and motives are neither breakdowns of the system requiring artful repair, nor signs of moral frailty requiring the positing of regulative counterfactual ideals. On the contrary, all these are precisely the features of naturally-occurring and sublunary—as distinct from artificial or angelic—languages that make them, as systems, responsive and dynamic rather than regular (that is, regulated, orderly, and invariant) and inert. But, again, we have a coin with two sides. For this, the inevitable difference of our verbal histories and motives and the un-fixable instability of our verbal practices, is also why no speaker can predict exactly the effects of her words on any of her audiences or, for better or worse, *control* all such effects: not poet, preacher, lover, teacher, ruler, or revolutionary, and not with all the verbal artistry, logical-moral rigor, political power, or technological wizardry in the world. I repeat: for better or for worse.

5

Unloading the Self-Refutation Charge

Philosophers, logicians, and those whom they have instructed demonstrate recurrently—in classrooms, at conferences, in the pages of professional journals—the "incoherence" of certain theoretical positions: for example, relativism, skepticism, perspectivism, constructivism, and postmodernism. They often do this by exposing to their audiences—students, colleagues, and readers—how such positions are self-refuting. The positions so exposed are, characteristically, those that diverge from the relevant philosophical orthodoxy. Though presumably not impossible, it is certainly not common to find a neo-Platonist or neo-Kantian charged with self-refutation. Defenses of orthodox positions are, to be sure, sometimes charged with hollow arguments, but the charge here is characteristically that of begging the question: that is, circular self-affirmation rather than specular self-refutation. The classic agents and victims of self-refutation, however, are Protagoras, the relativist, Hume, the epistemological skeptic, Nietzsche, the perspectivist, and, in our own era, postmodernists such as Kuhn, Feyerabend, Foucault, Derrida, Lyotard, Goodman, and Rorty, whose individual and collective incoherence, self-contradiction, and self-refutation have been demonstrated by numerous defenders of more orthodox philosophical positions.[1]

As the foregoing list suggests, the agents/victims of self-refutation are also usually philosophical innovators: that is, theorists who have articulated original substantive views on various matters of philosophical interest: knowledge, language, science, and so forth.

73

When their self-refutation is being exposed, however, they are seen primarily in their role of negative critics of orthodox thought: that is, as deniers, rejecters, and abandoners of views that are widely experienced as intuitively correct and manifestly true. Indeed, even prior to and independent of any formal demonstration of their self-refutation, the views of such theorists tend to be experienced by disciplinary philosophers—and those whom they have instructed—as self-evidently absurd.

Because various elements of the orthodoxies in question—that is, those from which the views of the skeptic/relativist/postmodernist diverge—are also widely seen as sustaining important communal goods (for example, the authority of law, the possibility of moral and aesthetic judgment, the progress of science) and as averting corresponding evils (for example, social anarchy, moral paralysis, aesthetic decline, intellectual chaos), the questioning or denial of those elements is also widely seen as, at the least, communally perilous and often morally criminal as well. It is not surprising, then, that the theoretical innovators mentioned above have often been demonized. Nor is it surprising that much of the energy of disciplinary philosophy has been and continues to be devoted to demonstrating—as the self-refutation charge itself proclaims—that the apparently dangerous demons are actually impotent, self-deceived fools. That, in fact, seems to be the point of the self-refutation charge: to show, so to speak, that the devil is an ass.

What officially justifies the charge of self-refutation is a manifestly self-canceling, self-disabling statement: "All generalizations are false," "Relativism is (absolutely) true," "It is wrong to make value judgments," and so forth. What more commonly elicits the charge, however, is some set of analyses and arguments that is said to "come down to" such a statement or, duly paraphrased, to have the "logical form" of such a statement. The justice of the charge, in either case, may be more or less readily acknowledged by the person accused, who may then attempt to eliminate the problem through some appropriate self-qualification. For example, the distinctly alarming "All generalizations are false" may be amended to the relatively unexceptionable "Most generalizations have exceptions." Or, as in the recent case of the sociology of science, acknowledgment of the justice of the recurrent charge of self-contradiction may have important effects on the development of an entire field of study.[2]

Charges of self-refutation do not always, however, yield genial or self-transformative resolutions. On the contrary, although a particular charge may be manifestly on target from the perspective of many members of some immediate audience, it may also appear empty and irrelevant to the alleged agent/victim and to his or her partisans. Indeed, a charge of self-refutation is, often enough, a sign of head-on intellectual collision and an occasion of especially dramatic non-engagement or impasse. Accordingly, an examination of its general operations—logical, rhetorical, psychological, and to some extent institutional—will serve our larger purposes here and, perhaps, make the charge of self-refutation, in some quarters, somewhat less automatic.

Tricks of Thought

In the dialogue that bears his name, the good-natured, mathematically precocious Theaetetus offers, in reply to Socrates's questions about the nature of knowledge, the teachings of Protagoras: "Man is the measure," and so forth. Through cross-questioning, certain implications and difficulties of the doctrine are explored. Protagoras himself is imagined risen from the grave and arguing in his own defense. Other difficulties, notably an "exquisite" self-contradiction, are drawn out. These are acknowledged by Theaetetus, now delivered to better understanding.[3]

This is the archetypal exposure of self-refutation, both in its dramatic, triangular form—student, false teacher, true teacher—(to which I return below) and in the logical/rhetorical details of the turnabout. Through the explications and applications of subsequent commentators, Socrates's exposure of self-refutation becomes the authority for charging, and the model for exposing, the incoherence of latter-day Protagoreans.

Man is the measure of all things, says the Protagorean, or *Each thing is as it is perceived.* Thus he denies the possibility of (objective, absolute) truth and (objectively) valid knowledge. But then he cannot claim that his own doctrine is (objectively, absolutely) true or the product of (objectively valid) knowledge. Thus also he declares the (objective, absolute) truth of the views that disagree with his own. But, then, he acknowledges that what he says is false and worthless. His doctrine refutes itself.

These moves are simple enough. So also is the problem with

them, namely that they hinge on dubious paraphrase and dubious inference. For the self-refutation charge to have logical force (as officially measured), the mirror reversal it indicates must be exact: What the self-refuter explicitly, wittingly denies must be the same as what he unwittingly, implicitly affirms. Accordingly, the charge fails to go off properly, and the supposed demonstration is declared a trick or an error, if the restatement diverges too obviously or too crucially from the original[4] or if the supposedly implied affirmation is itself questionable: if, for example, Protagoras had actually said "*It appears to me that* man is the measure of all things . . .," or obviously meant his doctrine to be taken as only *relatively* true, or obviously meant to affirm only that each thing is as it is perceived *to those who perceive it that way*. Similarly, in the case of the related tu quoque charge, the trait evidently condemned by the self-refuter must be the same as that thereby exhibited, as in the (social) scientific theory that claims: "Scientific theories are (mere) reflections of the social interests of those who produce and promote them." Here the charge fails if the supposed self-refuter disavows the "mere," and the presumably self-*excepting* claim is revealed as (or transformed into) an explicitly and flagrantly self-*exemplifying* one: "You charge my theory of the social interests of all theories with reflecting social interests? But *of course* it does: it could hardly prosper otherwise!" Thus, as in the schoolyard exchange, the target of the taunt ("You, too. So *there!*") turns the tables back again ("Me, too. So *what?*").

An error or perhaps trick of this kind—that is, dubious paraphrase and/or dubious inference—occurs, according to most classical scholars, in the course of Socrates's examination of Protagoras's doctrine in *Theaetetus.*[5] Almost all of those scholars, however, read the charge of self-refutation as redeemed—both there and more generally—on shifted grounds. Thus it is said that Protagoras *must* claim the *absolute* truth of his doctrine because all assertions are implicit claims of absolute truth and that otherwise there would be no point to anyone's listening to or believing him. One commentator, for example, after extensive consideration of the text, concludes that Protagoras's doctrine and "relativism" more generally are self-refuting "for reasons that go deep into the nature of assertion and belief."[6] "No amount of maneuvering with his relativizing qualifiers will extricate Protagoras from the commitment to truth absolute which is bound up with the very act of assertion. To assert is to assert that *p* . . . —that something is the case—and if *p*, indeed if and only if *p*, then *p* is true (period)."[7] Another commentator assures his readers, "Relative rightness is not rightness at all . . . The relativist cannot regard her beliefs or her relative truths as warranted or worthy of belief."[8] Yet another, acknowledging Socrates's dubious paraphrase of Protagoras's thesis, insists on the ignominious outcome of the examination: for, he observes, "if what [Protagoras] says is right he has no claim on our attention."[9]

It will be noted that, in all these recuperations, the assumption is that the particular conceptions of "truth," "assertion," "rightness," and so on, to which they appeal are not themselves contestable, that those concepts and also the discursive/conceptual ("logical") connections among them could not be seen, framed, or configured otherwise. The assumption is crucial and, when joined with the other common but dubious convictions discussed below, gives the self-refutation charge much of its logical/rhetorical force.

In explications of *Theaetetus* and elsewhere, the supposed self-refutation often hinges on what is taken to be an *egalitarian* claim implied by the unorthodox doctrine at hand: that is, a claim seen as erasing all differences of (presumably inherent, objective) better and worse, superiority and inferiority. Thus one commentator writes: "[T]he point of Protagoras's theory which is to be attacked [in the dialogue] is its implication that no man is wiser than any other." This supposed implication leads to a self-refutation because, "according to his own theory [Protagoras] cannot himself be any better judge of truth than the ignorant audience he mocks."[10] Indeed, much of the sense of intellectual and moral scandal evoked by the charge of "relativism" derives from a supposed implication of this kind: that is, the idea that, according to the skeptical or unorthodox doctrine in question, everything—every opinion, every scientific theory, every artwork, every social practice, and so on— is "just as good" as every other.

I call this general supposition and argument the Egalitarian Fallacy.[11] It is a fallacy because, if someone rejects the notion of validity in the classic (objectivist) sense, what follows is not that she thinks *all* theories (and so on) are *equally* valid but that she thinks *no* theory (and so on) is valid *in the classic sense*.[12] The non sequitur here is the product of the common and commonly unshakable conviction that differences of "better" and "worse" must be objective or could not otherwise be measured. When appealed to in the argument, the conviction is obviously question-begging. Thus, the supposed relativist could reply that her point is, precisely, that theories (and so on) can be and are evaluated in *other* non-"objective" ways. Not all theories are equal because they (including, significantly, her own) can be, and commonly will be, found better or worse than others in relation to measures such as applicability, coherence, connectability, and so forth. These measures are not objective in the classic sense, since they depend on matters of perspective, interpretation, and judgment, and will vary under different conditions. Nevertheless, they appear to figure routinely, and operate well enough, in scientific, judicial, and critical practice. Thus theories, judgments, or opinions (and so on) may still be seen as better or worse even though not, in a classic sense, as more or less objectively valid.

The second conviction of interest here could be called the Anything Goes Fallacy. This is the idea that a theory that does not ultimately affirm the absolute force of certain relevant constraints (for example, determinate meanings, an objective morality, or an objective reality) implies that, in the relevant domain, anything—any utterance or interpretation, any social practice, any belief, and so on—is acceptable. The fallacious assumption here is that there can be no *other* explanation for why we do not all talk nonsense, or run amok, or believe ridiculous things: that is, that no alternative accounts of the dynamics of communication, social behavior, or cognition are possible. The logic of "so anything goes" is identical to that of "so everything's just as good as everything else." Both depend on taking for granted as unquestionable or irreplaceable the orthodox concepts or explanations at issue. Hence, in all these cases, the recurrent (and technically proper) countercharge of question-begging; hence also the recurrent deadlocks, non-engagements, and impasses. Which brings us to what is, in my view, the heart of the matter here.

The classical scholars cited above, though close readers and scrupulous interpreters, operate within the closures of traditional epistemology and philosophy of language. The confinement is reflected in the strenuously self-affirming and self-absolutizing formulations that recur in their arguments. We recall, from one, "the commitment to truth absolute which is *bound up* with *the very act* of assertion."[13] He cites in support Husserl: "The content of such [relativistic] assertions rejects what is *part of the sense* . . . of *every assertion* . . ."[14] For another commentator, it is "*the very notion* of rightness" that is undermined by Protagoras and latter-day relativists.[15] He cites in support Hilary Putnam: "it is a *presupposition* of *thought itself* that some kind of objective 'rightness' exists."[16] A passage in the recent work of Jürgen Habermas is relevant here as well. He writes: "[In the process of] convincing a person who contests the hypothetical reconstructions [of the *inescapable presuppositions* of argument] that he is caught up in performative contradictions[,] . . . I must appeal to the *intuitive preunderstanding* that *every* subject competent in speech and action brings to a process of argumentation."[17] Two related ideas are notable in these formulations. One is that certain meanings, contents, forces, claims, or commitments inhere in (or are "bound up with," or are "part of the sense of") particular terms (or "concepts") and strings of words per se. The other is that certain concepts, claims, and commitments are deeply connected with ("presupposed by" or "fundamental to the nature of") our mental and discursive activities. Both ideas are recurrent; both, in my view, are dubious; and both, I think, are the product of cognitive tendencies—tricks of thought—that may be, as tendencies, endemic.

It appears from the formulations cited above and from the arguments in which they figure that the discursive/conceptual elements in question (concepts, meanings, claims, commitments) and also their interconnectedness are experienced introspectively by those who appeal to them as self-evident—intuitively right. This is not remarkable in view of the particular conceptual traditions in which, as philosophers, logicians, and classicists, they were presumably both formally educated and professionally disciplined, and in view also of the particular idioms with which, as scholars in those disciplines, they presumably operate more or less every day of their lives. What is worth remarking, however, is the move from *experiencing* one's own cognitive activities and their conceptual and discursive products (that is, one's own thought, beliefs, and linguistic usages) as self-evident or intuitively right to *positing and claiming* them as prior, autonomous, transcendentally presupposed, and properly universal.

It appears (on the evidence of, among other things, alternative introspections) that ideas such as "inescapable presuppositions," "intuitive preunderstanding," and "truth absolute" are neither universal nor inescapable. On the contrary, it is possible to believe (as statements in this book testify) that such concepts and the sense of their inherent meanings and deep interconnectedness are, rather, the products and effects of rigorous instruction and routine participation in a particular conceptual tradition and its related idiom. It is also possible to believe, accordingly, that instruction (more or less rigorous) in some other conceptual tradition, and familiarity with its idiom, would yield other conceptions and descriptions of "the fundamental nature" of "thought itself" and of what is "presupposed" by "the very act of assertion." Or, one might say (in the alternative idiom of one such alternative tradition), different personal intellectual/professional histories are likely to make different descriptions and accounts of the operations of human cognition and communication appear coherent and adequate.[18]

I pursue these points further below. First, however, a brief trip to the theater and to school, which are, in this neighborhood, not too far apart.

Theaters of Instruction

Foiled, exposed, and rejected, the devil in the old morality play exits stage left, muttering curses. The evocation of theater is not irrelevant here. The archetypal, exemplary self-refutation, *Theaetetus,* is, of course, dramatically scripted, and theatricality remains central to its re-productions. The dramatis personae are certainly among the most compelling in cultural history: the callow, showy, scoffing, hubristic truth-denier; the seasoned, gently ironic, ultimately martyred truth-deliverer; plus, as crucial parties to the scene, the mixed chorus of disciples and occasional interlocutors and, not insignificantly, the audience itself, motley representatives of the community at large.[19] The self-refuting skeptic recalls other self-deluded, self-destroying heroes and villains: Oedipus unwittingly condemning himself in his sentence on the killer of Laius; Hamlet's uncle, Claudius, "hoist with his own petard;"[20] Satan, self-corrupted and self-damned, his engines of unholy warfare recoiling upon himself.

The structural principle of self-refutation is turnabout, reversal— in logic, *peritrope*. It is the counterpart of *peripeteia*, the turn of fortune that Aristotle thought most conducive to the effects of tragedy: fear, pity, catharsis. The emotional effects of both—classical tragedy and classic self-refutation—are complex: anxiety and satisfaction, as fear yields to pity and terror to relief; the pleasures of formal symmetry (revenge and justice coincide, the punishment both fits and mirrors the crime) joined with the knowledge of a threat averted, an outlaw brought to book, order restored, orthodoxy vindicated. There is in self-refutation the satisfaction, too, of cognitive and pragmatic economy: the exposure and defeat of an adversary accomplished neatly, at his own cost. And, certainly, the frequency of suicides and self-mutilations in tragedy indicates that *self*-destruction has, as such, a certain frisson.

Self-refutation dramas—like all great artworks, or so we are told—can be experienced repeatedly without satiety. The effects are endlessly renewable here, perhaps because the threat involved is itself so strong and ineradicable. Every orthodoxy is to some extent unstable, vulnerable. And the skeptic's denial or countertruth is appalling: "All is flux," "It is as each man perceives it," "No knowledge is certain," "God is dead," "There is nothing outside of the text." A thrill of horror: What if it's *right?* Everything would be lost—rational argument, objective knowledge, truth itself, *and my life's work for naught.* But also, perhaps, another thrill, closer to desire: what if it's *right?* Everything would be permitted—anarchy, murder, mayhem, *and I, free at last of my life's work.*

The full tragic effect, it has been said, requires the spectator's identification with the hubristic hero: at least a moment of sympathy with him—or her—in opposition to all those gods, seers, kings, courtiers, and choruses of the orthodox. It may be that, among the audiences of self-refutation dramas, even among the disciples themselves, there are flashes of identification with the skeptic, even, sometimes, secret hopes for his triumph. Indeed, although the two lead figures described above—truth-denier and truth-deliverer—are familiar, their respective characterizations tend to blur (scoffer and ironist, tragic hero and martyr), and their respective roles can seem as reversible as the self-refuter's own argument. Thus Socrates can be seen as trickster and, perhaps, as the most radical of skeptics.[21]

Nor is it irrelevant here that the drama of self-refutation was originally produced as a pedagogic exercise for the betterment of the young. The "brilliant" (as he is called) but philosophically immature Theaetetus arrives in a state of enthrallment to dubious doctrines. He is delivered to better understanding—if not to the knowledge of knowledge itself—by witnessing and participating in the exposure of the self-refutation of those doctrines, thereby undergoing, through Socrates's midwifely ministrations, his own intellectual rebirth. The model is powerful and itself proves enthralling, the drama still re-produced, more than two millennia later, for the delivery of similarly bright, abashable seventeen- and eighteen-year-olds.[22] Are the doctrines not, after all, still the same, still seductive, and still false? Perhaps. In any case, the classic pedagogic exposure merges, along the way, with other stagings of demonic exposure and spiritual salvation, including exorcism.

As often observed, the enlightenment of the young in formal education operates through a process not dissimilar from other inductions into orthodoxy, from boot camp to monastery: a process of ordeal, alternating public punishment and public reward, that concludes with a welcoming by and incorporation into the special community. Given the institutional conditions under which this commonly occurs, that is, the regular convening in a theater of instruction of young men and women[23] in quasi-familial and semi-erotic relationships to—and rivalry with—both each other and the supervising master or mistress of the mysteries, it is not surprising that public humiliation has emerged as a favored technique. Moreover, in a company where status is measured by the development of intellectual prowess, there is probably no instrument of instruction more effective in that respect than the demonstration that one has unwittingly *refuted oneself*—the counterpart, no doubt, of the exposure, in other companies (athletic or military, for example), of more bodily self-disablings or self-foulings. It is no wonder, then, that the effects of such exposures (however gently, subtly, wittily, or ironically administered) remain, for those who receive or witness them, so powerful and profound, or that fear of a charge of relativism can haunt the spirits and buckle the knees of grown men and women, even the most sophisticated of them, even the most otherwise unorthodox of them.

Dreams of Reason

Like the devil, the skeptic is never finally vanquished or finally triumphant. No matter how decisively her self-refutation is demonstrated, she does not acknowledge or indeed believe that she has refuted herself. Nor does the orthodox believer regard the skeptic's evasion of his charge as proper, or acknowledge the justice of her countercharge that he has begged all the questions.[24] Alternatively, of course, it could be said that skepticism triumphant *is* orthodoxy.

But the question may still be asked: If orthodoxy is that which is manifestly true, self-evidently right, and intuitively and universally preunderstood, then how is it that its truth and rightness elude the skeptic? The orthodox answer to this question is familiar: profound defects and deficiencies of intellect and character—an innate incapacity for logical thinking, unregenerate corruption by false (or French) doctrine, domination by personal resentment and political ideology, or unfamiliarity with the best work on the subject in analytic philosophy.

The explanatory asymmetry here—that is, the orthodox believer's conviction that he believes what he does because it is true while skeptics and heretics believe what they do because there is something the matter with them—is a general feature of defenses of orthodoxy: political, aesthetic, and scientific as well as philosophical (or religious). Its recurrence seems to reflect the cognitive tendencies alluded to above: that is, the tendency to experience one's own beliefs as self-evident and, sometimes, to posit them as prior, necessary, and properly universal. The failure to believe what is self-evident is self-evidently folly; the failure to believe what is necessarily presupposed is necessarily irrational—or perverse.

The tendency to experience one's own thinking as inevitable and to experience its products as prior and autonomous is, in the conceptual traditions and idioms significant for this book, not a foundational intuition to be affirmed but a more or less intriguing phenomenon to be explained. Elements of the account of belief outlined in Chapter 3 are relevant here and can be recalled and extended accordingly.

Certain configurations of perceptual/behavioral tendencies ("beliefs") are strengthened and stabilized by our effective-enough and predictable-enough interactions with our environments (including other people and what they produce, for example, institutions and discourses). To the extent that this occurs, we (human, social, cultural, verbal creatures) may experience and interpret those configurations reflexively as "referring to" or "being about" specific, determinate features of an autonomous reality: features, that is, seen as (simply) "out there," prior to, quite separate from, and quite independent of, our own interactions, past or current, with our environments. This experience, so interpreted, is not either "illusion" or "delusion." Nevertheless, it could be *otherwise*—and, for some purposes, from some perspectives, more usefully, interestingly, coherently, and appropriably—described and interpreted.[25]

It is evident that, with some disciplined effort (by, for example, mystics, Buddhists, and deconstructionists), the experience of an autonomous reality may be subjected to reflexive scrutiny and to temporary denaturalization, destabilization, and dis-integration.[26] Descriptions of technologically induced "virtual reality" also make alternative interpretations of the experience easier to entertain. Subjects report that, after a certain amount of interactive feedback from computer-generated sensory stimuli—goggle-generated images that shift their shapes and size as the subject turns her head, glove-induced pressures that vary with the subject's hand motions—these modally diverse sensations will seem suddenly to integrate themselves and to surround the subject as a distinct and autonomous environment.[27] The cognitive dynamics of our ordinary experiences of "real" reality are, perhaps, not too different from the dynamics of such reported experiences of "virtual" reality.[28]

Human beings appear to have a strong tendency to protect their particular beliefs from destabilization, even in the face of what strike other people as clearly disconfirming arguments and evidence. We encountered this tendency in Chapter 3 as *cognitive conservatism*. As suggested there, although it often operates in technically "irrational" ways (as assessed by, say, decision scientists), cognitive conservatism is better regarded not as a flaw or failing but, rather, as the *ambivalent* (some times or ways good, some times or ways bad) counterpart of an also endemic and ambivalent tendency to cognitive flexibility and responsiveness.[29] For better and for worse, cognitive conservatism yields intellectual stability, consistency, reliability, and predictability; it also yields, for better and for

worse, powerfully self-immuring, self-perpetuating systems of political and religious belief. At its extreme, when played out in specifically theoretical domains, it can become *absolute* epistemic self-
privileging: that is, the conviction that one's convictions are undeniable, that one's assumptions are established facts or necessary presuppositions, that the entities one invokes are unproblematically
real, that the terms one uses are transparent and the senses in which
one uses them are inherent in the terms themselves, and, ultimately,
that no alternative conceptualizations or formulations are possible
at all, at least no adequate or "coherent" ones—at least not for
beings claiming to be "rational." Cognitive conservatism is an endemic tendency and a mixed blessing. Its hypertrophic development, absolute epistemic self-privileging, is a human frailty, common enough among common folk but, in rationalist philosophy,
honed to a fine art.

For those well instructed in traditional foundational epistemology, everything—each concept, each opposition, each link and each
move—hangs together comfortably and, it seems, self-evidently. It
hangs together in part because, perhaps, that's the way human cognition works, but also because the major project and achievement
of foundational epistemology is the maintenance, monitoring, and
justification of precisely that interdependency: the rigorous inter-
organization of everything that fits and the vigorous rejection (and
"refutation") of everything that doesn't. Indeed, disciplinary philosophy *as such* (I do not say every philosopher or every philosophical work) can be seen as the cultural counterpart and institutional
extension of individual cognitive conservatism—again, for better
and for worse.

The routines—rituals, habits—of rigorously taught, strenuously
learned conceptual production and performance come to operate
virtually automatically, to be experienced as necessary and autonomous, and, sometimes, to be posited as prior to and independent
of the activities of any mortal human agent.[30] The resulting coherence and interdependency of concepts, connections, distinctions,
and moves is what Derrida and other theorists speak of, with regard
to the history of Western philosophy, as "the closure of metaphysics."[31] It is not, however (as such theorists commonly stress), altogether closed, nor could any conceptual system ever be. Both individually and culturally, there is always noise and uncontrollable

play in the system. Individually, our beliefs are always heterogeneous and, though more or less effective and coordinated ad hoc, not globally coherent and always potentially conflicting.[32] Moreover, there are always glitches in cultural transmission. We never learn our lessons perfectly. The rigorous training is never rigorous enough. There is always someone who missed class that day, or got distracted, or came from somewhere else, or heard something else that she liked better first, or just didn't care: the class misfit—outlaw, heretic, devil, skeptic, spoiler.

None of this is to say that the postmodern skeptic has "discovered the objective truth of the inherent wrongness" of traditional epistemology. (To an orthodox epistemologist, any skeptic who claimed that would refute herself on the spot. To a postmodernist, any postmodernist who claimed such a thing would be a pretty problematic postmodernist.) The postmodern skeptic does not say or think that traditional epistemology is inherently wrong, an error, or a delusion. She observes and believes that the conceptual systems it sustains operate well enough for a good many people. Nevertheless, she also knows that those systems and that epistemology do not operate as well for her as other conceptualizations. That does not make them, in her eyes, all "equally valid" or "equally invalid." All are, and will be, measured and judged by, among other things, their applicability, coherence, and connectability. By such measures, different epistemologies and conceptual systems are found, and will be found, better or worse or, sometimes, congruent enough. But the measurements themselves, taken under differing conditions, interpreted from different perspectives, will vary. Equivalence and disparity, like commensurability and incommensurability, are, in her view, not absolute but contingent matters. As Protagoras might have put it, man is the measure of all the measures that man has.

The postmodern skeptic thinks that the interest and utility of all theoretical formulations are contingent. She is not disturbed, however, by the idea that, in order to be self-consistent, she must "concede" the "merely" contingent interest and utility of her own theoretical formulations. Nor is she embarrassed by her similar "obligation" to "concede" the historicity—and thus instability and eventual replacement—of the systems and idioms that she finds preferable to traditional epistemology and that she would, and does, recommend to other people. She is not disturbed or embarrassed—or, to her own way of thinking, self-refuted—by these things because she believes, in comfortable accord with the conceptual systems and idioms she prefers, that that's the way all disciplinary knowledge—science, philosophy, literary studies, and so forth—evolves. And she also believes that, all told (as she tallies such matters), that's not a bad way for it to happen.

Although the postmodern skeptic is not affirming (self-contradictorily) "the (objective) truth of the (inherent) wrongness" of traditional epistemology, a traditionalist may hear her affirming it, just as if those words were coming right out of her mouth. That is because, by his[33] logic, that's just what it means for someone to *deny* something. Thus, he hears her contradicting (and, in his terms, refuting) herself. By the postmodern skeptic's own logic, the traditionalist is mistaken. The traditionalist will not see his mistake as one so long as he remains a traditionalist. He may, however, become a postmodern skeptic himself—or, of course, the skeptic may become a born-again believer.[34]

This last point is significant: not the conversion (or corruption) of the believer (or the skeptic) per se, but, despite the reciprocal impasses indicated here, the general possibility of the transformation of belief. Nothing said here implies a permanent structure of deadlock. On the contrary, what has been said explicitly and implied throughout is that no orthodoxy—or skepticism—can be totally stable, no theoretical closure complete, no incommensurability absolute.

By the same token, one cannot *interact* with a theoretical closure and remain totally "outside" of it, even if the interaction is skeptical or adversarial. Thus one disputes "logic" with logic (or logic with "logic"), neither identical but each, over time, shaped by the other.[35] The process—that is, skeptical, adversarial interactions with traditional conceptual systems—is both rhetorical and cognitive: played out in public theaters (classrooms, conference halls, the pages of journals) and also in the private theater of the mind, where the "self" takes all the roles—truth-deliverer and truth-denier, master and disciple, chorus of mixed voices and motley audience—and every self-refutation is, simultaneously, the self's triumph and transformation.

6

The Skeptic's Turn:
A Performance of
Contradiction

It is said that, in the very speech acts through which the contemporary skeptic (poststructuralist, deconstructionist, anti-foundationalist, and so forth) denies things such as meaning, reason, truth, or value, she affirms those very things and thus performatively contradicts herself. For, it is explained, a meaningful denial of (determinate) meaning presupposes (determinate) meaning, to argue with (classic ideas of) reason is to appeal to (classic ideas of) reason, statements that question (absolute) truth necessarily claim (absolute) truth, the very condition of possibility of a rejection of (objective) value is a commitment to (objective) value, and so forth.[1] These explanations, however, are themselves subject to question.

As in classic self-refutation arguments, the force of the charge of performative contradiction depends on a paraphrase of the skeptic's skepticism that elides just what she questions.[2] Thus, the parenthesized modifiers above, required if the charge is to hit its target but typically omitted in statements of it, are crucial. For, when included, they make the skeptic's denial in each case duly specific (for example, what she denies is not meaning *per se* or *all* meaning but the classic idea of meaning as determinate) and expose as at least dubious the allegedly entailed presupposition (does a meaningful denial of the classic idea of determinate meaning necessarily presuppose *just that idea?*), thus depriving the charge of its immediate plausibility. The traditionalist elides the skeptic's speech acts

88

in this way not because he is being willfully deceptive but, commonly, because he does not appreciate the significance, for the skeptic, of the specificity of what she is questioning ("Meaning is meaning," he might say, "if it's not determinate meaning, then it's not really meaning *at all*"³), or, more generally and significantly here, because it is difficult for him to entertain the idea that the conceptualization in question *is* questionable. As with the classic charge of self-refutation, then, the logic that sustains the exposure of a performative contradiction (and gives it persuasive force for many audiences) coincides exactly with the network of traditional conceptualizations at issue—or, in classical terms, it is circular. That, however, is hardly the end of the story. Indeed, as we shall see, it is only the beginning—though, aptly enough for any circle (and many stories), it may, in fact, also be the end.

Much of the current authority of the idea of performative contradiction derives from Frankfurt School critical theory, where deployment of the charge serves a number of functions, ranging from the routine refutation of various contemporary ("counter-enlightenment") views to the validation of the specific norms of discourse ethics. This chapter considers the general operation of these efforts, beginning with the charge as framed by Karl-Otto Apel and, in that form, subsequently appropriated and extended by Jürgen Habermas. Along the way, we shall encounter a number of other issues of general interest here, among them, the resourcefulness of foundationalist logic, the elusiveness of the norms of discourse ethics, and the broader intellectual stakes involved in the particular controversies at hand.

The Skeptic's Norms

In *Moral Consciousness and Communicative Action*, Habermas cites Apel's analysis of communicative action as the most promising current argument for what he calls moral "cognitivism," explained as the view that normative rules for ethical conduct (e.g., *One should not deceive other people*), like "statements of fact and mathematical relations," admit of objective truth.⁴ Crucial to the argument supporting this position in Apel's work is his refutation of all arguments *contesting* it via the exposure of their performative contradiction. Apel frames the refutation/exposure in its relevant form in re-

sponse to an anti-foundationalist argument by the German philosopher, Hans Albert. Albert argues that foundationalism—specifically, the effort to ground the validity of certain norms on a priori
foundations—is logically untenable, being caught in an infinite regress (how are the grounds themselves grounded?) from which it
can escape only by making circular appeals to its own axioms or by
breaking off arbitrarily and thus dogmatically. In homage, presumably, to the legendary Baron who lifted himself out of difficult circumstances by pulling up on his own hair, Albert calls this set of
alternatives "Münchhausen's trilemma."[5]

Frankfurt School discourse ethics, which maintains that certain
norms of speech and argument can be grounded in the a priori
presuppositions of communication,[6] seems vulnerable to Albert's
objections. Seeking to refute the argument, Apel turns the tables
on Albert and anti-foundationalist skepticism more generally,
charging the latter with fatal self-contradiction. For, the counterargument goes, "[I]n putting forward his objection, the opponent
necessarily assumes the validity of at least those logical rules that
are irreplaceable if we are to understand his argument as a refutation."[7] In other words, the anti-foundationalist contradicts himself
because, in and through the very act of demonstrating the logical
untenability of foundationalism, he attests to the necessity of *the
very thing* that he rejects, namely the (a priori?) validity of certain
(in this case, logical) norms.

As indicated by my parenthetical question, this table-turning appears somewhat strained. For there is a significant difference between what the anti-foundationalist's objection explicitly questions,
namely the logical propriety of *a priori* justifications for ethical and
other norms, and what he thereby necessarily assumes, which seems
only to be the effective operation (validity, in that sense) of the
relevant logical norms. To be sure, the skeptic *would* contradict
himself if, in arguing that foundationalism was illogical, he claimed
or assumed that the logical norms to which his argument appealed
were valid in the foundationalist sense of demonstrable on a priori
grounds. There is, however, no reason to think that anti-
foundational skeptics would claim or do believe this. On the contrary, the idea of a priori foundations is just what such skeptics are,
by definition, skeptical about. But here is just where the special
twist of *performative* (self-)contradiction exhibits its force. For Apel

would insist that it makes no difference what Albert or any other anti-foundationalist (or, for that matter, anyone else) believes or doesn't believe, claims or doesn't claim: the (a priori) validity of logical norms just *is* presupposed by his argument, at least "if we are to understand" it as such, that is, "as a refutation." That type of necessity is just what it means to say that something is a priori. Accordingly, the anti-foundationalist's arguments are continuously and necessarily nullified by his very act of raising them.

A more Sisyphean torment than this could hardly be imagined, at least for a philosopher. But perhaps the anti-foundationalist can escape such a fate. Albert (or any other anti-foundationalist), in seeking to expose the logical problems of foundational demonstration, does assume certain logical norms. Given a non-foundational account of norms, however, there is nothing self-contradictory in these acts, performatively or otherwise.[8] The crux here is a familiar but significant disjunction. While the skeptic and the transcendental foundationalist may both "assume," in the sense of employ and appeal to, pretty much the same logical rules, each of them may *conceptualize* those rules and their operation in radically different ways. What is significant here is that acknowledgment of even the possibility of this disjunction (more or less same rules, more or less same uses, radically different conceptualizations) is excluded by the foundationalist's position, which not only posits the necessary validity of certain rules of argumentation but takes for granted as necessary and uniquely proper its own conceptions of the nature and operation of *all* argument and *all* logic.[9]

It is evident that Habermas and Apel give prior, tacit privilege, in their exposures of performative contradiction as elsewhere in their work, to a particular theory of communication, namely, the somewhat ad hoc "formal-pragmatic" linguistics they construct out of selected elements of Austin's speech-act theory (largely as mediated by John Searle),[10] selected elements of Chomsky's universal grammar, and H. P. Grice's explicitly neo-Kantian notions of conversational implicature.[11] Of interest here are not the particular problems with this theory of communication (though I think those problems are extensive), but just its contestable status in principle and the fact that virtually every element of it is currently contested.[12] Similarly and more significantly for the moment, the charge of performative contradiction privileges a particular theory of logical/

discursive norms, namely, the idea that such norms are logically prior to, and can be identified independent of, the occurrence of any actual acts or experiences (including the acts and experiences of any of the particular philosophers making those identifications). This idea, too, is both contestable in principle and strenuously contested in fact by a number of contemporary theorists.[13] Such theorists would, accordingly, be skeptical not only of the logical coherence of foundational moral theory (the skepticism specifically charged here with performative contradiction) but also of *each of the key constituents of the idea of performative contradiction itself.* Neither Apel nor Habermas considers, as such, the order of skepticism just mentioned: that is, the questioning of foundationalism coupled with the questioning of *both* the specific logic of its defense *and* what its defenders see and appeal to as the nature and authority of logic more generally. The point is significant here because the confrontation of strenuously defended classic beliefs with skepticisms of *that order* marks much contemporary theoretical controversy and is a virtual blueprint for deadlock.

In the alternative view of linguistic normativity outlined in Chapter 4, the norms of discourse (grammatical rules, conversational maxims, communicative conventions, laws of argumentation and logic, and so forth) are seen as formalized, standardized descriptions of recurrently emergent, relatively stable, institutionally reinforced social practices, acquired by the members of a community through social interaction and experienced by them as generalized tendencies and educated expectations. Accordingly, it could be said that an anti-foundationalist skeptic, in exposing the conceptual difficulties of foundationalist moral theory to a particular audience in a particular arena of debate, will harbor the educated expectation that certain discursive practices (a certain lexicon of philosophical terms, a certain range of intellectual-historical allusions, a certain set of logical/conceptual moves, and so forth) will be in play and that her critique will be interpreted and evaluated by at least a good part of that audience in relation to the norms associated with those practices in that sort of arena. The latter would include prevailing norms of logical propriety, which the skeptic may recognize and grant as exceptionally general in applicability. Unlike the neo-Kantian discourse-ethicist, however, the skeptic may conceive of the relevant norms of discourse as contextually responsive (and thus both contingent and variable), as operating with a certain degree of laxity (that is, in only *more or less* certain ways and only *often enough*), and as interacting with other relatively effective discursive practices that are commonly described and traditionally bracketed out as ("merely") rhetorical.

Apel's rebuttal of Albert's anti-foundationalist argument via the charge of performative contradiction *assumes* that the a priori validity of logical rules *must be assumed*. Thus, like the prodigious Baron, the defender of foundationalism lifts himself out of his difficulties by his own assumptions.[14] Is the feat successful? Well, that depends on how, and from what perspective, success is measured. If logical practices are sharply distinguished from rhetorical practices and logical norms are seen as absolute and noncontingent, then the foundationalist's rebuttal, being circular, must be seen as forfeiting all claim to logical/discursive propriety. If, however, like the contemporary skeptic herself, one sees the practices of logic and rhetoric as inevitably (and not condemnably) intertwined and conceives all norms as inevitably (and not undesirably) responsive and contingent in their operations, then one will expect and understand that Apel's table-turning charge, though logically circular, does not thereby lose its persuasive, restabilizing force, either for Apel himself or for a good part of his audience.[15] The (ironic) turn here is worth remarking: the foundationalist's argument is condemned absolutely by his own absolutist conception of logical norms, but relatively rescued (though in terms he would reject) by the contemporary skeptic's alternative ("relativistic") conception of them.[16]

Skeptical Confrontations

The vanquishing of skeptics is not only a continuously necessary adversarial operation for Frankfurt School moral theory but becomes, in Habermas's recent work, its redemption and justification. Specifically, he adapts and develops Apel's exposure of the anti-foundationalist's performative contradiction not only as a shield and weapon against critics and rivals but as a positive quasi-foundational method.[17] The method, its logical/rhetorical operations, and the rather vivid, dramatic terms in which Habermas illustrates it, will repay our attention here.

At a central point in *Moral Consciousness*, having rejected, as counter-intuitive, the major contending alternatives to transcendental moral theory,[18] Habermas turns to the validation of the specific claims of discourse ethics. The procedure, he explains, will take the form of "an imaginary debate between an advocate of ethical cognitivism and an advocate of moral skepticism" staged as "a seven-round debate," with the (hypothetical) skeptic bringing in objections and the (real) cognitivist, represented by Habermas, replying to them in turn (76–77).[19] For example, the skeptic, in view of what he[20] sees as the *"pluralism of ultimate value orientations,"* will say that he doubts whether consensus is possible at all, whereupon the cognitivist will reply that it is possible *in principle,* specifically on the principle of universalization, (U).[21] Then the skeptic will object "that (U) represents a hasty generalization of moral intuitions peculiar to our own Western culture," whereupon "the cognitivist will respond with a *transcendental justification* of his moral principle [i.e., (U)]." (76).

This sort of exchange will continue until the fifth round, when the skeptic raises objections to the whole idea of transcendental justification. The cognitivist "meets them with a more cautious version of Apel's argument" (76), the argument, that is, that the skeptic's unavoidable performative contradiction, in the very act of raising those very objections, is itself proof of the inescapability of just that mode of justification. Habermas observes that Münchhausen's trilemma—that is, the foundationalist's choice among circularity, arbitrariness, and infinite regress—is a problem for transcendental moral theory only if justification is seen as a logical *deduction.* Accordingly, the special value of Apel's argument from performative contradiction is not only that it disables the anti-foundationalist critique as such but that it "revives the transcendental mode of justification" by providing moral theory with a method of *nondeductive* but still *inescapable* proof (80). He continues: "In the sixth round, in the face of this promising justification of a discourse ethics, the skeptic can take refuge in a *refusal to enter into discourse.* But as we will see, by doing so he has maneuvered himself into a hopeless position (76)." Indeed, it is not only hopeless but, as will be seen, approaches a tragic denouement, and, as such, recalls the (self-)sacrifice of the agents/victims of self-refutation encountered in the previous chapter.

Initiating the debate, Habermas rehearses the key idea, namely that the skeptic, in the very act of "involving himself in a specific argument with the goal of refuting ethical cognitivism . . . must inevitably subscribe to certain tacit presuppositions of argumentation that are incompatible with the propositional content of his objection" (82). Accordingly, the inescapably valid rules of discourse and argumentation can be identified "through systematic analysis of [the] performative contradictions" of anyone who contests them. Habermas gives some examples of the sorts of tacit presuppositions he has in mind: *No speaker may contradict himself* and *Every speaker may assert only what he really believes.* Such rules, he stresses, are "not mere *conventions*" or just "definition[s] favoring an ideal form of communication," but the inescapable presuppositions of any speech community and, as such, constitutive elements of any ethics of discourse. (88–89).

Two steps are involved in the validation-by-contradiction-analysis. First, one "appeal[s] to the intuitive preunderstanding that every subject competent in speech and action brings to a process of argumentation" (89–90). Second, one convinces anyone who is skeptical of the norm that he cannot contest it without self-contradiction.[22] Habermas illustrates the method with an example which, as it happens, is ill-chosen for his purposes but instructive for ours. The rule in question is: *To convince someone of something, you must do it with reason, not lies.* To demonstrate that this is an inescapably presupposed norm and not just a matter of conventional practice or privileged definition, the cognitivist presents the skeptic with the following two sentences:

1. Using good reasons, I finally convinced H that *p*.
2. *Using lies, I finally convinced H that *p*.

According to Habermas, it will be intuitively clear to the skeptic as to everyone else that only statement (1) is proper. That, he explains, is because of "the internal connection between the expressions 'to convince someone of something' and 'to come to a reasoned agreement about something' " (90). Conversely, statement (2), because it implies conditions that "contradict the pragmatic presuppositions" that hold good "not only for particular instances but inevitably for every process of argumentation," is manifestly "nonsensical" (ibid.). At the most, he adds, you can legitimately say:

3. Using lies, I finally *talked* H *into believing* that *p*.[23]

Significantly enough, however, the demonstration will falter here for many speakers of English, who will have little difficulty supplying linguistically proper and intuitively acceptable instances of the supposedly nonsensical statement: for example, Iago's possible confession or boast, "Using lies, I finally convinced Othello that Desdemona was unfaithful to him."[24]

The translators' note at this point is quite pertinent. They remark: "Habermas contrasts *überzeugen* and *überreden*, here translated as 'convince' and 'talk into.' The contrast is more emphatic in German than in English; *überzeugen* implies the use of argument, while 'to cause to believe by argument' is one but not the only meaning of 'convince.' "[25]

But if *überzeugen* already implies, in German, the use of argument (meaning, as Habermas always glosses it, "reason" or reasoned argument), then the supposedly inescapable presupposition and rule of discourse ethics illustrated by statement (1)—that is, *To convince [überzeugen] someone of something, you must do it with reason, not lies*—is just a tautology or, at most, a specification of certain of the conditions under which a particular verbal form tends, currently, to be used by speakers of a particular language. If the validation of that rule depends on the skeptic's and everybody else's intuition of the *un*acceptability of statement (2), and if, as appears to be the case, speakers of German and English have rather different intuitions in this regard, then the validity of the rule is, precisely, a *matter of convention*. To be sure, if people do not in fact routinely lie to other people in order to convince them of things, it is not a matter of (mere) linguistic convention. If they do not *speak* of doing so in those terms, however, it is at least in part because of the conventional practices of linguistic usage, in accord with which we do not, at least not if we are German-speaking, use the word *überzeugen* to describe that communally disagreeable but nevertheless not impossible (and perhaps, in a sense, inescapable) possibility.[26]

Just Accidents and Mere Conventions

Habermas strenuously rejects in advance the suggestion that statement (2), above (Using lies I finally [*überzeugt*] H that *p*), may not sound right because that's not the way we (members of the relevant verbal community, here speakers of German) commonly use the word *"überzeugen."* It is not, he insists, just a matter of dictionary definitions or mere semantic convention, but because of "the *internal connection* [*internen Beziehung*] between the expressions 'to convince someone of something' and 'to come to a reasoned agreement about something' " (90, my emphasis): "I can refer someone to a dictionary to look up the meaning of the verb 'to convince.' But that will not explain *why* statement (2) is a semantic paradox ... In the *final* analysis [*letzlich*], convictions rest on a consensus that has been attained discursively," i.e., in Habermas's terms, through reasoned argument (90, his emphasis).

The issue here, clearly a central one, may be illuminated by consideration of a related argument in a recent work by the British analytic philosopher, L. Jonathan Cohen. Cohen is concerned with the distinction between the concepts *belief* and *acceptance*. His major claim is that, while "believing that *p*" (as in "I believe that the Mississippi will flood tomorrow" or "He believes that monarchy is the best form of government") implies a passive, involuntary cognitive state, "accepting that *p*" (as in "I accept that you meant no harm," or "He accepts that monarchy is the best form of government") implies a cognitive state that is voluntary and morally responsible.[27] *Beliefs*, he explains, are thought of "as resulting from the operations of relevant causal factors, such as sensory stimuli or the transmission of information," while *acceptances* are thought of "as outcomes of reasoning in conformity with rules."[28] These distinctions, he suggests, may be of some philosophical importance, reflecting and revealing fundamental aspects of mental life and, perhaps, of ethics as well. They are not, Cohen insists, "just an accident of linguistic idiom."[29]

But what does it mean for something to be *just an accident* of linguistic idiom or, as in Habermas's formulations, just a matter of dictionary definitions or *mere* convention? Such phrases, and the contrasts they imply to something else that is necessary, nonarbitrary, and deep, are familiar. They figure recurrently in defenses of rationalist epistemology and in claims made for the distinctive significance and irreplaceable functions of so-called conceptual analysis, commonly over and against more empirical investigations or naturalistic accounts of cognition and verbal or other social norms. It could be argued, however, that such demoting phrases and contrasts reflect dubious distinctions, dubious assumptions re-

garding the relations between concepts and verbal usage, and severely confined notions of the historical and social operations of
language.

The differences that Cohen observes in the usage and implications of the expressions *"believe* that *p"* and *"accept* that *p"* are, to
be sure, neither totally arbitrary nor strictly local features of a particular language.[30] It does not follow, however, that they reflect universal or necessary features of human mental life. The two terms,
the expressions in which they commonly figure, and what Cohen
spells out as their perceived implications all operate within a dense,
extensive, and highly ramified network of interrelated ideas *about*
mental life, including (as in his explication of them) the idea that
beliefs have propositions as their contents, that propositions can be
either (and only) true or false, that cognitive acts are either (and
only) voluntary or involuntary, and that reasoning is a special type
of cognitive process. The question here is whether, as Cohen implies, the two terms—or what he might insist were prior, autonomous, perhaps language-independent *concepts*—operate that way
anywhere, anytime, for all human beings as such (at least all adult,
sane, sober, rational, and competent ones), or if, as could otherwise
be suggested, the linguistic patterns and related conceptual operations he describes are culturally and otherwise limited.

The provisos just indicated—adult, sane, sober, rational, competent—are routine features of the formulations of rationalist philosophy, required because of the obvious or sooner-or-later troublesome *exceptions* to the generalizations (or presumptive universals)
put forth in the name of logical presuppositions. If one asked how
many such provisos would have to be added to make those generalizations empirically valid, the answer would seem to be *a great
many* and, more significantly, that a number of them would have
to be of precisely the kind explicitly rejected in these analyses as
merely conventionalist or culturally relativistic:[31] that is, specifications of class, formal and informal education, historical moment,
acculturating practices, and particular discursive/conceptual idioms. The network of ideas concerning mental life described just
above is, to be sure, not confined to contemporary, philosophically
instructed speakers of British English; it can be seen to operate,
with variations, across a relatively broad range of Western conceptual idioms.[32] There is, however, no independent (that is, non-

question-begging) reason to believe that just that set of ideas, and just those discursive distinctions and logical implications, characterize human thought as such, or, in the phrase sometimes used, "the architecture of *the* mind."

In a characteristic passage, Cohen writes: "We *think* of our beliefs as states of mind that are *normally* responsive to the truth . . . Belief is not *thought of* as being *normally* achieved at will because it is *thought of* as being *regularly* caused . . . by something independent of the believer's choice; factual beliefs are *typically* reactions to . . . [etc.].[33]

The questions that could be asked here are not only *who* is doing all that thinking (all of us? with how many exceptions or provisos?), but how Cohen himself *knows* what we are all thinking, and how either he or we *determine* all those matters of normality, regularity, and typicality. Although the fact is obscured to some extent by the objectifying effects of the passive constructions here ("is [or is not] thought of," etc.), these observations are by no means self-evident nor, it appears, are they the product of any systematic lexicographical surveys. It appears, rather, that the data for Cohen's generalizations, as for those of conceptual analysis more generally, are the analyst's personal introspections, amplified and reinforced by his observations of usage in his own more or less specific verbal and intellectual communities. As such, these data and the generalizations they yield may be of interest and use: for example, to a sociolinguist or, perhaps, as enrichments and refinements of the work of professional lexicographers.[34] My point here is not that the (often, as here, painstaking) conceptual analyses of academic philosophers are without interest or value but that, contrary to claims sometimes made for them, they do not yield unique insights into the supposed fundamental structure of human thought or the supposed inescapable presuppositions of human speech and action.

The force of logical/conceptual analysis, like that of Habermas's "*final* analysis" (see quotation above), depends on a distinction drawn between, on the one hand, the deep, necessary connections among concepts intuitively known to ("competent") speakers and revealed or reconstructed by such analysis and, on the other hand, the superficial, contingent ("just accident[al]") relations of linguistic convention. That distinction, however, though a commonplace of rationalist language theory, is itself questionable. Neither an analytic philosopher nor anyone else could identify the conceptual and discursive operations of a particular verbal form (*convince, believe, accept, salt,* or *rain*) *without* considering particular patterns of verbal usage, even if only those he or she discovers through personal introspection. Nor, it appears, does anything *other than* some set of relatively stable patterns of usage authorize the normative rules and objectifying claims that attend such analyses, including Cohen's suggestion that *acceptances,* as distinct from *beliefs,* are "thought of as outcomes of reasoning in conformity with rules," and Habermas's rule that only a belief that "rest[s] on a consensus that has been attained discursively" counts as a *conviction.* In short, the analysis in each case seems to depend on what it claims to transcend, namely, specific and contingent patterns of verbal usage—or, as we commonly say, linguistic convention.

Münchhausen Proofs

We may return now to the moral cognitivist's (or discourse-ethicist's) ongoing demonstration to the skeptic that the rule in question *(Convince people only with reasoned argument, not lies)* is inescapable. Observing that the defiantly contrary statement (2) (Using lies I finally convinced H that *p*) "contradict[s] the pragmatic presuppositions of argumentation as such," Habermas continues:

> I can prove this by making a proponent who *defends the truth* of statement (2) aware that he thereby gets himself into a performative contradiction. For as soon as he cites a reason for the truth of (2), he enters a process of argumentation and has *thereby accepted the presupposition,* among others, that he can never *convince* an opponent of something by resorting to lies . . . But then the content of the assertion to be justified contradicts one of the presuppositions the proponent *must operate with if his statement is to be regarded as a justification.* (90–91, emphases, except for *convince,* added)

Two points, highlighted by the emphases above, are crucial here. First, it is clear that the strictly hypothetical skeptic constructed by Habermas for his own purposes must operate in technically very specific ways. Among other things, his questioning or denial of some proposition must be understood as equivalent to his *defense of the truth of its negation.* So characterized, the speech-acts of the hypothetical skeptic are quite distinct from those of the real-enough postmodern skeptic evoked at the conclusion of Chapter 5, who, we recall, does not, when she denies things, necessarily (to her mind) assert the truth of their negatives nor (to her mind) ever assert the truth of things in the assumed traditional (Platonic or Fregean) sense of either *truth* or *assertion*. Indeed, Habermas's hypothetical skeptic, even if different in other ways from the postmodern skeptic, could question this supposed rule of discourse ethics without defending the truth of its negation (and without performative contradiction) by simply observing that, as formulated here, the rule requires, dubiously enough in each case, that *lies* be seen as distinct and clear-cut entities and that the meaning of *reason* be always already known.

Second, the hypothetical skeptic must *already accept* the cognitivist's preemptive definition of *justification* in order to agree that the rule in question (you must not use lies to convince people of things) *must* be presupposed if his argument in defense of the acceptability of statement (2)—his reminder, let us say, that Iago did use lies to convince Othello—is to count as a justification. But, then, the cognitivist's supposed proof of the inescapability of this rule of discourse ethics is pure tautology. For all that has been demonstrated here—and, correspondingly, for any other of his presumptively inescapable rules—is that anyone who *already accepts* the general network of assumptions and definitions that constitutes Frankfurt School discourse ethics will contradict himself if he denies any of the specific claims that may be deduced from it.[35]

The Skeptic's (Self-) Slaughter

In the sixth round of the debate between the cognitivist and the hypothetical skeptic, the stakes become higher as well as more complex. It is no longer, here, just the existence and identity of specific discourse norms that the skeptic questions but the possibility of discourse ethics altogether: the effectiveness of its methods, the validity of its remaining claims, and its very dignity as an enterprise. Accordingly, the moves become more aggressive, the weapons grow sharper, and the Habermasian conception of argument as (ideally) a cooperative, non-strategic, non-success-oriented, mutual search for truth is harder to keep in view.

Habermas asks us now to imagine that the skeptic, anticipating his (self-) defeat if he plays this "game of wits" by the usual rules, just refuses to continue.[36] What immediately becomes clear, however, is a certain paradoxical and potentially catastrophic dependency. For, given the crucial function of the skeptic's performative contradictions in *validating* the norms of discourse ethics, it follows that *unless* he voices his skepticism regarding those norms, the norms cannot be validated. As Habermas puts it: "The *consistent skeptic* will deprive the transcendental pragmatist of a basis for his argument" (99). He notes as well certain forms this stubborn or spiteful uncooperativeness might take. The skeptic could, for example, not "argue" his position at all but just sit the controversy out, behaving, Habermas remarks, like "an ethnologist" who observes the practices of his own community "as though he were witnessing the unintelligible rites of a strange tribe." Nietzsche, he adds, "perfected this way of looking at philosophical matters, and Foucault has now rehabilitated it" (ibid.).[37] In any case, a fainthearted cognitivist (not Habermas) is imagined as "throw[ing] up his hands" when faced with a skeptic whom he cannot lure into argument: "[A] willingness to argue ... must really be presupposed," he (the other cognitivist) exclaims, "if the whole concern of moral theory is not to become pointless" (ibid.).

A postmodern skeptic would have an obvious comeback here: "Precisely," she could reply, "that is just what I and many of my fellow skeptics have been saying all along: moral theory, at least the way foundationalists define and pursue it, *is* pointless—which is why those of us interested in questions of ethics are developing alternative ways to formulate and pursue them."[38] Habermas does not write such a line into the skeptic's script, perhaps because he has already anticipated and disarmed it by *defining* moral theory in such a way that any pursuit of it other than foundationalist cognitivism is disqualified in advance.[39] In any case, he goes on to explain what the moral cognitivist *should* have said instead of throwing up his hands, namely that the skeptic, in dropping out of the debate, had thereby "voluntarily terminate[d] his membership in the community of beings who argue—no less and no more" (100).

No less and no more. What this means, Habermas observes, is that the skeptic now cannot, strictly speaking, "deny" anything, and just this incapacity will be his fatal undoing and the cognitivist's ultimate triumph. For, since the skeptic "cannot, even indirectly, deny . . . that he grew up in a web of communicative action, and that he reproduces his life in that web," then his very existence, mute though it may be, testifies to the inescapability of the presuppositions of discourse ethics. Indeed, "[a]s long as he is still alive *at all*," Habermas stresses, the skeptic cannot drop out of "the communicative practice of everyday life," to the presuppositions of which he remains bound (100). And, since the presuppositions of the practices of everyday life are "partly identical with the presuppositions of argumentation as such" (101), then it follows that *the skeptic performatively refutes his own skepticism simply in being alive.* Habermas does not hesitate to press the point home: "[N]ot unless he is willing to take refuge in suicide or serious mental illness," can the skeptic "extricate himself" from the bonds of those presuppositions or, therefore, maintain his skepticism without self-contradiction (100). The debate is over. The cognitivist has won. It has been proved that there are no live skeptics with valid arguments, or at least no live sane ones. Cognitivism as a general moral theory, and all of the specific norms it identifies, *must* be valid. And yet . . .

The hypothetical skeptic, who may remain both alive and sane to his own mind, could still object to the idea that, just because he declined to participate in a debate in which all his moves were stipulated and lines dictated in advance by his adversary, he had excommunicated himself from human society. Moreover, he could deny (precisely—refusing the cognitivist's restrictions on his mental or discursive activities) that he need sacrifice his life or sanity to retain his skepticism regarding the unique value and inescapability of transcendental moral theory. For, he could observe, while it may be true that, in order to operate effectively as a member of "the community of beings who argue," he must act in accord with certain instructed expectations concerning the likely acts and reactions of other members of that community and, in that sense, was bound to certain norms of discursive and more general social interaction, it did not follow that he was bound to those norms *as described and theorized* in Frankfurt School moral theory. It did not follow, that is, unless "the community of beings who argue" were *defined* as just those who are bound to those norms so described and so theorized—which is, in fact, exactly how it is defined by the inexorable logic of the discourse of discourse ethics.[40]

It could be said, then, that beyond the existence, identity, or validity of discursive or ethical norms, the crucial issue in this debate is the claim of a particular system of conceptualizations to absolute epistemic authority. The staged exchanges between the cognitivist and the skeptic are shadowed at every point by that larger claim and contest. They are also shadowed, accordingly, by the broader epistemological question of in/commensurability. For, of course, it is not given in advance how the outcome of that contest will be determined, or by which or whose norms of theoretical validity, or, indeed, whether such norms will be involved at all.[41]

At the end (there is, as mentioned above, a seventh round), Habermas imagines the hypothetical skeptic realizing that his attempts to evade the rules of discourse ethics lead to a "dead end" but, unregenerately unenlightenable fellow that he is, continuing to snipe and carp. Indeed, in a last desperate gesture (taking his cue here, Habermas remarks, from Hegel), the skeptic turns on the whole show, "question[ing] . . . the meaning of a formalistic ethics of this kind" altogether (102). The implications of the skeptic's final turn here are significant, but best appreciated in the context of Habermas's larger project in *Moral Consciousness and Communicative Action,* that is, his defense of rationalist philosophy more generally—or, as he sees it, of Reason itself—in the face of a range of contemporary challenges. I consider his handling of those challenges in the next chapter, where I also offer some related speculations on the curious union-in-opposition of philosophy and skepticism.

7

Arguing with Reason

Unless ye believe, ye shall not understand.
Isaiah 7.9

Reason, whether understood as the exercise of a certain mental faculty or as due conformity with a certain set or system of rules, is classically seen as a privileged way of knowing and arguing. It is privileged because, it is said, reason and reason alone—as distinct from thought, argument, or belief based on sentiment, habit, desire, interest, mere experience, mere preference, or mere authority—permits us to arrive at objectively valid judgments, unconditional truths, and genuine consensus. A number of theorists have "argued with reason" in the sense of questioning this set of claims and ideas, usually in conjunction with more general critiques of the conceptual systems through which they have been formally articulated (for example, transcendental moral theory or rationalist epistemology) and in conjunction also with the development of alternative intellectual projects, such as constructivist accounts of knowledge or pragmatist theories of political and social interaction. It is currently argued, however, in accord with a logic examined in the preceding chapter, that this skeptical questioning of reason is fatally self-contradictory. For, it is explained, in the very act of arguing—at least if it is serious argument, which means argument oriented toward genuine agreement, which means agreement arrived at through reason—the skeptic necessarily and inescapably presupposes reason and thus affirms performatively what she otherwise denies. As one such defender of reason puts it, post-structuralists, postmodernists, and others who reject the claims of classical rationalism are "in pursuit of an understanding whose possibility has in fact already been ruled out on a priori grounds."[1]

This ability to rule out in advance all skeptical or adversarial views is a considerable advantage for any system of ideas. As might be expected, however, those whose views are thus ruled out don't see it that way themselves. What they do see is the unbreachable circularity of the reasoning just given, each link of which depends on the prior acceptance of the claims, concepts, and definitions at issue. But, as might also be expected, the defenders of reason are neither defeated nor disheartened by counter-charges of circularity. Rather, they draw on other logical and rhetorical resources (elaborations, corroborations, qualifications, supplements, and so forth) in renewed support of their arguments. We need not pursue further the exchange of moves in this controversy. Its evidently perpetual dynamics may be summed up as follows: given the rationalist's rationalism, the skeptic's argument with Reason appears demonstrably self-contradictory; and, given the skeptic's skepticism, the rationalist's argument "with"—in the sense of via or by means of—Reason appears demonstrably self-affirming and thus hollow.

This symmetry is bemusing and I return to it later. First, however, I want to consider a significant entry in the debates over reason, namely Habermas's response, in *Moral Consciousness and Communicative Action*, to what he acknowledges as the serious contemporary challenge not only to foundationalist moral theory but to rationalist philosophy as such.[2] Certain perplexities that seem to beset his efforts here are, I shall suggest, indexes of more general quandaries which, in turn, may help illuminate those perplexities and also certain more general features of intellectual life.

Cognitive Self-Stabilization

A number of passages in *Moral Consciousness* are of interest here. The first comes from its opening pages, where Habermas evokes the Enlightenment idea of philosophy as the disciplined defense of rationality and indicates his troubled response to Richard Rorty's explicit rejection of this idea in his *Philosophy and the Mirror of Nature:*

> While I find myself in agreement with much of what Rorty says, I have trouble accepting his conclusion, which is that . . . [phi-

losophy] must also surrender the function of being the "guardian of rationality." If I understand Rorty, he is saying that the new modesty of philosophy involves the abandonment of any claim to reason . . . [H]e also unflinchingly accepts the end of the belief that ideas like truth or the unconditional *with their transcending power* are a necessary condition of humane forms of collective life. (3, my emphasis)

The passage is interesting along several lines. First, Habermas's casual (that is, unargued) attribution of "transcending power" to "ideas such as truth and the unconditional" indicates not only his own conviction that such ideas have such power but his failure to note or perhaps inability to believe that anyone could believe otherwise. It is, however, just the notion or claim of such power that Rorty questions most strenuously in *Philosophy and the Mirror of Nature*.[3] Habermas's failure to register this disparity of belief has important rhetorical effects here. For if, like Habermas himself, Rorty *did* grant transcending power to such ideas, then his "unflinching[] . . . accept[ance of] the end of the belief" in their ethical or political value would appear curiously unmotivated or, so to speak, irrational. Since, however, Rorty does *not* grant them such power, then his rejection of the idea of their necessity as a condition of "humane forms of collective life" follows readily and, so to speak, reasonably enough.[4]

What is notable here is not just the logical (and even, in a sense, discourse-ethical) lapse involved in Habermas's question-begging formulation, but the cognitive operation it seems to indicate, that is, his ignoring, forgetting, or resisting the possibility of anyone's seriously rejecting the ideas at issue. The claims and concepts invoked by Habermas in the passage just quoted (the transcending power of ideas such as truth, the necessity of such ideas as a condition of humane forms of collective life, and the crucial role of philosophy as the guardian of just such claims and ideas) are sustained here and in his larger opus by the more general system of concepts, definitions, distinctions, and arguments in which, since Kant, they have classically figured: a system that Habermas identifies as, simply, "philosophy" and to which, of course, he has himself contributed significantly. It could be said, accordingly, that the rejection of those ideas and claims is, for Habermas, literally inconceivable: that is, he could not himself do any conceiving (at least none that he would recognize as genuinely philosophical) without them, and, given the exclusive legitimacy that particular conceptual system awards to its own ideas, he does not and cannot believe that anyone else could do so either.

I speak specifically of Habermas, but his responses figure here as an example of a more general phenomenon that could be illustrated in the work of many other philosophers as well as theorists in a number of other fields, including law, literary studies, political theory, and theology . The phenomenon, commonly signalled by what we call circular reasoning, is the pursuit of cognitive self-stabilization through recursive self-affirmation. Here as elsewhere, the believer perceives, conceives, and articulates the skeptic's skepticism in terms that construct that skepticism as necessarily absurd and (not irrelevantly here or elsewhere) as morally or politically irresponsible, thus securing and restabilizing his own beliefs and vanquishing the skeptic's skepticism—at least to the believer's own satisfaction—at least until the next time skepticism must be engaged.

A second passage of related interest follows immediately the one just quoted:

> Modernity is characterized by . . . a belief in procedural rationality and its ability *to give credence to our views* in the three areas of objective knowledge, moral-practical insight, and aesthetic judgment. *What I am asking myself is this:* Is it true that this (or a similar) concept of modernity becomes untenable when you dismiss the claims of a foundationalist theory of knowledge? (3–4, my emphasis)

The answer to the question Habermas asks himself here (and evidently asks himself repeatedly, or so the iterative verb suggests) seems to be yes. That is, when classic foundationalism is seen as conceptually unworkable, then the idea that procedural rationalism (or anything else) can "give credence" to people's views in the classic foundationalist sense of grounding their validity-claims unconditionally is also seen as (or "becomes") untenable. Although this conclusion appears obvious enough (it is a simple restatement of the import of anti-foundationalism as such), it is evidently very difficult for Habermas to accept. Thus he continues to ask himself that question, and thus he continues to resist that seemingly inevitable answer, seeking instead to re-ground classic foundationalism on other newly fortified or not-quite-foundational foundations.[5]

Tradeoffs, Ambivalences, Equivocations

A number of these re-grounding attempts were discussed in Chapter 6. Others will concern us here. Especially relevant to the dynamics of cognitive self-stabilization is Habermas's effort to strengthen discourse ethics through an alliance with the social sciences. Thus Lawrence Kohlberg's developmental psychology and Noam Chomsky's generative linguistics are invoked as providing "corroborative supplements" to discourse ethics in the form of reconstructions of the supposed universals of, respectively, moral reasoning and communicative action. Given the virtually defining claim of rationalist philosophy to an epistemic authority superior to that of (merely) empirical science and its traditional denial of normative relevance to empirical research more generally,[6] the alliance is inevitably awkward. Of particular interest here is Habermas's negotiation of those difficulties through repeated sequences of careful distinction, due concession, and renewed affirmation.

For example, Habermas acknowledges (or insists)[7] that Chomskian linguistics and Kohlbergian moral psychology are quite special sciences, the products, he writes, of "fertile minds" which, though working in "nonphilosophical disciplines," are nevertheless willing to "give . . . a try" to "[e]mpirical theories with strong universalistic claims" (15). He explains the characteristic method of such sciences as follows: "Starting primarily from the intuitive knowledge of competent subjects . . . and secondarily from systematic knowledge handed down by culture, [they] explain the presumably universal bases of rational experience and judgment, as well as of action and linguistic communication" (15–16). In short, these empirical theories and reconstructive sciences are not quite empirical or scientific, as Habermas acknowledges (or insists or equivocates) in his term for them, "hybrid discourses." Given the special features of those sciences as just described, Habermas can make a further important distinction, insisting that, although he is gratified by the "cooperation" between discourse ethics and these particular sciences, he neither anticipates nor endorses any "convergence" between philosophy and science more generally. "It makes better

sense," he writes, to see discourses such as Chomsky's linguistics
and Kohlberg's psychology "as stages on the road to the philoso-
phization of the sciences of man . . . than as stages in the triumphal
march toward objectivist approaches, such as neurophysiology, that
quaint favorite child of the analytic philosophers" (15). This vision
of the course of intellectual history *from* empirical science *to* rationalist philosophy is, at the end of the twentieth century, rather
remarkable. But Habermas is neither daunted nor impressed by
alternative expectations or contrary trajectories, and he pointedly
disdains the efforts by other (for example, analytic) philosophers to
naturalize philosophy via anything as "quaint" as "neurophysiology."[8]

I return later to Habermas's negotiations between the claims of
philosophy and science. At this point, however, I would note the
recurrent and perhaps fundamental dilemma to which he responds
in handling their strained relationship: that is, the choice or tradeoff
between conceptual purity (here, the definitive but empirically ungrounded universalist claims of rationalist moral theory) and empirical force (here, the classically contaminating elements of contingency, difference, uncertainty, and contestability introduced by
any appeal to the empirical). The general dilemma haunts his efforts
throughout *Moral Consciousness* and is reflected in his often elusive
explanations of the limited practical and political applicability of
discourse ethics.

As Habermas recognizes, the uncompromising purity and aloof-
ness of transcendental moral theory create problems for ethical and
political practice. For example, rehearsing the major claim of discourse ethics, which is (only) to provide a procedure for testing the
validity of whatever norms are proposed, he acknowledges (or insists) that the actual content of ethical norms, as distinct from their
validity, must come from "outside": "real conflicts," "concrete situation[s]," and "specific social group[s]" (103).[9] All discourse ethics
can do, he cautions, is prove that norms that are "not susceptible
to consensus" through rational discourse are invalid and must therefore be discarded. As he also grants, however, there is considerable
question as to whether anything survives the process: that is,
whether any norm is good enough to pass the U-test or, as he puts
it, "whether this very selectivity [of the test for universalizability]
might not make the procedure unsuitable for resolving practical
questions" (ibid.).

An especially vivid but still equivocal acknowledgment of these problems occurs a few pages later. Noting the rarity and vulnerability of patterns of (procedurally proper) "consensual conflict resolution" in "the sea of [actual] practice" ("islands threatened with inundation," "means of reaching agreement thrust aside by the instruments of force"), Habermas observes: "Hence action that is oriented toward ethical principles has to accommodate itself to imperatives that flow not from principles but from strategic necessities" (106). His notice of this required accommodation appears to be a substantial concession to the operations of contingency and context, but its implications for transcendental moral theory are quickly whittled away and, in fact, appear to be withdrawn in the very moment of being articulated. He continues:

> These limitations of practical discourses testify to the power history has over the transcending claims and interests of reason. The skeptic for his part [, however,] tends to give an overdrawn account of these limits. The key to understanding the problem is that moral judgments, which provide demotivated answers to decontextualized questions, require an offsetting *compensation*. If we are clear [, however,] about the feats of abstraction to which universalist moralities owe their superiority to conventional ones, the old problem of the relationship between morality and ethical life appears in a different, rather trivial light . . . [and] . . . the relevance of the experiential context of [one's] lifeworld tends to pale. (106–107, his emphasis)

It is, I think, impossible to say whether this sequence of observations is intended to operate as a "key" to *solving* that "old problem"—that is, the practical limits of deontological moralities—or, as the argument could also be read, as a simultaneous (or alternating) acknowledgment of the problem and refusal to grant its force.[10]

Ambivalence and equivocation of the sort exhibited in these examples are likely wherever tradeoffs are required in practice but prohibited by theory: for example, where two goods are reciprocally related so that both cannot be obtained (at least not maximally) at the same time, but both are posited as absolutely necessary or unauthentic unless total. In moral theory, generality and practical force can be seen as reciprocally related goods of this kind. The very degree of generality or vagueness that makes it plausible to claim universality or universalizability for an ethical rule (for example, *It is wrong to take human life unnecessarily*) also leaves its practical application open or unclear; conversely, the very degree of specificity that would be required to give a rule critical bite in any particular situation (for example, *abortion is wrong; the death penalty is wrong; lethal warfare is wrong; euthanasia is wrong*) also makes it more controversial and, accordingly, any claim of its universal(izabil)ity less plausible.

The perplexed situation of Frankfurt School moral/critical theory can be understood accordingly.[11] If specific practical application and critical force are demanded of a moral theory (as, for example, by activists), then the requirement of universal(izabil)ity must be significantly modified. Conversely, if such application and force are *not* of primary significance (as, for example, to moral theorists as such), then the transcendental requirements can be strenuously affirmed—with, perhaps, an appended claim to the effect that such rigorous criteria, though problematic for practice, are nevertheless valuable as inspirational regulative ideals. This latter is a classic response to the perplexity and arguably the solution most congenial for Habermas; but it is cold comfort to feminists, post-colonial critics, and others who look to critical theory for concrete application and substantive critical edge.[12]

The formal moves that define discourse ethics, its idealizing procedures, totalizing requirements, bracketing-out of contingency, and refusal of irreducible difference, make it unwieldy in an impure, contingent, differentiating world. Indeed, as Habermas repeatedly acknowledges but does not *acknowledge* acknowledging, the only way to make the norms, procedures, and imperatives of discourse ethics workable in such a world is to attach duly particularizing qualifications and conditions to them: for example, clauses specifying the communities for which, or circumstances under which, the imperatives in question do (or might, or should) apply; or codicils to the effect that the requisite procedures will be (or may be, or must be) modified in response to emergent conditions or "strategic necessities." It seems, in other words, that discourse ethics can be adapted for specific and effective ethical/political application only by being historicized, contextualized, and conditionalized, or, in short, relativized. But that would mean turning it into its own classic adversary (relativism), or at least conceding a more complex relation between the two than is usually granted: more complex, that is, than the relation between two mutually exclusive doctrines, an orthodoxy understood as inherently and absolutely necessary and a heresy understood as fundamentally and dangerously flawed.

It is not surprising that resolute defenders of deontological moral theory would find such self-transformation (or self-reconception) difficult, and, even where something like it is actually achieved (as it is, I think, at many points in Habermas's work), that explicit acknowledgment of it would be impossible, severely muted, or highly unstable.[13] Indeed, one might expect that, here as elsewhere, longtime believers, even as their beliefs *are* responsively transformed, would continue to affirm the fundamental validity of the orthodox belief *as such* and continue to indict the intellectual insufficiency of all conceivable alternatives and the morally and politically suspect character of any immediate rivals. During periods of profound transformation, moreover, one might expect longtime believers to devise conceptual/discursive techniques to handle both the resulting condition of cognitive instability and such other practical/rhetorical problems as answering skeptics and critics, satisfying the needs of loyal disciples and followers, and transmitting the belief—in whatever old/new form—to new generations of believers. Among these techniques would be equivocation: that is, the alternating avowal, disavowal, and re-avowal of crucial claims, the virtually simultaneous granting and cancelling of crucial concessions, and the strenuous affirmation of mutually incompatible doctrines.[14]

Philosophy's Necessity

We may return now to Habermas's handling of the difficulty created by rationalist philosophy's need to invoke the authority of empirical science to bolster its own claims but, simultaneously, to deny that authority in maintaining its own definitive epistemic privilege. His acknowledgment of the difficulty takes the form, at one point, of a rhetorical question: "If it is true that philosophy has entered upon a phase of cooperation with the human sciences, does it not run the risk of losing its identity?" (16). The answer comes obliquely by way of a grim characterization of the compartmentalization of knowledge in (post)modern times and, especially, the "disgorging" by empirical science of some eminently desirable features of *pre*-modernity, including "elements of religion" and a concern for "issues of the good life" (17).[15] The only thing, Habermas observes, that can mediate the now isolated compartments of knowledge and repair the "sundered . . . unity" of reason is philosophy—and, moreover, philosophy precisely "to the extent to which [it] keeps at least one eye trained on the topic of rationality, that is, . . . keeps inquiring into the conditions of the unconditional" (17–18). In short, the answer to the question he poses—and, accordingly, the solution to the dilemma he both acknowledges and dismisses—is that (transcendental rationalist) philosophy need not fear losing its identity in its obligatory interactions with science so long as it insists on its identity as *transcendental rationalist* philosophy and, thereby, on its fundamental epistemic supremacy.

This answer, however, does not dissolve the dilemma but only postpones acknowledgment of the cost of the choice made. The resolute grasping of one horn (the necessity of the claim of unconditionality) at one point requires an accommodation or equivocation of the other horn (the severe limits on practical application entailed by that claim) down the road, as the irrepressible skeptic will be sure to point out, setting up the need for further resolute reaffirmations, further accommodations or equivocations, and so forth without obvious resolution. Reflecting on the anti-foundational arguments of Rorty and other postmodern theorists, Habermas predicts that, without the absolute underwriting that only "justificatory discourse"—and thus transcendental philosophy—can provide, they "will not be able to find a resting place" (14). That may be true, but Habermas himself, even with such a discourse, seems unable to find one; and "a resting place" may not be what postmodernists seek, or what any of us will find this side of the moon or short of the grave.

Habermas believes that rationalist philosophy is crucially necessary not only because it is uniquely qualified to mediate fractured knowledge but also because issues of the good life must be resolved, and their resolution can consist only of the moral justification of particular practices, and practices are (genuinely) morally justified only where it can be shown that they are in conformity with unconditionally valid norms, and unconditionally valid norms can be arrived at only through the establishment of the conditions of the unconditional, and establishing the conditions of the unconditional is the defining role of rationalist philosophy. Or, one could say,

Habermas believes rationalist philosophy is necessary because Habermas believes rationalist philosophy.

Even in the midst of these strong reaffirmations and recirculations of claims and convictions, however, the philosopher is haunted by the recollection and anticipation of challenges from critics and skeptics. Won't some "critic of the master thinkers," he wonders, raise objections, demanding to know "[what] gives the philosopher the right to offer his services?" (17). Habermas's reply on this occasion is a model of rhetorical/intellectual aplomb, simultaneously conciliatory and intransigent. What gives philosophy (meaning, again, transcendental rationalist philosophy) its special authority is just its handle on the unconditional, the inescapable necessity of which is attested to, he argues, by the very positions from which such skeptical questions arise, namely "pragmatism and hermeneutics":

> I think pragmatism and hermeneutics have joined forces to answer this question by attributing epistemic authority to the community of those who cooperate and speak with one another. Everyday communication makes possible a kind of understanding that is based on claims to validity and thus furnishes *the only real alternative* to exerting influence on one another in more or less coercive ways. The validity claims that we raise in conversation— that is, when we say something with conviction—transcend this specific conversational context, *pointing to something beyond* the spatiotemporal ambit of the occasion . . . [B]uilt into the structure of action oriented toward reaching understanding is *an element of unconditionality.* And it is this unconditional element that makes the validity . . . that we claim for our views different from the mere de facto acceptance of . . . habitual practices . . . [W]hat we consider justified is not a function of custom but a question of justification or grounding. (19–20, my emphasis)

A number of turns deserve notice here. First, although Habermas treats pragmatism and latter-day hermeneutics[16] elsewhere in the book as false upstart alternatives to Enlightenment philosophy, he seems to enlist them here, in spite of themselves as it were, in the service of its defense and rehabilitation. He characterizes both positions, however, in ways that strip them of their critical force and indeed of their identity as alternative theoretical projects. Rorty's pragmatism explicitly rejects the notion of transcendently valid truth, redefining epistemic validity as local, conditional acceptability in the context of ongoing practices. Habermas accepts *ongoing practices*, but cancels *local* and *conditional.* Similarly, latter-day hermeneutics rejects the idea of transcendently correct interpretations, deriving interpretative authority from specific cultural traditions in the context of particular purposes. Habermas takes over *cultural traditions*, but cancels *specific, context*, and *particular.* Thus, in the very course of appropriating these rival projects, he reaffirms just those absolute, universalist elements of his own position that proponents of either would most strenuously reject and, at the same time, deftly excises just those particularizing (or relativizing) elements of their alternative positions that give them their specific and more or less radical character.

Second, we may note Habermas's strong claim and evident conviction that to speak "with conviction" is to claim unconditional validity for one's statements. A less strenuous supposition might be that, when we speak with conviction (as signaled, for example, by our use of unqualified terms), we believe (and mean to imply) that the reasons for our judgments are quite substantial and that the judgments themselves will hold up across most relevant domains and under most relevantly comparable conditions—including, significantly here, conditions relatively distant in space and time and, in that sense, "beyond the spatiotemporal ambit of the occasion." Habermas's extension of conditions beyond the immediate occasion to *all conditions without exception* is a crucial leap, based, it appears, on his own unselfconsciously universalized introspections. It may very well be, of course, that when Habermas himself says something with conviction, he has the sense (and means to imply) that he is claiming its unconditional validity. What is notable here, however, is the move from a perhaps quite strong personal sense or "intuition" to a posited necessary and universal "claim," and the invocation of that now presumptively inherent claim as a ground for awarding legitimacy to, or withholding it from, other people's intellectual lives.[17] For what Habermas suggests here, of course (and elsewhere explicitly insists), is that *unless* one is making a claim of unconditional validity for one's statements, then one is not speaking with (genuine) conviction.

Sequences or chains of moves of this kind are familiar in rationalist argument and significant in accounting for the difficulties of arguing with Reason. In Habermas's case, the particular chain just described readily sets up an argument from performative contradiction. If the skeptic claims to speak "with conviction," then her questionings and alternative formulations, in necessarily claiming unconditional validity, are self-contradictory; but if she denies that she is claiming unconditional validity in her speech acts, then she has confessed that she is not "oriented toward genuine agreement," and thus not engaged in "genuine communication," and thus not a member of "the community of those who cooperate and speak with one another"—that is, "rational" persons. Given this set of alternatives (Habermas, we recall, adds two others: committing suicide and going mad), it is not surprising that many skeptics take the self-excommunication option. That is, they avoid getting into arguments with rationalists or, like Feyerabend, declare themselves epistemological anarchists or dadaists and bid "farewell to reason."[18]

Before moving on to more general observations, I want to consider one further point of interest in the passage quoted above, namely the choice evoked in Habermas's contention that agreement reached through reason—meaning the raising of claims to universal validity—"furnishes the only real alternative to exerting influence on one another in more or less coercive ways." The alternatives are familiar: rational *Right* or barbarian *Might;* the presumptively justifiable claim of unconditional validity or the flourishing of fist, club, or gun. Perhaps, however, there is another alternative—perhaps, indeed, a whole range of alternatives obscured by the absolute, binary terms in which this (coercive enough) set is framed. In opposing rational agreement to exerting influence "in more or less coercive ways," Habermas suggests that it makes little difference whether the "exerting" in question is more coercive or less coercive. But it could make quite a bit of difference to those involved— enough, for example, to cause a somewhat *less* coercive method to be experienced as effective persuasion and another relatively *more* coercive method to be experienced as grievous intimidation. Where differences of *degree* are not acknowledged or are treated as insignificant, then binary opposites—pure reason versus brute force— do indeed *become* "the only real alternatives." Conversely, where such binary opposites are seen as "the only real alternatives," then the real-enough significance of *other* alternatives may not be recognized. Those who question and reject the appeal to *unconditional* Right or Reason are obliged, of course, to devise or describe other methods of exerting influence, whether as social agents, attempting to affect other people's views and actions, or as social theorists, seeking to explain such observed changes more generally. Fist, club, or gun—barbarian Might—is one such alternative method and explanation; but there certainly are and, historically, certainly have been others. There are, for example, forms or sources of might (or, in less inflammatory terms, effectiveness[19]) that are not especially barbarian, and reasons or reasonings that are sublunary rather than transcendent: that is, responsive to considerations, such as prior experiences, general goals, relevant conditions, expected outcomes, and long-term implications, that may be quite subtle, informed, broadly shared, and otherwise more or less judicious but still historically contingent and more or less particular.[20] For a number of contemporary social theorists and social agents, what recommends "pragmatism and hermeneutics," along with such other nonfoundational projects as genealogies of morals, archeologies of knowledge, and anthropologies or sociologies of science, is not their possible service as auxiliary launching pads for "transcendental modes of justification" but, rather, their efforts to identify and work through just such alternative reason(ing)s and alternative forms of practical, including political, effectiveness.[21]

Webs of Reason

The current re-grounding of transcendental rationalism centers on the demonstration of the inescapable necessity of (its conception of) reason as validated by the exposure of the inescapable performative contradiction of anyone denying it. Since the force of those demonstrations and exposures depends, as we have seen, on the prior acceptance of just the system of ideas, claims, and definitions at issue, the supposed re-grounding is thoroughly circular. Nevertheless, such arguments for Reason through Reason are evidently powerful and persuasive for many people, largely, it seems, *because* they are circular: that is, because they appeal to established ideas, ideas that skeptics question and reject but that rationalists accept and believe and, in accepting and believing, also believe cannot be questioned or rejected.

For those who conduct their intellectual lives primarily or exclusively through transcendental rationalism, that set of densely interconnected, mutually reinforcing ideas (claims, concepts, definitions, and so forth) operates as a virtually unbreachable cognitive and rhetorical system, or, one might say, as a continuously self-spinning, self-repairing, self-enclosing web. We have already observed, in this and earlier chapters, a number of its nodes and threads. One such thread of particular significance here is the chain or interlinked series that defines *argumentation* as rational discourse oriented toward the reaching of agreement, *agreement* as rational understanding achieved through argumentation, *rationality* as argumentation in conformity with the norms of discourse, *norms of discourse* as the presuppositions of every competent speaker, and communicative *competence* as the ability to engage in (rational) argumentation—which is to say, around again to the beginning.[22]

Three aspects of these definitions—aside from their considerable distance from idiomatic usage outside rationalist circles (in both senses)—are notable: first, they are individually extremely rigorous; second, they are altogether mutually consistent; third, they are thoroughly recursive. Habermas's arguments and, though less rigorously or consistently, those of his disciples,[23] tend to proceed almost exclusively through the deployment, rearrangement, rehearsal, and intervalidation of just this set of preemptively defined concepts and their mutually confirming definitions. The supreme intellectual virtue of such a system (transcendental rationalism is not the *only* such system, though perhaps the most nearly perfect one) and the source of its conceptual power is its rigor, which is to say, its severe consistency and coherence, in every move, at every level. Everything in the system fits together tightly and securely. Whatever does not fit *into* the system is identified by the system as irrelevant or unauthentic. Any question about the system raised *in the system's terms* can be answered *by* the system readily, rigorously, and consistently, and all such answers endorse the system unconditionally. No question about the system raised in any other terms is recognized by the system as legitimate or coherent.

The rigorous, unremitting work of Reason creates a tight, taut web, intertextual and interconceptual. Tighter and stronger than the shifting, contingent, partial, and always contestable ideas and claims produced and justified by mere experience or mere sentiment, preference, desire, imagination, faith, custom, or convention, the ideas and claims delivered and justified by Reason are unconditional, universal, and, for better or worse, inescapable. "For better or worse" because, as I have been suggesting, the certainty or stability of belief promised and delivered by such a system becomes, for the believer, the inescapability of belief *from* the system.

Mirrors of Circularity

A final set of reflections is suggested by a curious rhetorical phenomenon recurrent in arguments with and about Reason, namely the reversibility—indeed *double* reversibility—of the rationalist's charge of the skeptic's self-contradiction. What I have in mind here is the tendency on the part of those persuaded of the fatal self-contradiction, incoherence, and inconsistency of so-called postmodern theorists to *berate* those theorists for, precisely, their coherence and consistency, now, however, re-labeled "relentlessness" (as in "relentless negativity") or "totalization" (as in "totalizing suspicion of the concept of truth"), and, at the same time and often in the same breath, to *celebrate* the inconsistencies, self-contradictions, and equivocations of more conceptually congenial theorists, now, however, labeled "flexible recognitions," "dialectical mediations," "constructive tensions," and so forth. Thus, for example, Christopher Norris applauds the equivocations ("flexibility") of Roy Bhasker's politically agreeable "scientific realism"[24] in contrast to Stanley Fish's consistent ("relentless") but, in Norris's view, politically disagreeable anti-realism;[25] and Peter Dews warns of the "profoundly menacing . . . aspect" of "an unqualified hostility to the universal in the domain of ethics and politics" and, especially, of "the politically disastrous implications" of "a mode of thought [post-structuralism] which prides itself precisely on *a reckless integrity and consistency.*"[26]

This sort of double-talk is familiar in any polemics, but my point is not just to indict it as such. For what interests me in these equivocal charges and recurrent reversals are the more fundamental cognitive/pragmatic ambivalences that produce them and, perhaps, make them inevitable. The connections here can be suggested in fairly general terms. It appears that the greater the degree of coherence in an established system of ideas, the more secure the cognitive stability it offers but also, thereby, the more conceptual and practical confinement it risks. Conversely, for a system of ideas to retain significant cognitive plasticity and practical responsiveness, it must forego a certain degree of theoretical purity and, thereby, the rhetorical advantage of claims to completeness, unique necessity, or, where that is sought, the power to ground the validity of norms or judgments.[27] *Self-sameness* and *self-variance* are, of course, reciprocal and, indeed, exhaustive possibilities of all theory, discourse, and argument, though each acquires different valences from different perspectives and, accordingly, different names: "coherence" rather than "circularity," for example, in the case of self-sameness, or "flexibility" rather than "self-contradiction" in the case of self-variance. Indeed, these logical/rhetorical terms appear to name the irreducibly reciprocal operations of *all* epistemic life, that is, the ongoing processes of both individual cognition and public argumentation: stabilization and destabilization, defense and critique, the effort to conserve belief and the pressure to transform it. Hence, in arenas of public controversy, the familiar dance of Skeptic and Believer. Hence, in the arenas of internal controversy or *psychomachia,* the recurrent episodes of doubt that are the believer's cross and agony but also, it seems, the sign of his or her activity as a functioning intelligence.

It could be said that the communal mission of philosophy as "the guardian of rationality" has been to establish the conditions under which certain valued qualities of conceptual and discursive practices—for example, reliability, applicability, communicability, appropriability, and connectability—may be maximized. This is a worthy mission in some respects, and its pursuit and products have no doubt had important inspirational, fortifying, and otherwise desirable effects over the course of its history. But, it appears, that mission becomes self-defeating and communally hazardous precisely when and insofar as it is pursued *hypertrophically* as pure, absolute, and across-the-board maximization: that is, when the need for tradeoffs is not acknowledged; when the heterogeneous, gradient, and reciprocally variable qualities just mentioned (reliability, applicability, etc.) are absolutized, reified, and mystified (as, for example, Truth Itself), and their pursuit becomes the search and demand for unassailable conviction, fail-proof proof, and unconditional validity; when it is supposed that procedures for securing those often subtle, elusive, and highly contingent qualities can be determined beforehand and codified once and for all (as, for example, *the* canons of logic, *the* rules of discourse, or *the* scientific method); and when the conditions that secure those socially and pragmatically interactive qualities are located either totally outside our heads (as, for example, a state of conformity to an absolutized, reified, and mystified Reality Itself) or totally inside our heads (as, for example, the proper exercise of a faculty of Reason).

It is possible, accordingly, to see the communal desirability of an *alternative* project, symmetrical and reciprocal to that "critical theory" currently pursued in the name of Reason and Philosophy: an intellectual project, that is, that would seek not to maximize the stability of valued claims and concepts but, rather, to expose their forgotten instabilities; not to justify the necessity of accepted norms and practices but, rather, to reveal their repressed or equivocated costs. This reverse or mirror critical theory would operate as a dis-authorizing, de-sedimenting, counter-regulative ideal, prepared to be "critical" through thick and thin: critical not only of all and any established *practical* (social, political, technological) practices, but also of the *conceptual* (logical, discursive, rhetorical) practices of all and any established theories, including established (as might certainly happen) versions of itself. This alternative critical theory does exist, and has existed, it seems, from the time there was theory of any kind. Like the devil, it has many names, including the devil's own names: nihilism, atheism, relativism, anarchism, deconstruction, and postmodernism. One of its most ancient names is, of course, Skepticism.

If, as I have suggested here, skepticism and belief are reciprocally implicated, then their essentially antagonistic energies cannot be reconciled, synthesized, or transcended, nor can there be any agreeable-to-all "middle way" between them. That is why the adversarial embrace of Skeptic and Believer may indeed be eternal. Their deadlock, however, may not be as total as it sometimes appears. To be sure, there remains no reason to expect any *final* argument or agreement, either way; no time when it will be determined who was, after all and all along, really right; no conversion to belief without the possibility of doubt; no doubt that cannot itself become dogmatic. But these mutually abrasive engagements are not, I think, either pointless or sterile. On the contrary, it appears to be out of the endless dance and clash of skepticism and belief that all knowledge emerges: that is, all the particular theories, contingent claims, contestable judgments, local discourses, and provisional practices that we generate through and *as* the very process of living in an irremediably sublunary world.

APPENDIX: WEBS OF REASON

The definitions below are based on Habermas's usage or explicit definitions, primarily in the pages of *Moral Consciousness and Communicative Action*. Virtually all the terms discussed here, however, along with the interconnected, intervalidating senses indicated, recur throughout his writings and in the work of his colleagues and disciples. The weblike properties of the set will emerge most clearly if the reader, starting with any one of the entries, follows each of the cross-referenced terms as indicated.

Argumentation: reaching agreement through the raising of presumptively valid (q.v.) claims. [*Not* verbal dispute or the explanation and defense of positions as such.]

Cognitive: transcendentally (q.v.) demonstrable as true or false. [*Not* relating to the processes of knowledge and perception naturalistically conceived.]

Communication: action oriented toward reaching agreement through the raising of mutual claims to validity (q.v.). [*Not* verbal exchange as such.]

Competent/ce: conforming to valid (q.v.) norms (q.v.).

Discourse: rational (q.v.) argumentation (q.v.).

Ethical: relating to universalizable norms (q.v.) of action or speech.

Intuitions: the (pre)knowledge of the norms (q.v.) presupposed (q.v.) by action, communication (q.v.), and argumentation (q.v.) that is possessed by every competent (q.v.) actor and speaker.

Justify: demonstrate to be transcendentally (q.v.) valid (q.v.).

Moral: universalizable; raising claims of validity (q.v.) in the sphere of practical (q.v.) matters.

Norms: unconditional and historically and culturally universal imperatives presupposed (q.v.) by speech and action and known intuitively (q.v.) by every competent (q.v.) speaker and actor.

Philosophy: transcendental (q.v.) philosophy; the justification (q.v.) of norms (q.v.) and reconstruction (q.v.) of presupposed (q.v.) conditions.

Practical: relating to action or speech; ethical (q.v.).

Practical discourse: rational (q.v.) argumentation (q.v.) about the validity (q.v.) of norms (q.v.) of action or speech. [*Not* verbal exchanges about everyday, concrete, or, in the idiomatic sense, "practical" matters.]

Presupposed: necessary, as demonstrated by transcendental (q.v.) analysis or reconstruction (q.v.).

Rational: conforming to or derived from inescapably presupposed (q.v.) norms (q.v.), intuitions (q.v.), or transcendental (q.v.) principles.

Reason/ing: the capacity for rational (q.v.) thought; philosophy (q.v.); argumentation (q.v.).

Reconstruction: demonstration, through rationalist techniques (e.g., the analysis of intuitions [q.v.]), of empirically non-demonstrable but inescapably necessary laws, rules, and norms (q.v.).

Theory: philosophy (q.v.).

Transcendental: universal and unconditional; demonstrable, without recourse to empirical knowledge, as inescapably presupposed (q.v.); pertaining to such demonstrations.

Valid/ity: justifiability (q.v.); satisfying the transcendental (q.v.) requirements of reason (q.v.).

8

Microdynamics of Incommensurability: Philosophy of Science Meets Science Studies

A number of themes and issues significant in previous chapters converge in this analysis of the dynamics of nonconvergence. My immediate focus here is a recurrent failure of intellectual engagement in encounters between traditional philosophy of science and the critiques and alternative views of theorists, historians, and sociologists working in the relatively new field of "science studies." I am also concerned, however, with the more general issue of in/commensurability, which has occupied these pages virtually from the beginning and, not incidentally, figures centrally in the exchanges just mentioned. The question is whether, as is traditionally maintained, rival theories are always ultimately measurable against a common standard of truth so that, at least in principle, their divergent claims may be compared and the superior ones chosen accordingly; *or* if, as is argued by a number of contemporary philosophers and historians of science, there are conditions under which evidently conflicting theories cannot be measured or compared that way: when, for example, they assume radically divergent but (arguably) equally credible conceptions of the universe, or, as in the case of these epistemological debates themselves, when part of what divides the parties is how to understand the standards (*truth, rationality, evidence,* and so forth) by which the merits of

125

their divergent theories could be measured—if, indeed, merits, measurements, or even choices, as classically conceived, are relevant to the outcomes of such conflicts (if, indeed, those divergences need be seen as conflicts).

As is clear from this description, the situation that concerns us here has a distinctly reflexive quality: that is, certain evidently rival views of knowledge and science differ on, among other things, how to describe, explain, compare, and assess rival views. The reduplicative—echoing, mirroring—structure of this situation is intriguing and, I think, instructive in several ways. For it not only indicates an important source of the difficulty in these failed engagements, but it also raises the more general question—very general, I would say, with ethical and political resonances as well as extensive theoretical implications—of how to understand the cognitive intractability (or, as it may be seen, the blindness, stubbornness, and folly) of those who disagree with us.

In exploring these questions here, I focus on the epistemological controversy as played out in the pages of a recently published book by the Anglo-American philosopher of science, Philip Kitcher.[1] In a move quite familiar in these debates, Kitcher seeks, in the name of a "middle way" between two allegedly "extreme" positions—one a familiar and more or less established account, the other a relatively novel and currently controversial alternative—to redeem precisely the former: in this case, the set of interrelated ideas about science shared over the past century or so by most academic philosophers, many scientists, and much of the educated public. It is to this set of ideas, currently challenged in a number of quarters, that Kitcher alludes in the "legend" of his subtitle; and, indeed, he does display a certain ambivalence or affectionate irony toward some of its hoarier features. Nevertheless, his clear and intermittently explicit aim is to rehabilitate and ultimately to reaffirm the established account in all its crucial elements.[2]

Citing the "old-fashioned virtues" of the "broadly realist" conception of science he defends, Kitcher rehearses those elements as follows: "[S]cientists find out things about a world that is independent of human cognition; they advance true statements, use concepts that conform to natural divisions, [and] develop schemata that capture objective dependencies" (127). His defense of this set of ideas could claim its own virtues as well. Unlike other defenders of besieged orthodoxy who snipe and snort at often unnamed, commonly unquoted, and largely unread "postmodernists," Kitcher identifies his adversaries explicitly, quotes from their texts directly, gives evidence of having read them in some sense carefully, and frames his objections politely and painstakingly. Moreover, he sets forth his own views of science through patient rehearsals of standard arguments, detailed reconstructions of classic cases in the history of science, elaborate analogies and thought experiments, and established models drawn from other fields, including economics and evolutionary biology.

These are substantial virtues from most perspectives and, in Kitcher's own understanding of intellectual history, decisive ones. That is, they embody and exhibit what he calls "well-designed" and "properly activated cognitive propensities" from what he calls "dysfunctional" or "improperly activated" ones and which, accordingly, yield propositions "likely to prove true" rather than false (178–218). Given the epistemic criteria that Kitcher promotes and seeks to satisfy in his book and the cognitive procedures he describes and seeks to exemplify there, *The Advancement of Science* should carry the day in competition with the more skeptical, revisionist accounts of science he seeks to refute. And, indeed, as indicated by appreciative reviews in the *New York Times* and elsewhere, it does carry the day for a number of readers—especially, it appears, those who already grant the decisive authority of those epistemic criteria and the propriety of those pointedly rational cognitive procedures.[3] As indicated by more critical reviews in other journals, however, it does not carry the day for all readers, especially not, it appears, those already persuaded (or, as it may be seen, seduced and deluded) by more skeptical revisionist accounts.[4] This divergence of *critical judgments* regarding the success of Kitcher's efforts could be explained in various ways, but the explanations of that divergence would themselves probably diverge in more or less strict accord with the tenor of those judgments. This familiar self-doubling, self-confirming regress of judgment and justification recalls the reflexive echo noted above in traditional and revisionist views of the commensurability of traditional and revisionist views. It thereby exemplifies as well the more general structure of cognitive and rhetorical circularity which, as suggested in earlier chapters, is a crucial feature of the dynamics that concern us here.

Construing Constructivism

Among the critiques of, and alternatives to, traditional realist/rationalist philosophy of science that Kitcher seeks to defuse or rebut, some are clearly more provocative for him than others. Thus, while he takes issue on some points with other philosophers, notably Larry Laudan, Hilary Putnam, and Bas van Fraassen, he is most seriously exercised by the ideas of a particular group of historians and sociologists of science, many of whom are institutionally as well as intellectually affiliated with each other and a number of whom, not insignificantly here, are or have been Kitcher's colleagues at the University of California San Diego. The group in question includes Barry Barnes and David Bloor, founders of the "strong programme" in the sociology of science at Edinburgh; their British and American associates, Simon Schaffer, Andrew Pickering, Steven Woolgar, and Steven Shapin (the latter now at San Diego); and, perhaps preeminently, Bruno Latour, the classification-resistant anthropologist, sociologist, and theorist-at-large from Paris who was, for a time, also Kitcher's colleague in California. I return later to the significance of these institutional overlaps and intersections, but my major concern here will be the dynamics of Kitcher's engagement—or non-engagement—with the ideas of this group.

The question that Kitcher himself sees as most fundamental is whether, in the last analysis, the propositions of science reflect "stimuli from external asocial nature" or if, as some revisionists seem to claim, they are the product of something else distinctly social and verbal, such as "social forces," "conversations with peers," or "remarks made by teachers, friends, colleagues, and adversaries" (166, 162, 164). The crucial issue, he writes, is "the constraining power of . . . nature": whether or not, "given the actual social structures present in scientific communities, the input from asocial nature is sufficiently strong to keep consensus practice [i.e., the generation of scientific knowledge as such] on track" (166, 165).

The alternatives posed by Kitcher's formulations here—namely, asocial nature versus mere social exchange, empirical observation versus mere conversation, and the inexorable progress toward truth versus the deflecting pressure of mere exterior forces—are certainly familiar, and so is the structure of distinction and opposition through which he frames them. There is some question, however, as to whether, as he maintains, the crucial issue is the *choice* between those alternatives or, as his adversaries would see it, the *coherence* of just that notion of choice, of just that set of alternatives, and of the entire system of concepts and conceptual routines marked out by just such familiar but, in their view, dubious distinctions and oppositions. In a revealing footnote, Kitcher declares himself baffled by Latour's rejection of *both* "nature" *and* "society" as explanatory concepts in the history and sociology of science. "I find myself," Kitcher writes, "quite at a loss in understanding what resources are left for understanding the genesis and modification of scientific cognitive states" (166, note 52). The sense of perplexity he expresses here—the feeling that something obvious and necessary has been arbitrarily removed, a conceptual space suddenly evacuated, an indispensable resource inexplicably annihilated—is a recurrent and perhaps inevitable result of a collision of ideas of this kind and order.

Read from a post-Legendary perspective, Latour does not, of course, reject Nature or Society per se. Rather, he exposes the instability of the classic dualism that defines and constitutes each of these concepts by mutual contradistinction—or, to put it another way, what he rejects is just the idea of their *per se-ness.*[5] Similarly (and contrary to common charges), Latour and other revisionists do not reject Reason or Rationality per se. What they reject, rather, is the conception of reason as a distinct, ortho-tropic process that can be separated from—or ideally, as in science, purified of—the supposed pressures and distortions of such supposedly exterior forces as the reasoner's individual embodiment, immediate situation, prior intellectual investments, and ongoing verbal interactions. It is clear that part of the difficulty here—as elsewhere in current epistemological controversies—is a crucial divergence of conceptions of *concepts,* especially with regard to their relation to language. In the view of Latour and a number of other epistemological revisionists (or, as they are sometimes called in this respect, "constructivists"), the classic concepts in play in these debates—*nature, reason, reality, knowledge,* and so forth—are best understood as, precisely, constructs, that is, as variable discursive and conceptual products of our ongoing interactions with the physical, cultural, and verbal worlds in which we live and act. For Kitcher and most traditional realists, however, those classic concepts are properly understood as autonomous entities, that is, as the ontologically prior and independently determinate "referents," as it is said, of the words that merely name them.[6] Other important differences of conceptualization are closely related to this one. For example, Kitcher sees what he calls "the effects of nature" as exclusively unidirectional—informational "inputs," he also calls them—and, in relation to the formation of scientific knowledge, as necessarily prior and causal. For Latour and other constructivists, however, the effects of nature are, precisely, *effects;* that is, what we call Nature can be seen as the relatively stable product of the ongoing reciprocal coordinations of our perceptual, conceptual, verbal, manipulative, and other practices, formed and maintained through the very processes of our acting and communicating in the worlds in which we live.

Reciprocal coordination is the key idea here: not social interaction or discourse alone, and not social interaction or discourse simply *added to* empirical evidence, as the latter is classically understood, but a complex interactive process that is simultaneously dynamic, productive, and self-stabilizing. When Kitcher goes on to suggest what he calls a "moderate" version of "extreme" sociology of science, a version in which the beliefs of scientists are caused "jointly" by nature and society, it is clear that reciprocal coordination is not what he has in mind. Rather, as he indicates, his compromise here is analogous to the familiar supposed resolution of the nature/nurture debate, in which, as Kitcher puts it, "extreme" genetic determinism and environmentalism give way to a "middle ground" where scientists determine the "relative contributions" of genes and environment to various human traits (164).[7] This analogy, however, just duplicates at another level of description the dualistic structure of asocial nature (read "genes") and social forces (read "environment") at issue in his disagreement with the sociologists. Indeed, the biological model to which Kitcher appeals here, in which the traits of an organism are seen as the product of the combined "contributions" of genotype and environment, is currently challenged by more subtle and dynamic models of developmental systems, models in which one of the key mechanisms is, precisely, reciprocal determination.[8] I shall have more to say about this process later. What is significant for the moment is that the sources of Kitcher's bafflement appear to be more complex than he recognizes and that they reflect a divergence of ideas more radical than he might be willing to grant as possible. But this, of course, is just the issue of incommensurability.

More generally, I would suggest that what sustains the recurrent impasses in these and related epistemological controversies are not, as is sometimes said, just differences of "vocabulary" or conflicts between limited sets of already charted "positions," but, rather, systematically interrelated divergences of conceptualization that emerge at every level and operate across an entire intellectual domain. The exasperation and sense of intellectual (and sometimes moral) outrage that often attends these failed exchanges can be understood accordingly. Various scholars—historians and sociologists of science, epistemological theorists in related fields, and a number of philosophers as well—have, by one route or another, come to operate conceptually and to interact discursively with their professional and intellectual associates through currently heterodox conceptual idioms. For these scholars, the terms, concepts, and distinctions of traditional epistemology and philosophy of science are no longer either workable or, for the most part, necessary in conducting their professional and intellectual lives. For that reason, they find it usually difficult and sometimes (given the limits of mortal beings) impossible to answer theoretical arguments framed in the traditional terms or appealing to the traditional distinctions and oppositions—impossible, at least, to answer in ways that anybody finds gratifying or dignified. Conversely, traditionalist philosophers of science are, by definition, trained in, committed to, and in a sense intellectually and professionally constituted by a particular epistemological orthodoxy. Accordingly, they operate quite well with the traditional concepts, terms, and distinctions—at least within the orbits of the principal domains of their intellectual lives. And also accordingly, they are likely to find the critiques and alternatives elaborated by their heterodox colleagues absurd, arbitrary, and nihilistic: unmotivated rejections of what is commonsensical, solid, and well-established; irresponsible flattenings-out of what must be, and has been, carefully distinguished; reckless abandonments of what is most desirable and indispensable.

Given the matched and mirrored difficulties just described, it is not surprising that the misconnections in these exchanges are sometimes spectacular. A more extended example is Kitcher's reading and discussion of Latour and Woolgar's book, *Laboratory Life: The*

Construction of Scientific Facts, which is an ethnographic study of the day-to-day doings—technical experiments, casual conversations, formal meetings, preparations of scientific articles, and so forth—of a group of scientists in a particular laboratory at the Salk Institute. Explaining an important feature of their own work, Latour and Woolgar observe at one point, "We do not use the notion of reality to account for the stabilisation of a [scientific] statement . . . because this reality is formed as a consequence of this stabilisation."[9] Kitcher cites the remark as evidence of Latour and Woolgar's commitment to the "extreme view that inputs from nature are impotent" or, as he also paraphrases that supposed view, that scientific statements are the product only of the "social arrangement" of a particular laboratory and that "acceptance of [such] statements as firm parts of consensus practice is to be explained in a . . . fashion that makes no reference to the constraining power of stimuli from external, asocial nature" (164, 167, 165–166). The authors of *Laboratory Life,* Kitcher writes, want us to understand that "the encounters with nature that occurred during the genesis of [the scientists'] belief about TRF [the substance ultimately identified as a particular chemical compound] played no role" in the formation of that belief. In short, he concludes, in apparently aghast italics: *"However those encounters had turned out the end result would have been the same"* (166).

It could be argued, however, that, contrary to Kitcher's scandalized interpretation of it, the point of the observation he cites from Latour and Woolgar is neither that nature is impotent nor that reality is infinitely socially malleable but, rather, that to appeal to what the scientific community now accepts as an established fact in order to *explain* how that fact *came to be* established is to explain nothing at all: it is only to tell again the familiar (Legendary) story of scientific manifest destiny—that is, the story of how the truth always comes out in the end. But that story is, of course, exactly the one Kitcher himself would tell and seeks here most strenuously to defend.[10] Latour and Woolgar's forbearance from present-privileging assumptions is a significant methodological feature of Edinburgh-tutored sociology of science and constructivist science studies more generally. To Kitcher, however, that forbearance looks like gratuitous skepticism: an unnecessary and irrational refusal to credit the truth of established scientific knowledge (188). It is one of the ironies of the present scene of controversy that just this scrupulous self-skepticism on the part of constructivists—or what, mutatis mutandis, could be called, in the classic idiom, their "striving for impartiality and objectivity"—is routinely indicted by defenders of traditional realist epistemology as evidence of their scandalous "relativism."

Kitcher is persuaded by his own perception, interpretation, and report of Latour and Woolgar's ideas that those ideas are absurd. What is significant here is not simply that he misunderstands and misrepresents them but that, given his paraphrases of their specific claims and arguments in the idiom of his own intellectual tradition and disciplinary culture, he could hardly avoid doing so.[11] Throughout his book, Kitcher employs the idiom of realist/rationalist epistemology—"inputs from asocial nature," reconstructed "reasoning processes," "the constraining power of stimuli" versus "social forces," and so forth—as if its lexicon and syntax (terms, concepts, distinctions, oppositions, and so forth) were altogether unproblematic and, indeed, as if this idiom were the inevitable language of serious thought on questions of knowledge and science. Relevantly enough, he observes good-naturedly at one point that "[f]ew are born antirealists," that such ideas, strongly counter-intuitive as Kitcher experiences them, can only be the result of a certain line of argument being "thrust upon them" (131). But, of course, few—or none—are born realist/rationalist epistemologists either, however intuitively natural and inevitable that line of argument feels to those who argue it.

Loaded Observation

Kitcher finds the accounts of science and knowledge offered by constructivist social scientists scandalous and absurd. He is perplexed, however, not only by the accounts themselves but also by the fact that they are advanced by people he has reason to think are intellectually competent and indeed highly accomplished: several of them, we recall, including Latour and Shapin, are known to him as colleagues. Accordingly, he ventures a number of explanations for this curious situation. For example, he suggests at one point (perhaps humorously) that Latour's rejection not only of Nature (which might have been expected of a sociologist) but also of So-

ciety reflects an "admirable," though clearly misplaced, fondness for
"formal symmetry" (166, note 52). Or, he remarks at another point,
the social-political account of the ascendancy of the experimental
method offered by Shapin and Schaffer in their study, *Leviathan
and the Air-Pump*, derives from their exaggerated sense of the significance of the theory-ladenness of observation.[12] The latter suggestion bears some scrutiny for, from a constructivist perspective,
the significance of theory-ladenness in intellectual history is hard
to exaggerate. Moreover, the phenomenon itself appears to be
deeply implicated in the misconnections that concern us here. Both
points are illustrated in Kitcher's strenuously self-confirming reading of *Leviathan and the Air-Pump*.

Shapin and Schaffer seek to demonstrate that concerns about the
political authority of citizens and sovereigns in seventeenth-century
England helped shape the contemporary controversy between
Thomas Hobbes and Robert Boyle over the epistemic authority of
experimentation versus deduction; and, more significantly and con-
troversially, they suggest that the considerations involved in the
political debate were important in determining the *outcome* of the
intellectual debate. Commenting on their analysis, Kitcher writes:
"Because [Shapin and Schaffer] are so convinced of the power of
underdetermination arguments" (another way of stating the idea of
theory-ladenness),[13] they fail to focus on "the gritty details of the
encounters with nature" and "the complexities of the reasoning
about a large mass of observations and experiments"—details and
complexities, he suggests, that would, if focused on with "extrem[e]
car[e]," turn out to have been decisive in Boyle's victory (169, note
55). As Kitcher acknowledges, he has not himself undertaken this
purely hypothetical observation of those purely hypothetical gritty
details and complexities of reasoning, nor does he cite any alternative account of them. Nevertheless, so laden is he, so to speak,
with his theory of the *minor* significance of theory-ladenness and
the *decisive* significance of "encounters with nature" and proper
"reasoning" that he is prepared to affirm that "when that is done,"
Shapin and Schaffer's "thesis becomes implausible" and his own
view of the history of science is vindicated (ibid.).

The degree of unabashable conviction displayed in this argument
is remarkable, but more significant here is the self-affirming circularity through which it operates. The cognitive process exempli-

fied by Kitcher's resilience in the face of contrary argument and, arguably, contrary evidence is sometimes called the theory-ladenness of observation, sometimes the underdetermination of theory by fact, sometimes the hermeneutic circle, and sometimes the reciprocal determination of perception, belief, and behavior. That process or tendency—we have encountered it here before as "cognitive conservatism"—is, I believe, crucial to the dynamics not only of all theoretical controversy but of all theory, which is to say, all knowledge and cognition at both the micro and the macro level.[14] I return to these points below.

Reciprocal Coordinations, A/symmetrical Alternatives

In setting forth his own views of how to understand the *history* of science, Kitcher stresses that science is a definitively *epistemic* enterprise, with the single, uniform, and unchanging goal ("independent of field and time") of "attain[ing] significant truth," which he explains as "charting divisions and recognizing explanatory dependencies in nature" (157). Accordingly, he pays little attention to the historical and ongoing development of laboratory tools, skills, and techniques or to the historical and ongoing emergence of technological applications—all of which he evidently sees as incidental to the macrodynamics of science (or, in his teleological view of those dynamics, to its "advancement") and as irrelevant to the central goal of the *philosophy* of science, which is, in his view, the reconstruction of the reasoning processes of winning arguments.[15] Kitcher's views and practices in these respects have important consequences both for his understanding of revisionist science studies and for his rejection of them.

First, because laboratory techniques, technological applications, and other so-called non-cognitive matters are bracketed out in his own conception of science, Kitcher is not disposed to recognize their role in the alternative accounts developed by revisionist historians, philosophers, and sociologists. Thus he seems not to have noticed the important idea, associated with the more recent work of Latour, Pickering, Michel Callon, Ian Hacking, and others, of the complex relations between laboratory routines, technological extensions, and the formation of scientific statements themselves— all of which are seen in their work as reciprocally motivating, reciprocally determining, and (in Pickering's terms) mutually stabilizing practices.[16] In other words, the dynamics of science are understood in these accounts as neither the dis-covering (removing the covers from) a prior, autonomous truth nor the fabrication (making up whole-cloth) of a sheer collective fantasy but, rather, as the ongoing coordination (weaving together) of observation, theory formation, and material manipulation, each of these being continually adjusted in relation to the others. Thus, details of a theory are adjusted to details of technical manipulation and consequent observation; foci of observation are adjusted to extensions of both technological and theoretical application; material manipulations and details of theory are adjusted to emergent observations; and so on, around again.[17]

The situation of operative conceptual, discursive, and pragmatic stability that emerges from these kinds of ongoing reciprocal coordination is what we often call, in relation to the practices of science, *truth*.[18] In relation to the activities of individual cognition or belief formation, the corresponding situation of operative stability is what we usually call *knowledge*.[19] And, in relation to what can be seen as cognition in its broadest sense—that is, an organism's self-maintaining coordination with the domain of its operations—the corresponding situation is often called *adaptation* or biological *fitness*.[20] Of course, truth is commonly attributed not to sets of interactive practices but just to statements; and knowledge is commonly seen not as the global state of an organic system but as a specifically mental state; and fitness is treated often enough (as we shall soon see) not as a phenomenological feature of the ongoing interactions of organisms with their environments, but as an inherent property of organisms themselves. In each case, what *could* be seen as the name we give to the state of a dynamic system as viewed from a particular perspective is classically or commonly seen as an objective property of a logically and/or ontologically prior, autonomous entity.

These differing and perhaps rival conceptualizations of truth, knowledge, and fitness are commonly framed *asymmetrically* by the parties on both sides as Our enlightened truth versus Their error or illusion. But the alternatives could also be framed *symmetrically* on both sides as reflections of Our/Their differences of conceptual style and cognitive taste, differences that would themselves be seen as products of Our/Their more or less extensive differences of individual temperament and intellectual history, as played out within more or less different disciplinary cultures and sustained under more or less different epistemic conditions. Of course, these alternative and perhaps rival ways of describing and explaining alternative conceptualizations (symmetrically or asymmetrically) could *themselves* be described and explained either asymmetrically or symmetrically: either as (for example) Their hopelessly old-fashioned, asymmetrical realist dogma versus Our genuinely enlightened, symmetrical constructivist revelations or (reversing the perspective) as Their trendy, dangerous relativism versus Our established, crucially necessary, normative epistemology—or, again, as differences between Our/Their diversely shaped and situated conceptual styles and cognitive tastes. Thus the linked epistemological issues of—and commonly matched positions on—explanatory a/symmetry and evaluative in/commensurability could reduplicate themselves ad infinitum, at least theoretically. It is worth stressing, however, that they need not—and perhaps never can—do so in practice.

Indeed, it appears that a general intellectual taste for and commitment to unbroken epistemic symmetry ("relativism" in that sense) on the part of constructivist epistemologists may—and perhaps inevitably does—lapse (or rise) at certain psychologically or rhetorically significant points into an attraction toward asymmetry and an exhibition of unapologetic epistemic self-privileging. Thus Latour, distancing himself from an "absolute relativism" that he attributes to some of his science-studies associates, stresses that the *theoretically* presumptive epistemic symmetry (or equal credibility) of rival scientific (or other) accounts is actually always being broken by history and politics: that is, under the relevant prevailing conditions (institutional, intellectual, and so forth), one particular account will be more credible because it operates with a more powerful and extensive efficacy (of various kinds) than its rivals do. And, he suggests, the recognition of this historical and pragmatic asymmetry constitutes, in effect, a more enlightened "relative relativism."[21] Since, as Latour would no doubt grant, the superior efficacy of an account can be determined only after the fact, he would have to be seen as premature in maintaining the (relative) epistemic superiority of his own (relative) relativism *now*. On the other hand, the rhetorical energy and power that his account secures at the expense of historical modesty may turn out, in the long run, to be what makes it more effective (and credible) than the more scrupulously symmetrical or epistemically modest accounts of his rivals, sociological as well as philosophical.[22]

Ambivalent Processes, Normative Missions

Returning to Kitcher's state of conviction, it appears that, precisely because revisionist accounts of the reciprocal determination of conceptual and material practices in the history of science do not conform to his conception of science as unidirectional progress toward propositional truth, many of the substantive features of those accounts are, in effect, invisible to him. These include, significantly enough, "gritty details" (such as laboratory manipulations, technological extensions, and the effects of material tools and physical skills) that are quite at odds with the all-in-the-head, nothing-but-language, mere-social-forces caricatures of constructivist accounts that alarm traditionalists and are staples of current backlash publications. Because those features of revisionist science studies are invisible to Kitcher, however, they cannot affect either his conception of science or his understanding and evaluation of the revisionist accounts.

The negative route to self-confirming coherence and cognitive immobility indicated by Kitcher's reading practices—where prior theoretical commitment leads to conceptual bracketing-out, which leads to selective perception, which leads to sustained theoretical commitment, and so on, around again—is, of course, just the reverse side of the cognitive mechanism I have referred to in these pages as the hermeneutic circle, the theory-ladenness of observation, and the reciprocal determination of perception, belief, and behavior. But here we have a very curious and instructive situation. For, as already suggested, the self-securing circularity by which that unhappy—logically objectionable, cognitively confining—mechanism operates could be seen as duplicating, at the level of individual cognition, the complex processes of reciprocal determination and mutual stabilization that are, according to revisionist science studies, central to intellectual history and the dynamics of scientific practice and, according to revisionist theoretical biology, central to the dynamics of all living systems. What I would emphasize here is not only the evident importance of forms of circularity in everything we call cognition and knowledge, but also the evidently irreducible *ambivalence* of all the relevant mechanisms or processes, where what is most problematic (circular, self-immuring) duplicates what is most essential (coherence-maintaining, life-sustaining), and what appears positive from one perspective or at one level of analysis appears negative from another perspective or at another level of analysis—or, in other words, where it is difficult to say, simply or finally, what's good and what's bad.

But this brings us back to Kitcher's book, one of the major goals of which is to affirm both the normative mission of traditional philosophy of science—that is, precisely its effort to say what is epistemically good and bad, to distinguish genuine science from pseudoscience and right thinking from wrong thinking—and its related "meliorative" project, which he explains as "the delineation of formal rules, principles, and . . . informal canons of reasoning, [which,] when supplemented by an appropriate educational regime, can . . . make people more likely to activate propensities and undergo processes that promote cognitive progress" (186). Kitcher defends these normative ambitions by way of a parallel to evolutionary biology—under, it must be added, the strongly progressivist and heavily adaptationist interpretation of evolution favored by most realist epistemologists.[23] "Darwinians," Kitcher writes, "want not only to claim that successful organisms are those that leave descendents, but also to investigate those characteristics that promote reproductive success"; and analogously, he claims, philosophers of science, reviewing the historical fortunes of various competing scientific theories, want to identify what it is that "confers explanatory and predictive success" on those that succeed (155–156, 156–157). The key to that success, he observes, is clear to the *realist:* just as certain organisms succeed because they are adapted to their environments, certain theories in science succeed "because they fasten on aspects of reality," which is to say, because they are true (156).[24]

These parallels between traditional, normative philosophy of science and evolutionary biology are, Kitcher remarks, "thoroughly Darwinian," the emphasis being required, perhaps, because significantly different interpretations of evolutionary theory could be offered and, as he acknowledges, significantly different analogies (and lessons) have in fact been drawn. It could be observed, for example, that since the biological fitness of an organism can be specified only in relation to a particular, contingent, environmental situation, the idea of *general* "sources of fitness" makes little sense and the search for *inherent* traits that "endow organisms with high Darwinian fitness" or "dispose them to survive" (156) is pointless. Analogously, we are no more able to devise a method for distinguishing or producing "cognitively progressive," or *inherently* more-likely-to-be-true, beliefs than to devise one for distinguishing or producing *inherently* more-likely-to-be-fit organisms . . . or people. Indeed, if biological fitness is taken as a metaphor for epistemic truth, then the meliorative project of traditional epistemology would have to be seen as the eugenics of philosophy.

Kitcher rejects such alternative understandings of biological fitness and their implications for the philosophy of science as "shallow," "pessimistic" (156), and "close to [a] caricature" of the views of "[r]eal evolutionary biologists" (156, note 39). Philosophers, he insists, *can* identify the cognitive strategies and propensities "designed [presumably by natural selection] for the promotion of cognitive goals" (196). The way for them to do it, he maintains, is by continuing to reconstruct the manifestly successful reasoning of good scientists, that is, the ones like Galileo and Darwin who make (or made) discoveries that turn(ed) out to be significantly true, and by examining closely the manifestly dysfunctional cognitive behavior of those of their scientific colleagues who, along with various cardinals, bishops, assorted small clergy, and other cognitively intransigent lay persons, fail(ed) to acknowledge the truth of those discoveries after they are (or were) made.

Kitcher is persuaded that there are two distinct ways of thinking. One is the sort that gets us to where all thinking naturally (or rationally) wants to go, namely to *truth*. The other does not get us anywhere, at least nowhere we should (rationally) want to be. In providing updated scientific credentials for this ancient and familiar opposition, he appeals to empirical cognitive psychology or, rather, to certain philosophical appropriations of its findings.[25] Rationality, he observes, is not, as some versions of Legend claim, just an abstract matter of how people's beliefs are "logically connected" but also a matter of how they are actually "*psychologically* connected" (184). But, he insists, this does not lead to "relativism": "Nobody

. . . who believes (rightly) that changes in cognitive state have *causal explanations* . . . should go on to infer that there is no basis for distinguishing the types of processes that generate and sustain beliefs, actions, and decisions. Some types of processes are conducive to cognitive progress; others are not" (186, my emphasis).[26]

Kitcher evidently understands "relativism" here as the claim that all cognitive processes (or cognitive products) are equally progressive (or valid). And, as his assurances indicate, he is haunted by the traditional association of this epistemic egalitarianism with naturalistic efforts to *explain* beliefs *causally* as distinguished from the more properly philosophical task of *justifying* (or giving philosophically good reasons for) those beliefs that are properly epistemically privileged—for example (as is usually said), those that make up genuine scientific knowledge. A crucial implication of these traditional distinctions is that a thoroughly empirical or strictly naturalistic psychology, inasmuch as it does not strive to distinguish the conditions of true and false belief, is non-normative, hence presumptively relativistic, hence also, in the recurrent phrase, "not philosophically interesting." There is, however, a familiar dilemma here. In wanting to rehabilitate traditional philosophical epistemology by attaching it to cognitive science *and* simultaneously to retain its definitive normative ambitions, Kitcher is caught in a double bind: traditionally, only the *empirical* confers genuine scientific status but, by definition, cannot escape contingency; conversely, only the *normative* enjoys genuine philosophical status but, by definition, must escape contingency. Given, then, the traditional distinctions and definitions, it is, logically speaking, improper to appeal to the empirical to authorize the normative.[27] Nevertheless, that is just what Kitcher does here: insisting on the benefits and indeed necessity of an up-to-date scientific psychology for a contemporary understanding of mind, he extracts from it a strenuously normative, thus non-relativistic, thus desirably philosophical account of right thinking. There is some question, however, as to the long-range stability and general credibility of the achievement.[28]

Quasi-Naturalizing Reason

As distinct from more thoroughly empirical and naturalistic approaches, the cognitive science that girds Kitcher's normative epistemology is itself significantly mediated by work in rationalist philosophy of mind. Indeed, it could be said that his account of cognitive processing has already built into it all the concepts and distinctions required to sustain a traditional conception of right (rational) and wrong thinking.

Relatively early in the book, Kitcher observes that the best way to conceive the mind is "as a box whose contents are declarative statements or propositions" (61). He acknowledges some difficulties with this model (quite dubious from most contemporary naturalistic perspectives[29]), but affirms his conviction of its essential validity when fortified by ideas arising from research in artificial intelligence and cognitive psychology—or, rather, *certain* of those ideas. For he goes on immediately to reject what are arguably the major alternative models of mind now current, that is, neural-network or, as they are sometimes called, "connectionist" models. The reason Kitcher gives for "resist[ing]" these "challenge[s] to the propositional character of human cognition" is of considerable interest here: it is, he writes, "because I do not yet see how the envisaged alternative—thinking of cognition in terms of 'patterns of network activation'—can do justice to the articulation of propositions and reasons that is so prominent in the growth of scientific knowledge" (63, note 6).[30]

Clearly Kitcher takes for granted the prominence of "the articulation of propositions and reasons" in "the growth of scientific knowledge." But this is a distinctly rationalist presumption that would be questioned by, among others, the revisionist historians of science he seeks here to refute. (For the latter, the operations of other factors and forces—social, political, technological, and so forth—are at least as prominent in the history of science as the articulation of propositions or reasons, and perhaps even more significant in understanding its dynamics.) In short, Kitcher's justification for his convictions here begs the question. Or, to frame the observation another way, one apparent reason for his resistance to *both* thoroughly naturalistic models of cognition *and* revisionist accounts of the history of science is that the defining features of each are incompatible with the defining (one might say non-negotiable) features of rationalist epistemology and traditional philosophy of science.

A thoroughgoing connectionist might cite Kitcher's reason (or justification) for resisting connectionist models as just the sort of pre-scientific or "folk-psychological" explanation for a mental state that will ultimately be replaced by a genuinely scientific account in terms of, precisely, "patterns of [neural] network activation."[31] Accordingly, the connectionist would re-explain Kitcher's conviction of the inadequacy of naturalistic models as an organic state consisting of the decisive stabilization of certain of his neuronal patterns by certain prior formative experiences, for example, his evidently rigorous training and professional immersion in rationalist epistemology. In other words, precisely because of Kitcher's personal cognitive history vis-à-vis traditional models of cognition, he resists rival connectionist models; and this is also why he is unable to "see" (as he concedes) how a specification of neural connections "can do justice to" the articulation of propositions and reasons—including, presumably, his own articulation of his own reasons for rejecting such models. In short, the connectionist might conclude, Kitcher can neither understand connectionist models nor conceive or articulate connectionist explanations because his brain and nervous system have been decisively *in*scribed by the conceptual system to which (as he thinks) he rationally *sub*scribes.[32]

This last point raises the question of incommensurability fairly directly. There is certainly a significant difference between the presumptively *logically* linked "propositions and reasons" that Kitcher endorses and the presumptively *physiologically* linked (or perhaps co-excited) "patterns of [neural] network activation" that he rejects, or, to put this another way, between the characteristic reason-givings of rationalist epistemology and the characteristic cause-assignings of cognitive psychology.[33] But is it a *"world"* of difference? The question arises in this form because the idea of incommensurability is often identified with the claim—commonly seen as counter-intuitive and otherwise intolerable—that people who subscribe to radically divergent conceptual systems live in discrete and perhaps unbridgeable worlds. For some philosophers, one way of framing and simultaneously answering the question just posed is whether such manifestly divergent conceptual idioms (or "schemes") as rationalist philosophy of mind and connectionist neurophysiology are ultimately *intertranslatable.*[34]

To answer the question of intertranslatability in any particular case, one would, of course, have to specify both the perspectives

.

from which and the criteria of adequacy or success in relation to which a presumptive translation (in either direction) would be assessed. In the present case, for example, relevant criteria might be whether Kitcher's native Rationalese and the connectionist's native Naturalese are intertranslatable enough for native speakers of either idiom to feel that statements in one about patterns of network activation "can do justice to" statements in the other about propositions and reasons, and vice versa. Given Kitcher's testimony as just discussed, the answer is clearly no, at least for him. But such statements evidently *are* translatable for some connectionists, Paul M. Churchland for example, who, as his writings make clear, is happy to produce duly scientifically updated and pointedly deflationary translations of Rationalese into Naturalese at the drop of a hat.[35] To be sure, Churchland would not accept Kitcher's old Rationalese version of mental activity as adequate to the neuronal facts. Other intertranslators, however, such as philosopher/cognitive science experts Andy Clark and Owen Flanagan or theoretical neuroscientists William Calvin and Antonio Damasio, have produced subtle and detailed descriptions of mental-neuronal activity in a number of post-rationalist idioms that many readers find intellectually engaging and adequate for their particular purposes.[36]

It seems, then, that the intertranslatability of Rationalese and Naturalese—and thus, by implication, their commensurability—is fundamentally contingent, dependent on perspective and purpose, changing over time, varying in practice, and not otherwise determinable. And the same seems true more generally of the intertranslatability—and thus commensurability, so understood—of any set of conceptual idioms.

Cognitive Rights and Wrongs

We may turn now to the ways in which right and wrong thinking are actually separated in Kitcher's account of rationality. Insisting, as always, on the supposedly "relativism"-dashing availability of objective criteria for the assessment of cognitive activities and products, he writes: "People can make cognitive mistakes, perceiving badly, inferring hastily, failing to act to obtain inputs from nature that would guide them to improved cognitive states . . . Some types of processes are conducive to cognitive progress; others are not" (185–186).

To illustrate the difference between these types, Kitcher contrasts the ("reconstructed") reasoning of Darwin and his followers with the cognitive intransigence of nineteenth-century skeptics and present-day creationists. Reflecting on the latter's current debate with Darwinians (a debate, it should be stressed, in which Kitcher himself has participated extensively[37]), he writes:

> The behavior of creation scientists indicates a kind of inflexibility, deafness, or blindness. They make an objection to some facet of evolutionary biology. Darwin's defenders respond by suggesting that the objection is misformulated, that it does not attack what Darwinists claim, that it rests on false assumptions, or that it is logically fallacious. How do creation scientists reply? Typically, *by reiterating the argument.* Anyone who has followed exchanges in this controversy . . . sees that there is no adaptation to any of the principal criticisms. (195, his emphasis)

He means, of course, that there is no adaptation by creationists to the criticisms of their views by Darwinists.[38] But the "anyone" who sees this could not be quite anyone, since creationists could observe that, as far as adapting to criticism goes, Darwinists— blind, deaf, and inflexible as anyone can see they are—have not budged an inch either. Kitcher explains the overt cognitive conservatism of creationists as a sign of their underlying cognitive unwholesomeness. Creationists, however, could probably give a comparable array of reasons for their opponents' stubbornness in error: ignorance of the Bible, secular humanist prejudice, modern infatuation with evolutionary theory, plus, perhaps, certain sins of sloth and pride. My point here is not, of course, that the opinions of Darwinists and creationists regarding evolutionary theory are "equally valid," but that, for all the differences in their favored idioms and authorities, the explanation Kitcher offers for the intellectual obstinacy of his longtime adversaries exhibits the same asymmetrical structure as *their* explanation for *his*, which is to say the same tendency toward absolute epistemic self-privileging.[39]

Kitcher claims that the distinctions he draws between proper and improper activations of good and bad cognitive propensities are based on objective norms and criteria. There is reason to suspect, however, that, here as commonly elsewhere in the case of such objectivist claims, the judgments of goodness and badness, propriety and impropriety, *preceded* and were indeed *presupposed* by the framing of those norms and criteria. Latour remarks, in a passage that Kitcher quotes with some exasperation, that all efforts to separate rational and irrational claims are no more than *"compliments or curses,"* saying nothing about the claims in question but "simply help[ing] people to further their arguments as swear words help workmen to push a heavy load, or as war cries help karate fighters intimidate their opponents."[40] Kitcher objects that such remarks "disguise both the serious purpose and the genuine difficulties involved in appraisals of rationality" (185). But perhaps we have here just another (disguised) curse or compliment. For how, and from what presumptively objective perspective, can it be determined whether Latour is disguising a serious purpose and genuine difficulties or exposing an earnest but vacuous enterprise?

At the end of his analysis of creationist cognition, Kitcher displays a certain uncharacteristic vehemence, which, however, he makes a point of defending:

> There are limits to proper tolerance. In some cases, epistemic performance is so inflexible that we either view the cognitive systems in question as poorly designed for the promotion of cognitive goals or suppose that the goals that are being activated are not cognitive at all. Where the latter supposition is correct and the subjects in question profess cognitive goals, some form of deception or self-deception is occurring. (196)

It is not clear what Kitcher believes one is entitled to do at the limits of proper tolerance. What is clear, however, is that its justification slides significantly from a diagnosis of certain defects of *intellect* (poorly designed cognitive systems, the activation of non-cognitive goals) to a diagnosis of certain *character* defects (self-deception) and/or a charge of *moral* offense (downright deception). Given the familiar, evidently widespread, and perhaps endemic temptation to execute that sort of slide,[41] it is not surprising that normative epistemology is recurrently invoked to authorize it; given the duly credited authorizations of normative epistemology, the temptation may be all the harder to resist.

Epistemic Authority, Epistemic Domains

It will be instructive to draw together, now, a number of points touched on earlier. First, in connection with Kitcher's distinctly asymmetrical and often overtly self-privileging notions of mental fitness, we may recall that cognitive conservatism—the process or mechanism that produces what we call, under some conditions, circularity and stubbornness and, under other conditions, coherence and stability—is conceived here not as an inherent flaw in certain *(other)* people's cognitive design but as an endemic tendency of human, and perhaps not only human, cognitive operations. Indeed, it appears that hermeneutic circularity, the theory-ladenness of observation, and, more generally, the reciprocal determination of belief, perception, and behavior are crucial features of the complex set of cognitive processes that we call—depending on where we are standing and how we are cutting it—perception, reasoning, thinking, belief formation, theory formation, experiencing, responding, behaving, or living. The value ("fitness," "functionality," "progressiveness," "success") of those processes cannot be indicated or characterized independently of the domains in which they are played out or of the perspectives from which their products (that is, particular beliefs and related behaviors) are assessed. The cognitive processes that, on occasion, lead us (or is it only *them?*) astray and confine our thinking to circles of self-affirmation appear to be the *same* processes that give coherence to our individual beliefs, sustain and stabilize all scientific knowledge as such, and lead us to what we sometimes call *truth*.

Second, foregrounding the idea of cognitive or epistemic *domains*—that is, the spaces or, one could say, niches in which we play out our particular beliefs—we may recall here the institutional overlaps and interconnections noted earlier among the participants in these controversies. What can be stressed now is that the academic and professional arenas in which various parties play out their more or less divergent ideas may themselves diverge or coincide to greater or lesser degrees. Philosophers, historians, and sociologists of science, respectively, typically belong to distinct disciplinary cultures, publish in different professional journals, and train different graduate students. In these respects, their epistemic domains are relatively discrete. At the same time, however, they may be located in the same universities, attend some of the same interdisciplinary conferences, teach some of the same undergraduate students, and write for some of the same general interest magazines. In these respects, their epistemic domains will overlap, and they—and their respective beliefs—will inevitably, and for better or worse, bump into each other. Where the domains in question are relatively discrete, there is little occasion for the *divergences* of their beliefs to become *conflicts,* and their respective ideas and idioms can continue, so to speak, to live side by side. It is, of course, where those domains overlap or coincide that divergences of belief and conceptual idiom, and related differences of cognitive taste and disciplinary projects and practices, do become conflicts, as exhibited, for example, in the debates we have examined here and, in some places, in active, sometimes bitter, rivalries for intellectual and institutional authority.

Epistemic authority is involved in other ways as well in these quite general social and cognitive dynamics. Theories and accounts that are more or less incompatible with what we already take for granted as obvious, self-evident, or unquestionable are likely to appear inadequate, incredible, or incoherent to us, and, depending on our sense of the intellectual authority and sometimes other social characteristics of the people who offer them (e.g., their institutional credentials, age, gender, or class[42]), to appear also as ignorant, silly, outlandish, wildly radical, or fraudulent. We may resist accepting or even entertaining such theories or accounts even though they are presented with detailed arguments and defended with evidence that other people seem to find coherent and compelling; for, of course, those other people may, for that very reason, appear ignorant or intellectually inept to us and/or (depending again on our sense of them otherwise) gullible, trendy, brainwashed, or ideologically motivated. The *energy* with which we resist such theories or accounts will correspond, of course, to the significance to us of the particular ideas with which they are in conflict. The *form* of that resistance, however, is likely to be shaped by the type and degree of our own intellectual authority in the relevant epistemic domains, and it may range, accordingly, from perplexed and resentful withdrawal to elaborate condescension, detailed counterargument, virulent attack, or attempted suppression.

Since broader political resonances are inevitable here, a further general point can be added. In situations of intellectual rivalry, it sometimes happens that the only acceptable outcome for at least one of the parties is *absolute epistemic supremacy:* the claim is made, in other words, that there is but one truth, that the party in question is enlightened as to its essential nature and proper pursuit, and that it is universally desirable that all this be universally acknowledged. In such cases, any divergence of professed belief, conceptual idiom, or discursive practice in any domain whatsoever is seen as dangerous error requiring intervention and correction. Accordingly, all intellectual divergence is seen as deviation, all deviation becomes conflict, and, for the party (or parties: it may be both) so disposed, all conflict necessarily becomes zero-sum rivalry, with winners properly taking all, and taking it for all time, and losers properly disappearing forever. Indeed, it is precisely when institutionalized systems of ideas and related conceptual idioms and discursive practices claim absolute epistemic supremacy—or, of course (though there is often no difference), when they entail visions of universal *political* supremacy—that "wars of truth" become duels to the not always figurative death.

My description here is meant to be quite general, but it is not irrelevant that Legend insists on the unity not only of truth but also of epistemic domains. These indeed are its defining orthodoxies in relation to the contra-defining heresies of what it calls "relativism;" and, accordingly, they constitute a major source of the resistance by traditionalists to the idea of incommensurability and to the related notion of multiple "worlds"—which could also be understood as multiple epistemic domains.

Conflict, Commensuration, and Transformation

Returning to the issue of incommensurability as framed at the beginning of this chapter, we may ask where we stand at this point. Having lined up and compared these divergent accounts of science, are we now prepared to choose the better—that is, the epistemically superior—one? From the perspective of this analysis, the question is unanswerable and the choice irrelevant. This is not to say that we cannot or should not assess different ideas, theories, or beliefs; on the contrary, we can, must, and do assess them continuously, *in* and *as* the very process of playing and living them out in the relevant domains of our lives—pragmatic, intellectual, political, technological, religious, and so forth. It is to say, rather, that the occasions for such formal, discrete, and terminally decisive adjudications, as classically depicted, do not arise.[43]

We may recall here Kitcher's somewhat vehement insistence on "the limits of proper tolerance." One may agree that there are such limits, but observe, in accord with this analysis, that they are mundane—practical and quotidian—matters of social and institutional geography and politics, not matters for the high courts of epistemic adjudication. The point is illustrated well enough by the situation that evoked his vehemence, that is, the debate between creationists and Darwinists. As long as the domains in which their alternate accounts (of the origin of species, the mutability of life-forms, the age of the universe, and so forth) are played out remain effectively discrete, there is no reason for intellectual or political tolerance to be limited, nor, in fact, any occasion for it to be displayed—except, of course, as forbearance from invasive missionary activity by one side or the other. Conflict arises, however, when there is, or threatens to be, a coincidence of domains, as in the demand by some citizens that scriptural accounts of the relevant phenomena be taught in American public schools in place of, or as an "equal time" alternative to, evolutionary theory. It is quite a temptation but, from the present perspective, a conceptual mistake for Darwinian-minded citizens to imagine this conflict on the model of the struggle between Galileo and the pope or between Darwin himself and his nineteenth-century clerical adversaries. It is certainly a *strategic* mistake for them to play it that way at local school board meetings or in the nation's courts. For, unless Darwinists agree to having the issue framed in such terms, the relevant question is not whether evolutionary theory satisfies such arbitrary and arguably vacuous *general* epistemic criteria as "incontrovertible factuality" or "objectively determined truth" but, rather, which authorizing institutions are appropriate for evaluating the material to be taught specifically in American public schools. Given the constitutional separation of church and state, it could be argued that, although scriptural and other religious authority is appropriate enough in parochial schools, the only appropriate institutional authorities for assessing public school materials are secular. That would mean, in this case, that any theory of the origin of species, the mutability of life-forms, or the age of the universe (and so forth) taught in science classes in

American public schools is properly assessed in relation to currently established scientific knowledge and practice, where "established" is understood as *broadly accepted and highly reliably worked with* (that is, applied, extended, connected, and so on) *by members of the relevantly authorized secular epistemic communities*. Alternative interpretations of "established" as "incontrovertibly factual" or "objectively determined as finally, universally, and unconditionally true" could be seen, accordingly, as red herrings. Red herrings can be rhetorically effective, of course, at school board meetings and even in courtrooms. But the effectiveness of this one has depended, it appears, on the readiness of some Darwinists (including some biologists and philosophers of science) to rise to the epistemic supremacist bait dangled by their creationist opponents.[44]

There are, it appears, few particular occasions and no particular ways to select winners and losers in intellectual controversies, and, in a sense, no winners or losers either, at least no objectively determinate ones. It seems clear that none of the presently rival orthodox/heterodox accounts of science will survive or endure in any of their present forms. There will be "advancements" and retreats, of course, but only in the sense of the increased or decreased authority of one or another such account in various more or less restricted epistemic niches. In other words, the fitness, success, or survival of any theory of science will still be measurable only in relation to particular conditions and only from particular perspectives. And the same could be said of any theory or account whatsoever.

There can be no ultimate comparison of or decision between the epistemic merits of these rival theories, moreover, because each of them is being transformed by, among other things, the dynamics of their very rivalry. Academic philosophy of science has undergone substantial transformation at both the individual and the institutional level since at least the 1960s, when Kuhn and Feyerabend first presented their unignorable challenges to Kitcher's Legend. Claims, methods, and missions have been modified, in some respects drastically. Alliances have been formed with other disciplines, including the biological and physical sciences themselves, and new interdisciplinary fields, such as cognitive science, have emerged and become relatively well established.[45] The reciprocal of this is also occurring. Revisionist science studies keeps revising itself in response to, among other things, the resistances of traditional realist/

rationalist epistemology. To mention only one example here, but a telling one: Pickering's increased emphasis on "material practices" in his accounts of the history of particle physics and his related delineation and embrace of a position he calls "pragmatic realism" appear to have been shaped by, among other things, his prior and ongoing interactions with some persistently resistant philosophers of science.[46]

Incommensurability, it appears, is neither a logically scandalous relation between theories, nor an ontologically immutable relation between isolated systems of thought, nor a morally unhappy relation between sets of people, but a contingent, experiential relation between historically and institutionally situated conceptual/discursive practices. Some radically divergent ideas never meet at all, at least not in the experience of mortal beings. In other cases, meetings are staged repeatedly but never come off, ending only in mutual invisibility and inaudibility. Sometimes, however, meetings do occur, perhaps intensely conflictual and abrasive but also, in the long run, mutually transformative. Thus it may be that, at the end, on the real Judgment Day—if there is one—for which the philosophers are always preparing us, when all the stories are told and all the chips are in, counted, and compared, we will be unable not only to say who finally won but even to tell which was which.

Notes

1. The Unquiet Judge

1. Among those whose work along these lines has been especially significant in recent years are Paul Feyerabend, Jacques Derrida, Stanley Fish, Michel Foucault, Jean-François Lyotard, Richard Rorty, and Bruno Latour.

2. For instances of such charges, see S. P. Mohanty, "Us and Them: On the Philosophical Bases of Political Criticism," *Yale Journal of Criticism* 2 (1989): 1–31; Christopher Norris, *What's Wrong with Postmodernism: Critical Theory and the Ends of Philosophy* (Baltimore: Johns Hopkins University Press, 1990), and *Uncritical Theory: Postmodernism, Intellectuals & the Gulf War* (Amherst, Mass.: University of Massachusetts Press, 1992); Terry Eagleton, *The Ideology of the Aesthetic* (Oxford: Basil Blackwell, 1990), pp. 379–381; and Madhava Prasad, "The New (International) Party of Order? Coalition Politics in the (Literary) Academy," *Diacritics* 22 (1992): 34–46.

3. Thomas L. Haskell, "The Curious Persistence of Rights Talk in the 'Age of Interpretation,'" *Journal of American History* 74 (1987): 984–1012. The quoted passage appears on page 984. Haskell ultimately redeems the contemporary invocation of legal/political rights to his own satisfaction by redefining a "right" as the product of a quasi-objective "rational convention" (pp. 1002–1012).

4. Haskell cites, with satisfaction, what he takes to be anthropological evidence for " 'a set of basic predicaments which define what it is to be human' " ("The Curious Persistence of Rights Talk," p. 1004, note 37).

5. It is because this last point eluded Alisdair MacIntyre that he was able to generate the remarkable idea, crucial to his analysis of

153

postlapsarian moral discourse, that the way people use words such as "ought" and "duty" in these fallen times violates their original and thus, he suggests, inherent objectivist meanings (MacIntyre, *After Virtue: A Study in Moral Theory*, 2nd ed. [Notre Dame, Ind.: University of Notre Dame Press, 1984], esp. pp. 8–10). Haskell's anxieties about "rights talk" originate, as he indicates, in large part from his reading of MacIntyre's analysis ("The Curious Persistence of Rights Talk," p. 995). For further discussion of MacIntyre in a political and judicial context, see Barbara Herrnstein Smith, "Judgment After the Fall," *Cardozo Law Review* 11 (1990): 1291–1311.

6. Robin West, "Relativism, Objectivity, and Law," *Yale Law Journal* 99 (1990): 1473–1502. Subsequent page references to the article appear in parentheses in the text.

7. Barbara Herrnstein Smith, *Contingencies of Value: Alternative Perspectives for Critical Theory* (Cambridge, Mass.: Harvard University Press, 1988). West's article is, in part, a response to the book, which develops a critique of the foundationalist tradition in literary theory and aesthetics.

8. The notion that this sophomoric credo "follows" from non-objectivism is widespread but a strict non sequitur. I discuss it elsewhere as the Egalitarian Fallacy; see Chapter 5 and Smith, *Contingencies of Value*, pp. 98–101 and 150–152.

9. See Lynne V. Cheney, *Humanities in America* (Washington: National Endowment for the Humanities, 1988), and Larry Gordon, "Bennett Draws Fire in Stanford Talk Assailing Course Change," *Los Angeles Times*, 19 April 1988: 3.

10. "Objectivist moral/legal discourse, like any form of moral discourse, may be put forward in two very different sorts of contexts. First, objectivism may constitute a form of *critical* discourse. A moral critic of the political, legal, or social action taken by another might criticize that action on objectivist sorts of grounds; the act is at odds with what, morally, is objectively required" (West, "Relativism," p. 1489). The "objectivist sorts of grounds" West indicates here are given no substantive content and the repeated insertion of the term "moral" adds little more than a question-begging resonance. Are only *objectivist* arguments to be considered "moral"? In any case, Cheney and Bennett could have readily characterized themselves and their critiques as "moral": they were certainly regarded by many citizens as engaged in a profoundly moral battle against definitively immoral forces.

11. For applause and endorsements, see Roger Kimball, *Tenured Radicals: How Politics Has Corrupted Our Higher Education* (New York: Harper & Row, 1990), and the charter statement of the literally reactionary National Association of Scholars. For one set of contemporary rejoinders, see Barbara Herrnstein Smith, "Curing the Humanities, Correcting the Humanists," and "Reply to Lynne V. Cheney," *M[odern] L[anguage] A[ssociation] Newsletter* (respectively, Summer and Winter, 1988), and "Limelight: Reflections on a Public Year" [MLA Presidential Speech], *PMLA* 104 (1989): 285–293.

12. West sees as only practically difficult what is challenged as fundamentally problematic: "[I]t is surely possible that any particular attempt to construct an ideal based on human nature fails . . . But that there are or may be failed attempts does not imply that the project is intrinsically undoable. It only indicates . . . that the project is very difficult" ("Relativism," p. 1486).

13. Although West does not use the term, her efforts to defend a politically selective objectivism can be related to the idea of "strategic essentialism," that is, the claim that one or another feature of current political conditions makes it necessary to invoke essentialist concepts that are otherwise ("theoretically") criticized and rejected. There are occasions, of course, when virtually *any* rhetoric, including the assertion of what one knows are totally false statements, seems justifiable. Also, the public invocation of certain traditionally authorizing ideas ("fundamental needs," "basic rights," and so forth) may have the strategic effect of signalling to adversaries, and expressing for followers, the strength of a speaker's commitment to the project at hand. In view, however, of the long-range liabilities of objectivist appeals as discussed above (dogmatism, diminished responsiveness, group self-purging, handing weapons to adversaries, and so forth), their invocation must be counted as always strategically *risky* and as likely to be ultimately *politically* costly.

14. The pertinence of this analysis to specifically feminist political theory is highlighted if, here and below, one adds "women" to "we" or "us" and substitutes "*other* women"—or, with some adjustments, "men"—for "they" and "them."

15. For another example of the debate evoked in this section, see the instructive exchanges among Lynn A. Baker, " 'Just Do It': Pragmatism and Progressive Social Change," *Virginia Law Review* 78 (1992): 697–718; Richard Rorty, "What Can you Expect from

Anti-Foundational Philosophers?: A Reply to Lynn Baker," ibid., pp. 719–727; and William G. Weaver, "Richard Rorty and the Radical Left," ibid., pp. 729–757.

16. See Katharine T. Bartlett, "Feminist Legal Methods," *The Harvard Law Review* 103 (1990): 854–863, for a rigorous application of this point to specifically feminist legal theory.

17. West equivocates significantly. Any judge who based his decisions *only* on "the interests, preferences and 'economies' of the *interested parties*" ("Relativism," p. 1499, my emphasis) could be seen as irresponsible. Nothing, however, obliges the non-objectivist judge to do so. Like any other judge, he could just as readily (and altogether self-consistently) base his decisions on the broad values and general, long-range interests of, as West fleetingly allows, "the *relevant communities*" ("Relativism," p. 1500, my emphasis). Full acknowledgment of the latter possibility would rob her major charge here of its force.

18. See *Constant A. v Paul C. A.*, 344 PA Super 49; 496 A2d 1 (PA Super 1985).

19. *EEOC v. Sears, Roebuck & Co.*, U.S. District Court for the Northern District of Illinois, Eastern Division (Civil Action No. 79-C-4373, 1978).

20. The term "progressive" here complements West's usage of the term "conservative" and reflects my own sense of the general, long-term desirability of various projects and conditions.

21. Versions of such arguments were, in fact, offered by EEOC. The agency failed, however, to persuade the court that Sears's actual hiring and promotion practices—as distinct from the beliefs and presumptions of many employers—were discriminatory. It is not easy to say from the record the extent to which that failure reflected the rhetorical and/or evidentiary weakness of the agency's suit or the court's traditionalist bias. For a sample of documents and related discussion, see "Women's History Goes to Trial: *EEOC v. Sears, Roebuck and Company*," *Signs: Journal of Women in Culture and Society* 11 (1986): 751–779, and Joan Wallach Scott, "The Sears Case," in her *Gender and the Politics of History* (New York: Columbia University Press, 1988).

22. Among other such virtues, West lists "a humility toward her own conception of what the good requires, and an acknowledgment and appreciation of the worthiness of competing accounts"—all of

which (if they are not casual pieties) raises the question of whether a good judge would not, after all, have to be a good relativist too.

2. Making (Up) the Truth

1. For examples of constructivist history and sociology of science, see David Bloor, *Knowledge and Social Imagery*, 2nd ed. (Chicago: University of Chicago Press, 1991 [1976]); Bruno Latour and Steve Woolgar, *Laboratory Life: The Construction of Scientific Facts* (Princeton: Princeton University Press, 1986 [1979]); Karin D. Knorr-Cetina, *The Manufacture of Knowledge: An Essay on the Constructivist and Contextual Nature of Science* (Oxford: Pergamon Press, 1981); and Andrew Pickering, *Constructing Quarks: A Sociological History of Particle Physics* (Chicago: University of Chicago Press, 1984). For relevant studies of the relations among perception, cognition, and language, see discussion and citations in Chapters 3 and 4.

2. For examples of such adversarial conflation, see Paul R. Gross and Norman Levitt, *Higher Superstition: The Academic Left and its Quarrels with Science* (Baltimore: Johns Hopkins University Press, 1994), pp. 71–106.

3. An earlier version of this chapter was presented at a conference panel convened under that rubric.

4. For influential analyses, see Hayden White, *Metahistory: The Historical Imagination in Nineteenth-Century Europe* (Baltimore: Johns Hopkins University Press, 1973), and Jacques Derrida, "White Mythology: Metaphor in the Text of Philosophy," in *Margins of Philosophy*, trans. Alan Bass (Chicago: University of Chicago Press, 1982), pp. 207–272.

5. Examples include, for the respective fields, Latour, *The Pasteurization of France*, trans. Alan Sheridan and John Law (Cambridge, Mass.: Harvard University Press, 1988); Knorr-Cetina, *The Manufacture of Knowledge*; and Pickering, *Constructing Quarks*.

6. Steven Shapin and Simon Schaffer, *Leviathan and the Air-Pump: Hobbes, Boyle, and the Experimental Life* (Princeton: Princeton University Press, 1985), p. 60.

7. See the works cited in note 1 and, among other recent studies, Latour, *Science in Action: How to Follow Scientists and Engineers through Society* (Cambridge, Mass.: Harvard University Press,

1987); Brian Rotman, *Ad Infinitum—The Ghost in Turing's Machine: Taking God Out of Mathematics and Putting the Body Back In: An Essay in Corporeal Semiotics* (Stanford: Stanford University Press, 1993); and Shapin, *A Social History of Truth: Civility and Science in Seventeenth-Century England* (Chicago: University of Chicago Press, 1994). Rotman discusses the implications of "virtual witnessing" for the assumed reader and ideal(ized) subject of mathematical discourse.

8. Certification of social and, later, professional status has been crucial in the history of credibility, both juridical and scientific (see Shapin, *A Social History of Truth*). Social and professional self-certification are not incompatible, however, with gestures of *personal* self-effacement.

9. Issues of linguistic normativity are considered in Chapter 4. For discussion of the mimetic relations among fictive and other utterances, see (though the terms are a bit out-of-date) Barbara Herrnstein Smith, *On the Margins of Discourse: The Relation of Literature to Language* (Chicago: University of Chicago Press, 1978), pp. x–xii, 14–75. For relevant analysis of the "citationality" of all texts, see Derrida, "Signature Event Context," *Margins of Philosophy*, pp. 307–330.

10. Gertrude Himmelfarb, *On Looking into the Abyss: Untimely Thoughts on Culture and Society* (New York: Knopf, 1994), p. xii.

11. Ibid.

12. Terry Eagleton, *The Ideology of the Aesthetic* (Oxford: Basil Blackwell, 1990), pp. 378–379.

13. Christopher Norris, *Uncritical Theory: Postmodernism, Intellectuals and the Gulf War* (Amherst, Mass.: University of Massachusetts Press, 1992), p. 68. Norris maintains that the failure of intellectuals to protest American military actions in the Gulf War can be attributed to the effects of "pragmatist, anti-foundationalist or consensus-based theories of knowledge," theories, he claims, "which take it pretty much for granted that 'truth' in any given situation can only be a matter of the values and beliefs that happen to prevail among members of some existing 'interpretive community'" (16). It follows, he goes on, that "nothing could count as an argument against what the media or the government information-machine would presently have us believe" (20). He repeats these dubious claims and inferences in *What's Wrong with Postmodernism: Critical Theory and the Ends of Philosophy* (Baltimore: Johns

Hopkins University Press, 1990) and *The Truth about Postmodern-ism* (Oxford: Blackwell, 1993). Norris gets considerable righteous mileage out of a repeated identification of the views of Stanley Fish, Richard Rorty, and other (primarily American) theorists with Wil-liam James's definition of truth as "what is good in the way of belief" (Norris, *The Truth about Postmodernism*, pp. 283 ff.). There is little reason to think, however, that Fish, Rorty, or any other so-called postmodernist would endorse Norris's own understanding of that definition as an *equation* of truth with whatever anyone feels good believing. For Rorty's views of James's definition (which, duly de-contextualized and tendentiously paraphrased, has been scandaliz-ing academic philosophers for the past century), see Richard Rorty, *Consequences of Pragmatism: Essays, 1972–1980* (Minneapolis: Uni-versity of Minnesota Press, 1982), pp. xxv–xxvi, 162–166. For related discussion of the definition, see Barry Allen, *Truth in Phi-losophy* (Cambridge, Mass.: Harvard University Press, 1993), pp. 56–69. On Rorty's somewhat equivocal handling of the *term* "truth," see Barbara Herrnstein Smith, *Contingencies of Value: Al-ternative Perspectives for Critical Theory* (Cambridge, Mass.: Har-vard University Press, 1988), p. 218, note 10.

14. Similarly, Gross and Levitt are exercised throughout *Higher Superstition* by threats to what they see as the due epistemic au-thority of scientists per se and especially by the idea, which they evidently find outrageous, that persons other than established sci-entists (such as themselves) might seek either to study or interpret scientific practices or to evaluate any of the broader social operations of those practices.

15. For discussion of some of these difficulties, see Michèle Bar-rett, *The Politics of Truth: From Marx to Foucault* (Stanford: Stan-ford University Press, 1991).

16. For examples of such efforts, see Ernesto Laclau and Chantal Mouffe, *Hegemony and Socialist Strategy: Towards a Radical Dem-ocratic Politics* (London: Verso, 1985); Stephen A. Resnick and Richard D. Wolff, *Knowledge and Class: A Marxian Critique of Po-litical Economy* (Chicago: University of Chicago Press, 1987); Wil-liam E. Connolly, *Identity/Difference: Democratic Negotiations of Po-litical Paradox* (Ithaca: Cornell University Press, 1991); and Wendy Brown, *States of Injury: Power and Freedom in Late Modernity* (Princeton: Princeton University Press, 1995).

17. Jean-François Lyotard, *The Differend: Phrases in Dispute,*

trans. Georges Van Den Abbeele (Minneapolis: University of Minnesota Press, 1988; [1983]); see especially pp. 9–14, 32–33, and 56–58.

18. Norris, *Uncritical Theory*, p. 71.

19. Ibid., p. 68.

20. Norris's charges and evident perceptions here mirror those of Himmelfarb, who writes, "Only when history itself is 'problematized' and 'deconstructed,' when events and persons are transformed into 'texts,' when the past is deprived of any reality and history of any truth, does the distinction between history and fiction become blurred or elided" (*On Looking into the Abyss*, p. 146). It appears that, for Himmelfarb, history is a non-problematic concept, events and persons (and, perhaps, texts) can be apprehended independent of interpretations, and both the reality of the past and the truth of history are always already at hand. Accordingly, she sees indications of the complexity of the relevant concepts and analyses of the relevant mediating processes as acts of gratuitous "problematizing" or "deconstruction," as acts which themselves *bring about* the difficulties that (seen otherwise) they seek to bring into view.

21. Norris, *Uncritical Theory*, p. 72.

22. Norris evidently understands irreducible differences as "perpetual conflicts" and conflates two types of conflict as he himself frames them. His confusions on these matters may be both cause and effect of his failure to engage Lyotard's analyses adequately—or, one could say, of the irreducible differences of their respective conceptual idioms. See the following note.

23. Given his own descriptions, it appears that Norris himself is in the sort of unhappy position that Lyotard seeks to explicate; that is, Norris's arguments against what he sees as a prevailing discourse ("postmodernism") fall on deaf ears because the alternative discourse that he prefers (mainstream rationalist/analytic philosophy—he cites, repeatedly, Kripke, Davidson, and Putnam as well as Habermas) and which he believes would expose postmodernism as absurd, illegitimate, and perilous is disabled by the authority of just that (supposedly) prevailing discourse. Thus he rails against a predicament in which certain "figures on the postmodern scene" "can reckon on gaining a large and receptive readership for arguments whose blatant illogicality would leap off the page were it not for this lamentable down-turn in the standards of informed intel-

lectual exchange," and, at another point, protests helplessly: "That this is all sheer nonsense—a postmodern update on well-worn sophistical themes—should be obvious to anyone not wholly given over to the vagaries of current intellectual fashion" (*Uncritical Theory*, pp. 20, 15). Of course, so-called postmodernists could rail at *their* corresponding predicament; for, they could say (and sometimes do; see Jacques Derrida, *Points . . . : Interviews, 1974–1994*, ed. Elisabeth Weber, trans. Peggy Kamuf et al. [Stanford: Stanford University Press, 1995], pp. 399–454), their innovative ideas are routinely denounced by established intellectual authorities (including mainstream rationalist/analytic philosophers) who have evidently never read their works, or who grossly misrepresent them, or who appear incapable of understanding them. (Curiously enough, Norris, persuaded of the ethical and emancipatory impulses motivating Derrida's project, regularly exempts the latter from his strictures against postmodernism. He also exempts Paul de Man, in whose views he detects a similarly exculpating underlying commitment to realist epistemology. See Norris, *What's Wrong with Postmodernism*, pp. 45–46, and 113–116.) It is not clear, however, what tribunal is competent to hear these complaints or to remedy this *double* double-bind (a select panel of chairmen of the philosophy departments of major American and European universities?) or what judge could adjudicate impartially the opposed but symmetrical claims of the contesting parties. But, of course, even to characterize the situation in such terms is to acknowledge the relevance and power of Lyotard's idea of the "differend" (and thus, it could be charged, to view the contest prejudicially).

24. Thus Himmelfarb, at a rhetorical high point of her book, writes: "Postmodernist history, like postmodernist literary theory, celebrates 'aporia'—difference, discontinuity, disparity, contradiction, discord, ambiguity, irony, paradox, perversity, opacity, obscurity, anarchy, chaos . . . The modernist accuses the postmodernist of bringing mankind to the abyss of nihilism. The postmodernist proudly and happily accepts that charge" (*On Looking into the Abyss*, p. 155). She cites in support of this characterization a passage by Hayden White: "We require a history that will educate us to discontinuity more than ever before; for discontinuity, disruption, and chaos is our lot" (White, *Tropics of Discourse: Essays in Cultural Criticism* [Baltimore: Johns Hopkins University Press, 1978],

p. 50). Whatever else might be said about White's pronouncement (in which one might detect a certain degree of pride in the unflinching acknowledgment of our rather grim lot), it seems hard to fault it for *happiness*. To be sure, "postmodernist" history and literary theory do stress the positive values of difference, discord, and "perversity" where these are otherwise seen simply as negative states or set in simple contrast to supposedly obvious (and obviously desirable) states of commonality, agreement, or "natural"-ness. But, in these cases, the emphasis (or "celebration") is arguably quite ethically just as well as intellectually proper.

25. See Smith, *Contingencies of Value*, pp. 150–156.

26. I refer to the effects of sustained casual anti-Semitism (what "everybody" knows), which commonly operate in conjunction with those of its more obviously programmatic versions.

27. Of course, not all the sophomoric ideas uttered in the name of (or reported as the claims of) "constructivism," "deconstruction," or "postmodernism" issue from literal sophomores, and one may understand, accordingly, some of the scorn or hostility directed at what are *taken*, accordingly, to be the ideas or positions thus named. On the other hand, those who identify contemporary ideas only with third-hand versions and rush into denunciatory public statements on that basis might consider both the ethical implications and intellectual consequences of their own indiscriminateness, and, especially when such statements are issued in the name of science (see note 2), the intellectual or indeed scientific status of such rough sampling techniques.

28. I anticipate here the familiar charge of self-refutation routinely lodged against constructivist and so-called relativist accounts of truth and knowledge. For discussion of its dubious force, see Chapter 5.

3. Belief and Resistance

1. The supposed corrective resistance of brute facts to mistaken scientific theories has been assimilated, in literary theory, to the supposed corrective resistance of "the text itself" to mistaken literary interpretations. Thus Christopher Norris argues, *contra* (anti-)hermeneutic theorists such as Stanley Fish, that "the rhetorical structures" of texts offer "inbuilt resistance" to certain interpre-

tations. "[T]here is nothing absurd," Norris writes, "about the analogy between bumping up against recalcitrant facts in the realm of empirical knowledge and bumping up against anomalous details in the reading of familiar texts" (Christopher Norris, *What's Wrong with Postmodernism: Critical Theory and the Ends of Philosophy* [Baltimore: Johns Hopkins University Press, 1990], p. 115). The difficulty, however, is not in the analogy per se but in the idea, here doubled by analogy, of beliefs "bumping up against" autonomously recalcitrant entities. For discussion of (and disputes over) the epistemic status of anomalies in science, see Chapter 8, note 12.

2. The pedigree of the debate, at least in some of its key features, is as ancient as Plato's *Theaetetus* (see Chapter 5). Most intellectual historians date its sharpening in our own era to the publication of Thomas S. Kuhn, *The Structure of Scientific Revolutions*, 2nd ed. (Chicago: University of Chicago Press, 1970; orig. ed. 1962), and Paul Feyerabend, *Against Method: Outline of an Anarchistic Theory of Knowledge* (London: NLB, 1975), both of which challenge the logical empiricism of Vienna Circle philosophy of science and traditional Whiggish intellectual history. Since shifting labels and diversely characterized positions contribute to the difficulties here, a caveat is in order: what is meant by "constructivist-interactionist" accounts of knowledge is indicated by explicit description and exemplification in the present chapter. The term should not be taken, in other words, as the name of an otherwise specifically determined position, school, or movement.

3. Thus Hilary Putnam, positing a choice between supposedly self-refuting conventionalism and otherwise problematic metaphysical realism, asks, "Is there no middle way?" (*Realism with a Human Face*, ed. James Conant [Cambridge, Mass.: Harvard University Press, 1990], p. 26). In addition to Putnam's own proposed alternative ("internal realism"), recent mediating, synthesizing, and transcending efforts include Ian Hacking, *Representing and Intervening: Introductory Topics in the Philosophy of Natural Science* (Cambridge: Cambridge University Press, 1983); Richard J. Bernstein, *Beyond Objectivism and Relativism: Science, Hermeneutics, and Praxis* (Philadelphia: University of Pennsylvania Press, 1983); Arthur Fine, "The Natural Ontological Attitude," in *Scientific Realism*, ed. J. Leplin (Berkeley: University of California Press, 1984); Michael A. Arbib and Mary B. Hesse, *The Construction of Reality* (Cam-

bridge: Cambridge University Press, 1986); and Peter Galison, *How Experiments End* (Chicago: University of Chicago Press, 1987).

4. The term *symmetrical,* here and elsewhere in this chapter, glances at the so-called symmetry postulate of constructivist ("strong programme") sociology of science, in accord with which practitioners of that discipline undertake to give the same general account of beliefs currently accepted in their intellectual communities as *true* as they give of beliefs currently rejected as *false.* This section extends the postulate to theoretical accounts of belief as such (epistemology, anti-epistemology, cognitive science, and so forth) and, accordingly, exhibits the sort of reflexive self-exemplification required to escape a charge of self-refutation (see Chapter 5). On the symmetry postulate, see David Bloor, *Knowledge and Social Imagery,* 2nd. ed. (Chicago: University of Chicago Press, 1991), pp. 7, 173, 176–179. On the requirement of reflexivity (with a witty enactment of its implications), see Malcolm Ashmore, *The Reflexive Thesis: Wrighting Sociology of Scientific Knowledge* (Chicago: University of Chicago Press, 1989).

5. For theoretical biology, see Humberto R. Maturana and Francisco J. Varela, *Autopoiesis and Cognition: The Realization of the Living* (Boston: D. Reidel, 1980) and *The Tree of Knowledge: The Biological Roots of Human Understanding* (Boston: Shambhala, 1988). For cognitive/developmental psychology, see George Lakoff, *Women, Fire, and Dangerous Things: What Categories Reveal about the Mind* (Chicago: University of Chicago Press, 1987); and Esther Thelen and Linda B. Smith, *A Dynamic Systems Approach to the Development of Cognition and Action* (Cambridge, Mass.: MIT Press, 1994). For neurophysiology, see Gerald M. Edelman, *Neural Darwinism: The Theory of Neuronal Group Selection* (New York: Basic Books, 1987), and *The Remembered Present: A Biological Theory of Consciousness* (New York: Basic Books, 1989); William H. Calvin and George A. Ojemann, *Conversations with Neil's Brain: The Neural Nature of Thought and Language* (Reading, Mass.: Addison-Wesley, 1994); and Antonio R. Damasio, *Descartes' Error: Emotion, Reason, and the Human Brain* (New York: G. P. Putnam, 1994). For computer science, see Terry Winograd and Fernando Flores, *Understanding Computers and Cognition: A New Foundation for Design* (Reading, Mass.: Addison-Wesley, 1986); and Rodney Brooks, "Intelligence without Representation," *Artificial Intelligence* 47 (1991): 139–159, and "New Approaches to Robotics," *Science* 252 (13 Sep-

tember 1991): 1227–1232. For revisionist accounts of cognitive macrodynamics and specific examples of the transformation and stabilization of belief in the history of science, see Kuhn, *The Structure of Scientific Revolutions;* Paul K. Feyerabend, *Against Method: Outline of an Anarchistic Theory of Knowledge* (London: NLB, 1975); Bruno Latour, *The Pasteurization of France,* trans. Alan Sheridan and John Law (Cambridge, Mass.: Harvard University Press, 1988); and Andrew Pickering, *The Mangle of Practice: Time, Agency, & Science* (Chicago: University of Chicago Press, 1995).

6. The examples suggest why constructivist (anti)epistemology might not be *immediately* welcome in certain quarters. This is not to say, however, that the divergent sets of beliefs in question (for example, constructivism and commonsense intuitions of personal agency) are inherently incompatible or that the seemingly remote practical or political projects in question (for example, the furtherance of social justice) could not, in fact, find constructivist formulations both relevant and serviceable.

7. The operations of cognitive taste are often recognized informally by, among others, academic philosophers. Thus Putnam observes that the "cut between the observer and the system" implied by Niels Bohr's interpretation of quantum physics "would have been as distasteful to Kant as it was to be . . . to Einstein," and goes on to acknowledge the same taste in himself even as he confers dubious universal status upon it: "There is a part of all of us which sides with Einstein—which wants to see the God's-Eye view restored in all its splendor" (*Realism with a Human Face,* p. 18). For related discussion of taste and reason, see Barbara Herrnstein Smith, *Contingencies of Value,* pp. 72–77 and 104–107. On the generality of the domains of taste, see Pierre Bourdieu, *Distinction: A Social Critique of the Judgment of Taste,* trans. Richard Nice (Cambridge, Mass.: Harvard University Press, 1984), pp. 99–101. For a pertinent analysis of "mere," see Andrew Pickering, "Knowledge, Practice and Mere Construction," *Social Studies of Science* 20 (1990): 682–729.

8. See H. M. Collins, *Changing Order: Replication and Induction in Scientific Practice* (London: Sage Publications, 1985).

9. Stephen Jay Gould, *Wonderful Life: The Burgess Shale and the Nature of History* (New York: W. W. Norton, 1989), p. 283.

10. On the relation between the differentially selective (i.e.,

"winnowing") mechanisms of individual learning and natural selection, see B. F. Skinner, "Selection by Consequences," *Science* 213 (31 July 1981): 501–504, and Edelman, *Neural Darwinism,* pp. 291–311.

11. Stanley Fish, frequently the target of such charges (see, for example, Norris, *What's Wrong with Postmodernism,* pp. 77–133), has indicated some of the dubious assumptions that produce them; see Fish, *Doing What Comes Naturally: Change, Rhetoric, and the Practice of Theory in Literary and Legal Studies* (Durham, N.C.: Duke University Press, 1989), pp. 141–160. From the present perspective, however, he does not develop an altogether satisfactory alternative account of the dynamics of belief.

12. The extent to which any two creatures occupy the same environment (or "world") is just the extent to which they are structurally and functionally identical. As the phenomenon of biological symbiosis indicates, however, occupying (or "sharing") the same environment or world in that sense is not required for mutually coordinated interactions, and, as will be seen in Chapters 4 and 6, mutually effective verbal/social interactions and communal norms are possible without prior sharing or "commonality" in their usual senses.

13. The ubiquitous, complex operations of *culture* as just defined, and their continuous, subtle interactions with "nature" in the sense either of our natural environments or genetic constitutions, have, for the most part, eluded the theoretical programs of sociobiology, behavioral ecology, and so-called evolutionary epistemology, with consequences indicated below.

14. Various metaphors for this complex reciprocality have been proposed: especially apt is the evocation by Arbib and Hesse—commenting here on the relations among perception, observation language, and theory—of a "spiraling set of nested feedback systems" (Arbib and Hesse, *The Construction of Reality,* p. 8). The specific formulations in this section are my own but, along with many of the general ideas, significantly indebted to the works in biology, psychology, and neurophysiology cited in note 5, and to Susan Oyama, *The Ontogeny of Information: Developmental Systems and Evolution* (Cambridge: Cambridge University Press, 1985). For other related formulations encountered after this book was in press, see Horst Hendriks-Jansen, *Catching Ourselves in the Act: Situated*

Activity, Interactive Emergence, Evolution, and Human Thought (Cambridge, Mass: MIT Press, 1996).

15. See, for example, William G. Lycan, *Judgment and Justification* (Cambridge: Cambridge University Press, 1988), pp. 148–153. Lycan acknowledges the affinity of his unflappably teleological views with those of Dr. Pangloss and considers the difficulties presented by contemporary understandings of evolutionary mechanisms ("We must now think of Mother Nature as being in less than full control of the development of species . . . [S]he is somewhat at the mercy of chance events, mutation, drift, and so on"), but concludes: "I think it is still plausible to suppose that . . . Mother Nature does the best she can for her creatures . . . [and that] the effect of nonselectional factors in the evolutionary process has not . . . been great enough to deflect Mother Nature's basic strategy of maximizing [our] cognitive efficiency . . . All's for nearly the best, in this next-best of all possible worlds" (Lycan, *Judgment and Justification*, p. 153). The personalizing of a providential Nature is unusually explicit here, but not the interpretation of natural selection as purposive and optimizing. For an important critique of such interpretations, see S. J. Gould and R. C. Lewontin, "The Spandrels of San Marco and the Panglossian Paradigm: A Critique of the Adaptationist Programme," *Proceedings of the Royal Society of London* 205 (1978): 581–598. For controversies over optimality in the philosophy of biology, see John Dupré, ed., *The Latest on the Best: Essays on Evolution and Optimality* (Cambridge, Mass.: MIT Press, 1987).

16. Robert J. Richards, "Resistance to Constructed Belief," in *Questions of Evidence: Proof, Practice, and Persuasion across the Disciplines*, ed. James Chandler, Arnold I. Davidson, and Harry Haratoonian, (Chicago: University of Chicago Press, 1994), p. 156. Richards's essay comments on an earlier version of the present chapter ("Belief and Resistance: A Symmetrical Account," *Questions of Evidence*, ed. Chandler et al., pp. 139–153); some passages here are adopted from my reply to Richards (Barbara Herrnstein Smith, "Circling Round, Knocking Over, Playing Out," ibid., pp. 162–168). For other examples of evolutionary epistemology, see Gerard Radnitsky and W. W. Bartley III, eds., *Evolutionary Epistemology, Rationality, and the Sociology of Knowledge* (La Salle, Ill.: Open Court, 1987), and Kai Huhlweg and C. A. Hooker, eds., *Issues in*

Evolutionary Epistemology (Albany: SUNY Press, 1989). For pertinent commentary from revisionist perspectives, see Gonzalo Munevar, "Science as Part of Nature," in Huhlweg and Hooker, *Issues,* pp. 475–487; and J. N. Hattiangadi, "Physiological Foundations of Our Knowledge of the Mathematical Universe," in *Perspectives on Psychologism,* ed. Mark A. Notturno (Leiden, Netherlands: E. J. Brill, 1989), pp. 368–391. For discussion of other invocations of evolutionary theory in support of rationalist/realist epistemology and progressivist philosophy of science, see Chapters 4 and 8.

17. Are the immediate perceptions of all evolved creatures guaranteed valid by natural selection? Perhaps, in a sense, they are; i.e., if validity is understood as functional adequacy. But this would imply a cross-species epistemic relativism that Richards would presumably find otherwise unacceptable.

18. See R. E. Nisbett and L. Ross, *Human Inference: Strategies and Shortcomings of Social Judgment* (Englewood Cliffs, N.J.: Prentice Hall, 1980); Daniel Kahneman, Paul Slovic, and Amos Tversky, eds., *Judgment under Uncertainty: Heuristics and Biases* (Cambridge: Cambridge University Press, 1982); and P. N. Johnson-Laird and E. Shafir, eds., "Reasoning and Decision Making," special issue of *Cognition* 49 (1993). For a survey of such *pseudodoxia epidemica* from a staunchly realist/rationalist perspective, see Massimo Piattelli-Palmarini, *Inevitable Illusions: How Mistakes of Reason Rule Our Minds,* trans. Massimo Piattelli-Palmarini and Keith Botsford (New York: John Wiley & Sons, 1994). The normativity implied by my term "biases" here (see also the subtitle of Kahneman et al.) is located in other, more formally controlled, types of calculations; for example, mathematical ones. The normative veridicality of mathematics, however, is itself at issue in these controversies. For constructivist accounts, see David Bloor, *Wittgenstein: A Social Theory of Knowledge* (New York: Columbia University Press, 1983), pp. 83–111, and J. N. Hattiangadi, "Physiological Foundations of Our Knowledge of the Mathematical Universe."

The exposure by feminist theorists, among others, of the self-privileging biases commonly involved in *normative* invocations of supposed human universals has gone some distance, in some quarters, toward making any reference to general human traits ideologically suspect. I would stress, therefore, that the references here and elsewhere in this book to apparently endemic tendencies are not invoked to ground normative claims and cannot serve that purpose (or at least not without strain—as we shall see, foundationalists sometimes find putative grounds in what otherwise appear highly unlikely places) and that such references commonly operate in my arguments in pointedly *anti*-self- (or anyone-else-) privileging ways.

19. On the related idea of "belief perseverance," see Nisbett and Ross, *Human Inference*, especially pp. 175–179.

20. "Acquired" is, of course, crucial here: many feline perceptual/ behavioral tendencies are endemic, and, although acting in accord with them may, under certain conditions, be fatal to the individual cat, the tendencies will still be transmitted to her offspring if she survives long enough to have any. On the relation between genetics and human plasticity, see H. Ronald Pulliam and Christopher Dunford, *Programmed to Learn: An Essay on the Evolution of Culture* (New York: Columbia University Press, 1980); Robert Brandon, "Phenotypic Plasticity, Cultural Transmission, and Human Sociobiology," in James H. Fetzer, ed., *Sociobiology and Epistemology* (Boston: D. Reidel, 1985), pp. 57–73; and Oyama, *The Ontogeny of Information*.

21. For a piquant example, see Bruno Latour, "A Relativistic Account of Einstein's Relativity," *Social Studies of Science* 18 (1988): 3–44. Einstein's cognitive conservatism is stressed also (though not by that name) in Arthur Fine, *The Shaky Game: Einstein, Realism, and the Quantum Theory* (Chicago: University of Chicago Press, 1986).

4. Doing without Meaning

1. In evolutionary biology, see Humberto R. Maturana, "Biology of Language: Epistemology of Reality," in George A. Miller and Elizabeth Lenneberg, eds., *The Psychology and Biology of Language and Thought: Essays in Honor of Eric Lenneberg* (New York: Academic Press, 1978), pp. 27–63, and, with Francisco J. Varela, *The Tree of Knowledge: The Biological Roots of Human Understanding* (Boston: Shambhala, 1988), esp. pp. 205–235; John R. Krebs and Richard Dawkins, "Animal Signals: Mind-Reading and Manipulation," in *Behavioural Ecology: An Evolutionary Approach*, J. R. Krebs and N. B. Davies, eds. (Sunderland, Mass.: Sindver Asso-

ciates, 1978); and Michael Studdert-Kennedy, "Language Development from an Evolutionary Perspective," in Norman A. Krasnegor et al., eds., *Biological and Behavioral Determinants of Language Development* (Hillsdale, N.J.: L. Erlbaum, 1991).

In cognitive science, psychology, and neurophysiology, see Terry Winograd, "What does it Mean to Understand Language," *Cognitive Science* 4 (1980): 209–241; Raymond W. Gibbs, Jr., "Literal Meaning and Psychological Theory," *Cognitive Science* 8 (1984): 275–304; Benny Shannon, "Semantic Representation of Meaning: A Critique," *Psychological Bulletin* 104 (1988): 70–83; Gerald M. Edelman, *The Remembered Present: A Biological Theory of Consciousness* (New York: Basic Books, 1989), and *Bright Air, Brilliant Fire: On the Matter of the Mind* (New York: Basic Books, 1992) (though his work is relevant to the development of alternative linguistic theories, Edelman's own applications of it to language remain tied to standard accounts); Antonio R. Damasio and Hanna Damasio, "Brain and Language," *Scientific American* (September 1992): 89–95; Derek Edwards and Jonathan Potter, "Language and Causation: A Discursive Action Model of Description and Attribution," *Psychological Review* 100 (1993): 1–19; and William H. Calvin and George A. Ojemann, *Conversations with Neil's Brain: The Neural Nature of Thought and Language* (Reading, Mass.: Addison-Wesley, 1994).

For the outposts of linguistics, see Ronald W. Langacker, *Foundations of Cognitive Grammar*, 2 vols. (Stanford: Stanford University Press, 1986 & 1990); Paul Hopper, "Emergent Grammar and the A-priori Grammar Postulate," in Deborah Tannen, ed., *Linguistics in Context: Connecting Observation and Understanding* (Norwood, N.J.: Ablex Publishing Corp., 1988); Julie Tetel Andresen, *Linguistics in America, 1769–1924: A Critical History* (London: Routledge, 1990), and "The Behaviorist Turn in Recent Theories of Language," *Behavior and Philosophy* 20 (1992): 1–19; and Roy Harris, "On Redefining Linguistics," in *Redefining Linguistics,* Hayley G. Davis and Talbot J. Taylor, eds. (London: Routledge, 1990), pp. 18–52.

2. See Friedrich Nietzsche, *The Will to Power,* trans. W. Kaufmann & R. J. Hollingdale (New York: Random House, 1967), sections 480–544; Ludwig Wittgenstein, *Philosophical Investigations,* trans. G. E. M. Anscombe (Oxford: Basil Blackwell, 1953), sec-

tions 1–134; B. F. Skinner, *Verbal Behavior* (New York: Appleton-Century-Crofts, 1957); J. L. Austin, *How to Do Things with Words* (Cambridge, Mass.: Harvard University Press, 1962); V. N. Volosinov, *Marxism and the Philosophy of Language* (New York: Seminar Press, 1973 [1929]); and Erving Goffman, *Forms of Talk* (Philadelphia: University of Pennsylvania Press, 1981). For relevant discussion, see Sandy Petrey, *Speech Acts and Literary Theory* (New York: Routledge, 1990), and Richard Rorty, "Pragmatism and Post-Nietzschean Philosophy" and "Wittgenstein, Heidegger, and the Reification of Language," in Rorty, *Essays on Heidegger and Others* (Cambridge: Cambridge University Press, 1991). Others who have pursued significant alternative views of language along the lines indicated here include L. S. Vygotsky, Mixail Baxtin (M. Bakhtin), Kenneth Burke, Harold Garfinkel, John Gumpers, Dell Hymes, and Morse Peckham.

3. See Michel Foucault, "The Discourse on Language," in *The Archaeology of Knowledge*, trans. A. M. Sheridan Smith (New York: Pantheon Books, 1972); Jacques Derrida, *Of Grammatology*, trans. Gayatri C. Spivak (Baltimore: Johns Hopkins University Press, 1976), and *Limited Inc* (Evanston, Ill.: Northwestern University Press, 1988); Pierre Bourdieu, *Language and Symbolic Power*, trans. G. Raymond and M. Adamson (Cambridge, Mass.: Harvard University Press, 1991 [orig. *Ce que parler veut dire*, Paris, 1982]); and Jean-François Lyotard, *The Differend: Phrases in Dispute*, trans. Georges Van den Abbeele (Minneapolis: University of Minnesota Press, 1988).

4. I allude here to transformational-generative linguistics (see Noam Chomsky, *Aspects of the Theory of Syntax* [Cambridge, Mass.: MIT Press, 1965] and *Language and Mind* [New York: Harcourt, Brace, & World, 1968]), Frankfurt School moral-communication theory (see Jürgen Habermas, *Communication and the Evolution of Society*, trans. Thomas McCarthy [Boston: Beacon Press, 1979] and *Moral Consciousness and Communicative Action*, trans. Christian Lenhardt and Shierry Weber Nicholsen [Cambridge, Mass.: MIT Press, 1990]), and the analytic descendents of Fregean philosophy of language (see Saul A. Kripke, *Naming and Necessity* [Cambridge, Mass.: Harvard University Press, 1972], Hilary Putnam, *Reason, Truth, and History* [Cambridge: Cambridge University Press, 1981], and Donald Davidson, *Inquiries into Truth and Interpretation*

[Oxford: Oxford University Press, 1985]). In Anglo-American philosophy, a vindication of formalized versions of everyday conceptions of meaning and representation is the ongoing project of Jerry Fodor; see Fodor, *The Language of Thought* (New York: Crowell, 1975), *RePresentations: Philosophical Essays on the Foundations of Cognitive Science* (Cambridge, Mass.: MIT Press, 1981), *Psychosemantics: The Problem of Meaning in the Philosophy of Mind* (Cambridge, Mass.: MIT Press, 1987), and, with Z. Pylyshyn, "Connectionism and Cognitive Architecture: A Critical Analysis," *Cognition* 28 (1988): 3–71. In *Language, Thought, and Other Biological Categories: New Foundations for Realism* (Cambridge, Mass.: MIT Press, 1984), Ruth Garrett Millikan gives an account of the emergence of semantic and other linguistic norms in terms similar to those outlined here but, as her subtitle indicates, ultimately in order to underwrite epistemological realism. Although Millikan's analysis is richly detailed and admirable in many respects, her argument shares Panglossian and otherwise problematic elements with the more general efforts of evolutionary epistemology, as discussed above (see Chapter 3, notes 15–16). For a critique of Fregean conceptions of meaning from within Anglo-American philosophy, see G. P. Baker and P. M. S. Hacker, *Language Sense and Nonsense: A Critical Investigation into Modern Theories of Language* (Oxford: Basil Blackwell, 1984). For a summary and critical evaluation of Fodor's model of language in relation to rival models in connectionist neuroscience, see Andy Clark, *Associative Engines: Connectionism, Concepts, and Representational Change* (Cambridge, Mass.: MIT Press, 1993). For a discriminating assessment of Millikan's account from a perspective comparable to the one presented here, see Horst Hendriks-Jansen, *Catching Ourselves in the Act: Situated Activity, Interactive Emergence, Evolution, and Human Thought* (Cambridge, Mass: MIT Press, 1996), pp. 49–56, 149–151, 281–282. For other relevant discussion, see Henry Staten, "The Secret Name of Cats: Deconstruction, Intentional Meaning, and the New Theory of Reference," in *Redrawing the Lines: Analytic Philosophy, Deconstruction, and Literary Theory*, ed. Reed Way Dasenbrock (Minneapolis: University of Minnesota Press, 1989), pp. 27–48.

5. The continuities stressed here and below are significant for current controversies over plausible evolutionary scripts for the

emergence of what are traditionally seen as uniquely human and specifically linguistic behaviors. For an array of positions in the debate, see *Behavioral and Brain Sciences* 13, 4 (1990), a special issue that includes a target article by Steven Pinker and Paul Bloom, "Natural Language and Natural Selection," plus commentary and critique by language theorists of various persuasions. For an expanded and popularized version of the article (with, however, the possibility of alternative views no longer in evidence), see Pinker, *The Language Instinct* (New York: William Morrow and Co., 1994). For other perspectives on the controversy, see also Krasnegor et al., eds., *Biological and Behavioral Determinants of Language Development*.

It should be stressed as well that, given the reciprocally interactive operations of the language loop, familiar distinctions between (active, voluntary, conscious, willed, etc.) *acting* and (passive, involuntary, mechanical, unconscious, etc.) *reacting* are irrelevant to these descriptions of verbal agency and, in fact, cannot be sustained anywhere in the present account. See also the discussion below of listeners and readers (as well as speakers and writers) as agents.

6. "Verbal" is parenthesized here and in 2 to mark the continuity between verbal and all other responsive acts; in 3 and 4, the parentheses mark the continuity between verbal and all other perceived/discriminated forms. (Throughout this chapter, "verbal" means functioning as part of a communicative circuit. Accordingly, verbal acts are not *otherwise* distinguished from ongoing behavior or verbal forms from perceived/discriminated phenomena more generally.)

7. For convictions among ethical theorists of the inherent moral force of words such as "ought" and "duty," see Chapter 1, note 5. On philosophical invocations of the supposed inherent meanings of forms such as "t.r.u.t.h," "a.s.s.e.r.t.i.o.n," "r.i.g.h.t.n.e.s.s," and "c.o.n.v.i.n.c.e," see Chapters 5 and 7. On the resilience of the idea of inherent meaning in legal hermeneutics, see Robert Fishman, "The Futility of Theory?" *University of Colorado Law Review* 63 (1992), pp. 457–480.

8. The virtual infinity of the realm of the semiotic—or, perhaps better, of the process of semiosis—is often stressed in poststructuralist literary theory; see, for example, Morse Peckham, *Explanation and Power: The Control of Human Behavior* (New York: Seabury, 1979). The difficulties of precise demarcation here can be seen

to reflect the historical or conventional, as opposed to logical or a priori, ontology of the concepts and categories in question ("verbal," "linguistic," "semiotic," and so on). The idea that all concepts and categories are historical (or conventional, or constructed) rather than logical or a priori, is itself a key issue dividing poststructuralist (anti-hermeneutic, constructivist, and so on) conceptualizations of language from more traditional (formalist, rationalist, logicist, realist) ones.

9. Listeners usually assume (for good reason) that the utterance of *p* is an index not of the truth of *p* but of the speaker's intention to have the listener *believe p*—a quite different matter, of course.

10. For an influential though rather elusive version of this set of ideas, see Donald Davidson, "On the Very Idea of a Conceptual Scheme," in *Inquiries into Truth and Interpretation*. Significantly, in a more recent work Davidson calls for a radically alternative conception of language (see Donald Davidson, "A Nice Derangement of Epitaphs," in Ernest LePore and Brian P. McLaughlin, eds., *Truth and Interpretation: Perspectives on the Philosophy of Donald Davidson* [Oxford: Basil Blackwell, 1988], p. 446).

11. The observation is central to Wittgenstein's arguably (interpretations differ) revolutionary views of meaning in *Philosophical Investigations*. For the related idea of conceptual/semantic "prototypes," see Eleanor Rosch, "Cognitive Representations of Semantic Categories," *Journal of Experimental Psychology* 104 (1975): 192–233. For suggestive discussion of Rosch in connection with Lotfi Zadeh's distinctly post-rationalist perspective on logical concepts, see Daniel McNeill and Paul Freiberger, *Fuzzy Logic* (New York: Simon & Schuster, 1993), pp. 84–89.

12. "Patterns of verbal practice" are no more self-evident or objective, in an epistemological sense, than "underlying rules" or "presupposed maxims." Like any other phenomena indicated in this account or elsewhere in this book, they are understood here as distinguished as such by particular, situated observers, and described or theorized as such in a particular conceptual idiom. The difference between descriptions in terms of observable patterns of social behavior as against the positing of underlying rules or presupposed maxims is, of course, the difference between naturalistic and rationalistic accounts of the operations of language or communication.

13. Certain types of verbal production and response work out better *in the course of* social interactions as well as in their consequences for the individual parties involved. For discussion of how ongoing practices are shaped and sustained by subtle negotiations among the parties, see Harold Garfinkel, *Studies in Ethnomethodology* (Englewood Cliffs, N.J.: Prentice-Hall, 1967), Goffman, *Forms of Talk*, and Talbot J. Taylor, *Mutual Misunderstanding: Scepticism and the Theorizing of Language and Interpretation* (Durham, N.C.: Duke University Press, 1992), pp. 201–229. For the significance of such negotiations for current epistemological/linguistic debates, see Derek Edwards's two-way critique of rationalism and proposed alternatives (Edwards, "Categories are for Talking: On the Cognitive and Discursive Bases of Categorization," *Theory and Psychology* 1 [1991]: 515–542). George Lakoff, in his *Women, Fire, and Dangerous Things: What Categories Reveal about the Mind* (Chicago: University of Chicago Press, 1987), proposes, *contra* rationalist views, that verbal/conceptual categories are the products not of mental activities or a priori logical necessity but of broadly shared corporeal and pragmatic experiences. Edwards insists, *contra* both rationalists and Lakoff, that categories are constructed primarily through, and also in a sense *for*, specifically verbal transactions: that is, negotiated in the course of social/verbal exchanges for the purpose of facilitating those exchanges. Edwards's observations of the dubious realist implications of Lakoff's account are valuable, as is also his emphasis on the operations of dynamic *social* interactions as distinct from what Lakoff indicates as "shared" but evidently isolated and mutually independent *individual* experiences. From the present perspective, however, Edwards himself could be seen as overestimating the role of *ongoing* verbal interactions at the expense of the effects of *prior* verbal interactions—which, in fact, he seems to ignore. It is as if, in Edwards's account, every verbal transaction was, for each party, the first one, and no aspect of verbal behavior was ever "iterated" (Derrida's useful term for repeated-with-a-difference).

14. Formal language instruction does, of course, also take place. For example, where upward or outward social/cultural mobility is desired and the types of verbal interaction through which a native idiom is commonly acquired are not available, people may subject themselves and their (or other people's) children to strenuous and

explicit linguistic instruction. In learning their native idioms, however, children do not need to be praised specifically for using words appropriately and no one needs to give them grammar or elocution lessons.

15. For a dubious identification of social-science refusals of genetic determinism with a commitment to a supposedly "standard social science" tabula-rasa/environmental determinism, see John Toobey and Leda Cosmides, "The Psychological Foundations of Culture," in Jerome H. Barkow, Leda Cosmides, and John Toobey, eds., *The Adapted Mind: Evolutionary Psychology and the Generation of Culture* (New York: Oxford University Press, 1992), pp. 28–29. For an exposure of the inadequacies of genetic/environmental dualisms themselves and an alternative model of the emergence of human traits and abilities, see Susan Oyama, *The Ontogeny of Information: Developmental Systems and Evolution* (Cambridge: Cambridge University Press, 1985).

16. See Calvin and Ojemann, *Conversations with Neil's Brain*, and Damasio and Damasio, "Brain and Language."

17. See Massimo Piatelli-Palmarini, "Evolution, Selection and Cognition: From 'Learning' to Parameter Setting in Biology and in the Study of Language," *Cognition* 31 (1989): 1–44, for an example of the denial by generative linguistics of the formative effects of the individual histories of verbally interactive agents. Piatelli-Palmarini identifies "learning" with explicit instruction and goes on to argue that it has virtually nothing to do with language ability or, in fact, most human behavior. So defined, it may not: but the identification is itself gratuitous and, in relation to the issue (how to explain language acquisition), distinctly question-begging. The interpretation of biological evolution that supports Piatelli-Palmarini's larger argument involves a dismissal of the contingent, non-teleological operations of natural selection in favor of an array of supposedly non-Darwinian mechanisms (among them, Gould and Lewontin's "spandrels") invoked *ad hoc* to rescue key aspects of generative linguistics that are otherwise difficult to square with contemporary evolutionary biology. In effect, evolutionary theory is both raided and sacrificed to preserve the definitive innatist/rationalist claims of Chomskian linguistics. For related selective invocations of evolutionary mechanisms in the service of innatist/rationalist linguistic theory, see Pinker, *The Language Instinct*, pp. 332–369.

18. This latter feature of the operations of language has been stressed in poststructuralist language theory and related anti-hermeneutic literary theory, sometimes as the "indeterminacy" of meaning. Especially influential here are Derrida, *Of Grammatology* and *Limited Inc.*, and Stanley Fish, *Is There a Text in this Class: The Authority of Interpretive Communities* (Cambridge, Mass.: Harvard University Press, 1980), and "With the Compliments of the Author: Reflections on Austin and Derrida," in Fish, *Doing What Comes Naturally: Change, Rhetoric, and the Practice of Theory in Literary and Legal Studies* (Durham, N.C.: Duke University Press, 1989), pp. 37–67. For related discussion of the limits of linguistics-based literary hermeneutics, see Barbara Herrnstein Smith, *On the Margins of Discourse: The Relation of Literature to Language* (Chicago: University of Chicago Press, 1978), especially pp. 157–201.

19. Austin's analysis, in *How to Do Things with Words*, of the conditions governing the force and uptake of certain classes of utterance could be seen as supplementary along the lines described here, but, as suggested above, with ultimately more radical implications.

20. The point is stressed in different ways by a number of poststructuralist language theorists (for example, Bourdieu, *Language and Symbolic Power*, Derrida, *Limited Inc*, and Lyotard, *The Differend*). Thus Derrida writes: "ultimately there is always a police and a tribunal ready to intervene each time that a rule . . . is invoked [in such cases] . . . If the police is always waiting in the wings, it is because conventions are by essence violable and precarious, *in themselves* and by the fictionality that constitutes them, even before there has been any overt transgression" (*Limited Inc*, p. 105). The passage, much cited, is a memorable moment in the critique of classical understandings of "convention" as intrinsically binding presupposed rules, limits, or agreements. Understood, however, as the very *operation* of reciprocally effective interactions, the process of verbal "conventioning," as it might be called, involves no more—and, to be sure, no less—threat or history of violence than any other of our effective social interactions or, indeed, any other of our effective interactions with our environments more generally.

21. Though primarily politically and socially conservative, these conceptions of human motivation occur in both left- and right-wing versions.

22. The conception of the operative limits of semantic indeter-

minacy developed in this chapter is significantly different from Fish's "authority of interpretive communities" (see note 18). The latter—however intended by Fish or otherwise interpreted by some members of *some* communities—is often understood as itself a univocal and decisive external force. Accordingly, Fish's phrase (rendered as "the authority of *the* interpretive community") is often just slipped—without ruffle or other modification—into the slot previously (but now dubiously) occupied by "inherent/conventional meaning" in the classic formulas of semantic determinacy.

23. This negation is a significant implication of the "is/ought" gap familiar in moral theory. Attempted leaps across—or finesses of—that gap in so-called naturalized ethics do not, in my view, overcome the difficulties that give the naturalistic fallacy its name: that is, they smuggle in prior, ungrounded judgments (commonly those already accepted as ethical in the relevant community) or they make the logically and otherwise objectionable Panglossian assumption just indicated. Thus, either way, efforts to ground ethical and related political imperatives in naturalistic accounts typically (and, it appears, inevitably) end up with nothing more than they begin with—except, of course, for a claim, spurious from the present perspective, of scientific authority. See Chapter 8 for discussion of comparable general problems in current efforts to naturalize normative epistemology.

Humberto Maturana and Francisco J. Varela, whose work is otherwise of considerable value for contemporary reconceptualizations of cognition and language (and, as such, cited here repeatedly), are sometimes drawn to dubious grounding efforts and claims of this kind (see, for example, Maturana and Varela, *The Tree of Knowledge*, pp. 244–250). The efforts are clearly benevolent or even utopian in motivation and due recognition is given elsewhere in their work to the difference between the good (survival/autonomy) of a system and that of its individual components (ibid., pp. 198–199), but the specifically ethical claims and conclusions remain problematic along the lines just indicated.

24. For charges to the effect that systems theory generally or particular cybernetic or systems-centered theories are politically complicitous, inherently oppressive, or fundamentally anti-human(istic), see Danilo Zolo, "Autopoiesis: Critique of a Postmodern Paradigm," *Telos* 86 (Winter 1990–1): 61–80, Peter Gal-

ison "The Ontology of the Enemy: Norbert Weiner and the Cybernetic Vision," *Critical Inquiry* 21 (1994): 228–266, and N. Kathleen Hayles, "Making the Cut: The Interplay of Narrative and System, or What Systems Theory Can't See," *Cultural Critique* 30 (Spring 1995): 71–100. For critical discussion, see Cary Wolfe, "In Search of Post-Humanist Theory: The Second Order Cybernetics of Maturana and Varela," ibid., pp. 33–70.

On self-organizing, self-maintaining social systems more generally, see Niklas Luhmann, *Social Systems*, trans. John Bednarz, Jr., with Dirk Baecker (Stanford: Stanford University Press, 1995). In his analyses of social systems in this and other works (see also Luhmann, *Essays on Self-Reference* [New York: Columbia University Press, 1990]), Luhmann draws on various ideas of Maturana and Varela (autopoiesis, specification, reflexivity, and so forth) in interesting and productive ways. I would stress, however, that his conceptualizations of "communication" and "meaning" are significantly different from those outlined in this chapter and that some of his specific characterizations of linguistic communication—as, for example, a "transmission of information" or a "coincidence of self-referencing utterance, externally referencing information, and understanding" (Luhmann, "The Form of Writing," *Stanford Literature Review* 9 [1992]: 25–42, elaborated in *Social Systems*, pp. 157–163, 427–430)—seem to return us to the telegraphic model indicated in this chapter as problematic (and, as it happens, explicitly rejected by Maturana and Varela [see *The Tree of Knowledge*, p. 196]).

25. See Karl-Otto Apel, "The A Priori of the Communication Community and the Foundations of Ethics," in *Towards a Transformation of Philosophy*, trans. Glyn Adey and David Frisby (London: Routledge & Kegan Paul, 1980); Habermas, "Discourse Ethics: Notes on a Program of Philosophical Justification," in *Moral Consciousness and Communicative Action;* and H. P. Grice, *Studies in the Way of Words* (Cambridge, Mass.: Harvard University Press, 1989). Some qualified neo-Kantian elements can be found also in Talbot J. Taylor, "Normativity and Linguistic Form," in Davis and Taylor, *Redefining Linguistics*, pp. 118–148, and in Taylor, *Mutual Misunderstanding*, pp. 216–221.

26. For related discussion of the differing and possibly adversarial but interlocking motives of narrators and their audiences, see

Barbara Herrnstein Smith, "Narrative Versions, Narrative Theories," *Critical Inquiry* 7 (1980): 213–236. For detailed description of the formal features of pidgin languages, see Derek Bickerton, *Roots of Language* (Ann Arbor: Karoma, 1981). Bickerton's more recent hypothesis, that various features of pidgins are evidence of an innate and universal linguistic "bioprogram" (see Bickerton, *Language and Species* [Chicago: University of Chicago Press, 1990]), is dubious from the present perspective.

27. This could also be seen as an implication of Wittgenstein's notions of multiple "language games" and "forms of life" in *Philosophical Investigations*.

28. Peter Galison makes a similar point in his discussion of scientists working together on interdisciplinary projects (Galison, "Computer Simulations and the Trading Zone," in *The Disunity of Science: Boundaries, Contexts, and Power*, ed. Peter Galison and David J. Stump [Stanford: Stanford University Press, 1996]). He puts the point, however, in the rather strained service of a Davidsonian-type refutation of a "picture of science in total rupture between frameworks," a picture that he attributes, dubiously, to Carnap and Kuhn (pp. 157, 118) and that he claims—also dubiously, I think—dominates contemporary science studies. See Chapter 8, note 34 and discussion, for related commentary on Donald Davidson's views of intertranslatability, in/commensurability, and "conceptual [or, in Galison's term, 'framework'] relativism."

29. The present account is "non-normative" in the sense that it does not claim to ground, justify, or validate any norms of language or communication. Of course, since it depends on particular theoretical assumptions, involves particular intellectual judgments and choices, and promotes a particular approach, it is not non-normative in the (dubious) sense of "value-free." Contrary to common confusions, the observation of a gap between the empirical and the normative ("is" and "ought") is not equivalent to maintaining the possibility of purely objective (and, in that sense, value-free) observations or descriptions.

30. For a genial effort of that kind, see Taylor, *Mutual Misunderstanding*, pp. 186–200.

31. On the distinction, see Hopper, "Emergent Grammar and the A-priori Grammar Postulate."

32. See Chapters 6 and 7.

33. See, for example, Mary Louise Pratt, "Ideology and Speech-Act Theory," *Poetics Today* 7 (1986): 59–72; and "Linguistic Utopias," in *The Linguistics of Writing: Arguments Between Language and Literature,* ed. Nigel Fabb et al. (New York: Methuen, 1987); and Nancy Fraser, "How Critical is Critical Theory?: The Case of Habermas and Gender," in *Feminism as Critique: On the Politics of Gender,* ed. Seyla Benhabib and Drucilla Cornell (Minneapolis: University of Minnesota Press, 1987), pp. 31–56.

34. See note 24 for related charges directed against systems-theoretical or naturalistic (versus humanistic) accounts more generally.

35. Differences and connections of these kinds also seem involved in the mutually self-distinguishing contrasts drawn by practitioners of adjacent and to some extent competitive disciplines or intra-disciplinary approaches: contrasts. for example, between sociology and psychology, literary theory and philosophy, clinical and experimental psychology, biological and cultural anthropology, and, in many scientific fields, between (mere, genuine) "theory" and (mere, real) "bench research."

36. The effectiveness of our verbal practices in serving our *individual* interests and projects is what Habermas and others would see as their "strategic" value, understood as ethically suspect. But, as my parentheses suggest, there is no reason why our individual interests and projects cannot themselves be far-sighted, communally responsible, and otherwise ethically commendable. (The reply will be: yes, they *can* be; but that's not the same as saying they *should* be or showing they *must* be. To which one can only say, in turn: to be sure.)

5. Unloading the Self-Refutation Charge

1. Individual instances are cited where discussed, below. For rehearsals, collections, and surveys, see Harvey Siegel, *Relativism Refuted: A Critique of Contemporary Epistemological Relativism* (Dordrecht: Reidel, 1987); Michael Krausz, ed., *Relativism: Interpretation and Confrontation* (South Bend: University of Notre Dame Press, 1989); and Larry Laudan, *Science and Relativism: Some Key Controversies in the Philosophy of Science* (Chicago: University of Chicago Press, 1990).

2. The crucial charge against constructivist sociology of science has been *tu quoque* (you, too), that is, unwarranted self-exception and thus, if condemnations are involved, implicit self-condemnation. For the effects of the charge on the field, see Steve Woolgar, ed., *Knowledge and Reflexivity: New Frontiers in the Sociology of Knowledge* (London: Sage, 1988); Malcolm Ashmore, *The Reflexive Thesis: Wrighting Sociology of Scientific Knowledge* (Chicago: University of Chicago Press, 1989); and Andrew Pickering, "From Science as Knowledge to Science as Practice," in A. Pickering, ed., *Science as Practice and Culture* (Chicago: University of Chicago Press, 1992), pp. 1–26.

3. Plato, *Theaetetus* (170a–172c, 177c–179b). The translation by M. J. Levett is appended to Myles Burnyeat's study of the text, *The Theaetetus of Plato* (Indianapolis: Hackett, 1990). I draw also on the following: Edward N. Lee, " 'Hoist with His Own Petard': Ironic and Comic Elements in Plato's Critique of Protagoras (Tht. 161–171)," *Exegesis and Argument*, ed. E. N. Lee, A. P. D. Mourelatos, and R. M. Rorty (Assen: Van Gorcum, 1973), pp. 225–261; Myles Burnyeat, "Protagoras and Self-Refutation in Plato's Theaetetus," *The Philosophical Review*, 85 (1976): 172–195; David Bostock, *Plato's Theaetetus* (Oxford: Clarendon Press, 1988); and Rosemary Desjardins, *The Rational Enterprise: Logos in Plato's Theaetetus* (Albany: State University of New York Press, 1990).

4. When the texts of fertile and original theorists (Nietzsche or Foucault, for example) are paraphrased as one-line "theses," "claims" or "*p*'s", the assumption is that specific analyses, examples, and counterproposals are irrelevant to the identity of a theoretical position, and also that particulars of verbal idiom—diction, voice, imagery, style, and so on—are irrelevant to its force, uptake, interest, and appropriability. This assumption, fundamental to the operations of formal logic, is implicitly contested by the rhetoricist/pragmatist line in poststructuralist language theory discussed in Chapter 4.

5. G. B. Kerferd, "Plato's Account of the Relativism of Protagoras," *Durham University Journal* 42 (1949): 20–26; Gregory Vlastos, ed., *Plato's Protagoras*, trans. B. Jowett (Indianapolis: Liberal Arts Press, 1956), introd. The trick or error is noted and discussed in all the commentaries cited in note 3, and also by Siegel, *Relativism Refuted*.

6. Burnyeat, *The Theaetetus of Plato,* p. 30.

7. Burnyeat, "Protagoras and Self-Refutation," p. 195. For a (self-exemplifying) reply to this formulation and argument, see Barbara Herrnstein Smith, *Contingencies of Value: Alternative Perspectives for Critical Theory* (Cambridge, Mass.: Harvard University Press, 1988), pp. 112–114, 205.

8. Siegel, *Relativism Refuted,* pp. 8, 20.

9. Bostock, *Plato's Theaetetus,* p. 95. Lee, " 'Hoist with His Own Petard,' " argues the same point as Bostock.

10. Bostock, *Plato's Theaetetus,* pp. 89, 85.

11. See Smith, *Contingencies of Value,* pp. 98–101, 150–152.

12. "Validity" is especially pertinent here, but the analysis applies to the rejection of any classic measure—truth, beauty, virtue, and so on—in an absolute or objectivist sense.

13. See Burnyeat, quoted above (my emphasis).

14. Edmund Husserl, *Logical Investigations,* 2nd ed. (1913), trans. J. N. Findlay (London: Routledge and Kegan Paul, 1970), p. 139 (my emphasis), cited by Burnyeat, *Theaetetus of Plato,* p. 30.

15. Siegel, *Relativism Refuted,* p. 4 (my emphasis); similarly, later: " 'Relative rightness' is not rightness *at all* . . . To defend relativism relativistically is to fail to defend it *at all,*" pp. 8–9 (my emphasis).

16. Putnam, *Reason, Truth and History* (Cambridge: Cambridge University Press, 1981), p. 124.

17. Habermas, "Discourse Ethics: Notes on a Program of Philosophical Justification," in *Moral Consciousness and Communicative Action,* trans. Christian Lenhardt and Shierry Weber Nicholsen (Cambridge, Mass.: MIT Press, 1990), pp. 89–90 (my emphasis). The passage and argument are examined further in Chapter 6.

18. This is not to say that specific instruction in a particular discipline (philosophy, psychology, or sociology, etc.) is simply determinative: all education, formal or informal, is complexly interactive, and the effects of professional training are always diversely mediated by more or less individual cognitive tastes as well as by other aspects of personal/intellectual history.

19. We may recall, in *Theaetetus,* the figures Theodorus, senior mathematician and occasional participant in the dialogue, and Eucleides (142a–143c), its continuous witness and scrupulous recorder.

20. The appropriateness of Shakespeare's phrase to Protagoras is remarked by Lee, " 'Hoist with His Own Petard.' " Lee reads *Theaetetus* as fundamentally comic and, via the supposed punishment-fits-the-crime image of Protagoras reduced to a cabbage-like vegetable, as related in impulse to the *Divine Comedy*.

21. The irony in *Theaetetus* is exceedingly complex. Commentators note that it concludes with its ostensible central question— what is knowledge?—unanswered. Desjardins (*Rational Enterprise*, pp. 85–90) goes further, reading Socrates/Plato as ultimately endorsing the Protagorean thesis, appropriately interpreted.

22. See Hadley Arkes, *First Things: An Inquiry into the First Principles of Morals and Justice* (Princeton: Princeton University Press, 1986), pp. 78–80, for an unselfconscious report of triumphs along these lines by a professor of philosophy at a small, elite college.

23. Mostly young men, of course, in disciplinary philosophy. For instructive discussions of the historical and current significance of that bias, see Michèle Le Doeuff, *The Philosophical Imaginary* (Stanford: Stanford University Press, 1989), and Andrea Nye, *Words of Power: A Feminist Reading of the History of Logic* (New York: Routledge, 1990).

24. See James L. Battersby, "Professionalism, Relativism, and Rationality," *PMLA* 107 (1992): 63, for the (awkwardly stated) counter-counterargument that "self-refutation" (i.e., presumably, the charge) does not beg the question because it is (i.e., presumably, it appeals to) "a standard" that "belongs to the class of transparadigmatic criteria." Of course this only re-begs the question, though at a more elevated level. Similarly, Siegel argues that the charge by epistemological "naturalists" that the "incoherence argument" is question-begging "founders on the confusion . . . between truth and certainty," thus appealing (question-beggingly, as charged) to the classic conception of "truth" at issue (*Relativism Refuted*, p. 187).

25. Whether or not "it" is the same when otherwise conceived and described is a puzzle of which much has been made. It figures, for example, in the "dualism of [variable] conceptual scheme and [fixed] empirical content" alleged by Donald Davidson to be "essential to"—and thus, perhaps, crucially damaging of—certain views of Kuhn and Feyerabend (Davidson, "On the Very Idea of a Conceptual Scheme," in *Inquiries into Truth and Interpretation* [Ox-

ford: Clarendon Press, 1985], p. 189). Here as elsewhere, part of the issue is what sort of puzzle one thinks it is: whether "essentially" logical, as Davidson's term seems to indicate, or contingently discursive, conceptual, and rhetorical, as it could also be seen (and, accordingly, handled quite differently). Davidson's own position on the question appears ambivalent. It is certainly more elusive than is suggested by recurrent citations of this essay as decisive for debates over the epistemological claims of "conceptual relativism" and "postmodernism" and over the implications of the idea of incommensurability (see, for example, S. P. Mohanty, "Us and Them: On the Philosophical Bases of Political Criticism," *Yale Journal of Criticism* 2 [1989]: 1–31, and Christopher Norris, *What's Wrong with Postmodernism: Critical Theory and the Ends of Philosophy* [Baltimore: Johns Hopkins University Press, 1990], pp. 186–187.) For related discussion, see Chapter 8, note 34.

26. For descriptions of the effort among Buddhists, see Francisco J. Varela, Evan Thompson, and Eleanor Rosch, *The Embodied Mind: Cognitive Science and Human Experience* (Cambridge, Mass.: MIT Press, 1991), pp. 59–81. For discussion of the cognitive destabilizations effected in deconstruction, see Smith, *Contingencies of Value*, pp. 121–124.

27. Howard Rheingold, *Virtual Reality* (New York: Summit Books, 1991). Virtual reality technicians refer to the experience as "presence."

28. It should be recalled here that "cognitive" is not confined, in this book, to activities above the neck (i.e., the *entire* organism is always involved) and also that the stabilization and naturalization of belief are seen here as the products of interacting psychophysiological, social, and technological dynamics and practices. The latter point is elaborated in Chapter 8.

29. For relevant discussions, see Joan S. Lockard and Delroy L. Paulus, eds., *Self-Deception: An Adaptive Mechanism?* (Englewood Cliffs, N.J.: Prentice-Hall, 1988).

30. For the significance of that positing in mathematical theory, see Brian Rotman, *Ad Infinitum: The Ghost in Turing's Machine—Taking God out of Mathematics and Putting the Body Back In* (Stanford: Stanford University Press, 1993).

31. See Jacques Derrida, *Positions,* trans. Alan Bass (Chicago: University of Chicago Press, 1981), pp. 6–7, 13, 22. For extended

discussion of the idea, see Arkady Plotnitsky, *Reconfigurations: Critical Theory and General Economy* (Gainesville: University of Florida Press, 1992), pp. 194–211.

32. On this point, see also Smith, *Contingencies of Value*, pp. 147–149.

33. Here and elsewhere in this book, I use gendered pronouns (for example, masculine for "the traditionalist," feminine for "the skeptic") not to assign gender inflections to particular intellectual tastes or positions (many women theorists and scholars defend traditional conceptualizations, of course, and a number of notable skeptical theorists—ancient and postmodern—are men), but for variety, clarity (to help distinguish the personae in these debates), and, often enough, to acknowledge the present (female) author's association with one or another of the views in question.

34. "Traditionalism" and "postmodernism"—each of which comes in a variety of sizes and colors, not all represented here— are not, of course, the only epistemological positions possible, and one must not forget the multitudes of people who lead rich, full, lives without any articulated positions whatsoever on issues of epistemology. Also, here as in other contemporary intellectual controversies, various syntheses, middle ways, and transcendences have been proposed; see, for example, Richard J. Bernstein, *Beyond Objectivism and Relativism* (Philadelphia: University of Pennsylvania Press, 1983); Joseph Margolis, *The Truth about Relativism* (Cambridge, Mass.: Blackwell, 1991); and Susan Haack, *Evidence and Inquiry: Towards Reconstruction in Epistemology* (Oxford: Blackwell, 1995). While such efforts may be congenial and appropriable from some perspectives, most of them, if not just updates of traditional views, seem to strive simultaneously to hunt with the hounds and run with the fox(es), that is, to exhibit the solid home virtues of orthodoxy but also to claim credit for the cosmopolitanism (as it may be seen) of postmodernism. It is no coincidence that the pages in which they are developed are commonly strewn with charges of the "incoherence" and self-refutation of more unambivalently unorthodox positions.

35. The quotation marks here distinguish what are commonly seen as the fixed canons of formal logic from what could otherwise be seen as contingently, though very broadly, effective discursive/ conceptual practices. The parenthetical reversal acknowledges the

claims of each of these logics to priority: "logical" priority for the traditionalist; pragmatic/historical/psychological priority for the postmodern skeptic. Habermas and Karl-Otto Apel, among others, would see in this disputing of logic with "logic" a "performative contradiction" and, accordingly, a validation of both the "inescapably presupposed rules of argumentation" and the undeniability of "reason itself." In the next two chapters, I examine the questionable logical/rhetorical operations of such arguments as ("")rationally("") and ("")logically("") as seems necessary, under current conditions, to be persuasive.

6. The Skeptic's Turn

1. The idea of performative contradiction, anticipated by Kant and currently invoked by philosophers, theorists, and controversialists of various persuasions, is associated primarily with Frankfurt School "critical theory." See, especially, Karl-Otto Apel, *Towards a Transformation of Philosophy*, trans. Glyn Adey and David Frisby (London: Routledge & Kegan Paul, 1980 [Frankfurt-am-Main, 1972]), pp. 225 ff., and Jürgen Habermas, *The Philosophical Discourse of Modernity: Twelve Lectures*, trans. Frederick G. Lawrence (Cambridge, Mass.: MIT Press, 1987), pp. 185–186, and *Moral Consciousness and Communicative Action*, trans. Christian Lenhardt and Shierry Weber Nicholsen (Cambridge, Mass.: MIT Press, 1990), pp. 80–115. Several key terms involved in the idea, notably "speech act" and "performative," are derived by sometimes dubious mediation from J. L. Austin, *How to Do Things with Words* (Cambridge, Mass.: Harvard University Press, 1962). For recent invocations and alleged demonstrations of performative contradiction, see Peter Dews, *Logics of Disintegration: Post-Structuralist Thought and the Claims of Critical Theory* (London: Verso, 1987); Donald Guss, "Enlightenment as Process: Milton and Habermas," *PMLA* 106 (1991): 1156–1169; Thomas McCarthy, *Ideals and Illusions: On Reconstruction and Deconstruction in Contemporary Critical Theory* (Cambridge, Mass.: MIT Press, 1991); Steven Connor, *Theory and Cultural Value* (Oxford: Basil Blackwell, 1992), pp. 15–17; James L. Marsh, "Ambiguity, Language, and Communicative Praxis: A Critical Modernist Articulation," in *Modernity and its Discontents*, ed. James L. Marsh, John D. Caputo, and Merold

Westphal (New York: Fordham University Press, 1992), especially pp. 89–92; and Horace L. Fairlamb, *Critical Conditions: Postmodernity and the Question of Foundations* (Cambridge: Cambridge University Press, 1994).

2. The "skeptic" here is someone who currently questions standard philosophical (for example, Platonic, Cartesian, Kantian, Fregean) conceptualizations of *reason, truth, assertion, judgment, belief, validity, justification,* and related ideas. Correspondingly, the "traditionalist," below, is someone who currently accepts and defends those standard and more or less interrelated conceptualizations. (On my use of gender pronouns, see Chapter 5, note 33.) These definitions are designed to be minimal; individual questionings and specific defenses of such ideas vary more or less complexly along several lines. As the term is used here, contemporary (or "postmodern") skepticism is related to, but not identical with, various ancient or classic skeptical positions, such as Pyrronhism. For an instructive review of the latter, see Jonathan Barnes, *The Toils of Scepticism* (Cambridge: Cambridge University Press, 1990).

3. For comparable formulations, see Chapter 5, note 15.

4. Habermas, *Moral Consciousness,* p. 43. Subsequent page references to the book appear in parentheses in the text.

5. Hans Albert, *Treatise on Critical Reason,* trans. Mary Varney Rorty (Princeton: Princeton University Press, 1985 [1968]), pp. 16–21.

6. See Habermas, "What is Universal Pragmatics?" in *Communication and the Evolution of Society,* trans. Thomas McCarthy (Boston: Beacon Press, 1979), pp. 1–68, and Apel, "The A Priori of the Communication Community and the Foundations of Ethics," in *Towards a Transformation of Philosophy,* pp. 225–300.

7. This is Apel's rebuttal as summarized by Habermas (*Moral Consciousness,* p. 81).

8. Though an anti-foundationalist, Albert (a follower of Karl Popper and proponent of "critical rationalism") might not endorse the account of logical norms outlined below. If, however, he endorses any comparably non-foundational understanding of the operations of logic, he could escape the Catch-22 clause of Apel's argument.

9. Apel seems at one point to acknowledge the significance of this absolute self-privileging, but in a rather back-handed way.

Commenting on the possibly dismaying implications for transcendental foundationalism of Gödel's theorem, he writes: "I am more inclined to assume that the indirect self-referentiality [i.e., circularity] of argumentation which is contained in the transcendental-pragmatic discussion of . . . argumentation as such *only* becomes self-contradictory if it denies or fails to credit itself with its own truth, as is the case in radical scepticism" (Apel, *Transformation of Philosophy*, pp. 265–266, my emphasis). This seems to be saying that the (radical) skeptic's argument is self-contradictory precisely because it refuses to award itself absolute epistemic priority, and that foundationalism saves itself from self-contradiction precisely by *insisting* on so privileging itself, that is, by being circular. (As we will see in the next chapter, it is possible to posit a reciprocal relation between circularity and self-contradiction, but not quite the way Apel does here, nor for the same reasons.)

10. John Searle, *Speech Acts: An Essay in the Philosophy of Language* (London: Cambridge University Press, 1969). Apel cites Searle as "developing Austin's position in a systematic theory" (*Transformation of Philosophy*, p. 42, note 32). It can be argued, however, that the value of Austin's work for language theory is precisely its emphasis on the *limits* of systematicity.

11. [H.] Paul Grice, *Studies in the Ways of Words* (Cambridge, Mass: Harvard University Press, 1989). Habermas also cites R. Alexy, "Eine Theorie des praktischen Diskurses," in W. Oelmüller, ed., *Normenbegründung Transzendentalphilosophische* (Paderborn, 1978).

12. See Chapter 4, note 1, for alternative theories.

13. References here would include the work of not only the usual cast of anti-foundationalists but also of a number of language theorists, for example, Paul Hopper, "Emergent Grammar and the A-priori Grammar Postulate," in Deborah Tannen, ed., *Linguistics in Context: Connecting Observation and Understanding* (Norwood, N.J.: Ablex Publishing Corp., 1988).

14. Münchhausen maneuvers are not restricted to foundationalists. On the contrary, under different names (for example, "question-begging," "bootstrapping," or "the hermeneutic circle"), they could be seen as an element of all argumentation and crucial to the coherence of all systems of belief. I return to the suggestion in Chapters 7 and 8.

15. The centrality of *restabilization* as such is suggested by the following passage, in which Apel defends a classic conception of reason against the arguments of contemporary "irrationalists" (he specifies "followers of Kuhn, especially Feyerabend"): "It [reason] can always *confirm its own legitimation* through reflection on the fact that it presupposes its own self-understanding of the very rules it opts for" (Apel, "The Problem of Philosophical Foundations in Light of a Transcendental Pragmatics of Language," in *After Philosophy: End or Transformation?* ed. Kenneth Baynes, James Bohman, and Thomas McCarthy [Cambridge, Mass., 1987], p. 283, my emphasis).

16. The turning and re-turning of tables between traditional foundationalism and contemporary skepticism may continue virtually ad infinitum. Thus, Albert himself replies to Apel's table-turning in *Transzendentale Traumerein* (Hamburg, 1985) and to related attacks in "Münchhausen oder der Zauber der Reflexion," *Die Wissenschaft und die Fehlbarkeit der Vernunft* (Tübingen, 1982); Habermas undertakes the refutation of Albert's replies and anti-foundationalism more generally in *Moral Consciousness;* the present discussion responds to, even if it does not refute, Apel's and Habermas's refutations; and Habermas replies to various replies to his refutations of the refutations of foundationalism (though not to the present one) in a more recent work, *Justification and Application: Remarks on Discourse Ethics,* trans. Ciaran P. Cronin (Cambridge, Mass.: MIT Press, 1993).

17. It is *quasi*-foundational in that Habermas acknowledges the logical problems involved in classic, full-fledged transcendental (a priori) justification but believes something like it is both necessary and possible. The ambivalent playing out of that haunted conviction characterizes much of *Moral Consciousness.*

18. According to Habermas, ethical skeptics maintain "counter-intuitively" that people's "naive trust in the justifiability of norms and commands [is] an illusion" (54). He evokes a number of supposed skeptical positions here, including the view that ethical norms and imperatives reflect only the speaker's own values or that they operate for listeners merely as rhetorically embellished recommendations. These and other noncognitive approaches, he writes, "with a single blow . . . deprive the sphere of everyday moral intuitions of its significance" (55). For other (dubious) invocations of the force of moral intuitions, see Chapter 7, note 17.

19. The apparent symmetry here—"advocate of ethical cognitivism" versus "advocate of moral skepticism"—is misleading. Someone who finds various aspects of discourse ethics conceptually problematic or questions the coherence and workability of transcendental demonstrations more generally need not *advocate* "moral skepticism": that is, need not regard that dissatisfaction as a position, need not seek to promote it as such, and need not reject in advance all moral norms (non-prejudicially defined). Habermas's method here of justification via imaginary debate seems, additionally, to contradict his own earlier stipulation (*contra* John Rawls) that, for a justification of norms to be genuine, "a real discourse [must] be carried out and thus cannot occur in a strictly monological form, i.e., in the form of a hypothetical process of argumentation" (*Moral Consciousness*, p. 68).

20. I follow here Habermas's own pronoun usage, in which skeptic and cognitivist are both always masculine.

21. The (U) universalization principle (for justifying moral norms) is as follows: "*All* affected can accept the consequences and the side effects [that] its *general* observance can be anticipated to have for the satisfaction of *everyone's* interests (and these consequences are preferred to those of known alternative possibilities for regulation)" (*Moral Consciousness*, p. 65).

22. While Habermas insists that being *convinced* of something requires "com[ing] to a reasoned agreement" about it (see discussion), the process here is in some respects like a "knock-knock" joke, where someone, usually a young child, is led by someone else, often an older child or teasing adult, into saying something more or less embarrassing through an innocuous-seeming question-answer routine. But, of course, Socratic dialogues often operate that way too. The similarity between the two (i.e., Socratic dialectics and convincing-via-exposing-performative-contradictions) is highlighted by Habermas's use of the term "maieutic" to characterize his method here (*Moral Consciousness*, p. 97), recalling the midwife metaphor in *Theaetetus*, as discussed in Chapter 5. In both cases, a philosophical novice (or moral-theoretical incompetent) is brought by a philosophical expert to the recognition of what he (allegedly) always already knew.

23. The German text, discussed below, gives the alternatives as follows: [1] *Ich habe H schliesslich durch gute Gründe davon überzeugt, dass p* [. . .,] [2] **Ich habe H schliesslich durch eine Luge davon über-*

zeugt, dass p [. . . and] [3] *Ich habe H schliesslich mit Hilfe einer Lüge davon überredet, zu glauben (habe ihn glauben machen) dass p* (Habermas, *Moralbewusstsein und kommunikatives Handeln* [Frankfurt am Main, Germany: Suhrkamp Verlag, 1983], p. 100).

24. Austin seems to have had just this instance in mind in his illustration (without explicit allusion to Shakespeare's *Othello*) of how *any* utterance, issued "with or without calculation," may perform the perlocutionary act of *convincing:* "for you may convince me . . . that she is an adulteress by asking her whether it was not her handkerchief which was in X's bedroom, or by stating that it was hers" (*How to Do Things with Words,* pp. 109–110). Here as elsewhere, Austin's sense of the wide range, subtle modulation, and contextual contingency of the effects of verbal utterance seems at odds with subsequent formalized ("systematized") appropriations of his ideas (see note 10).

25. Lenhardt and Nicholsen, in Habermas, *Moral Consciousness,* p. 113, note 73.

26. Statement (2) probably sounds odd to speakers of English as well as German because, Iago notwithstanding, we don't expect people to confess quite that baldly to telling lies. This expectation and related verbal inhibition certainly reflect broader social/communicative norms that are, again, not just matters of linguistic usage. Such norms are not responsible, however, for the alleged "paradox" of the idea of convincing people of things by using lies.

27. L. Jonathan Cohen, *An Essay on Belief and Acceptance* (Oxford: Clarendon Press, 1992). The specific examples here are adapted from similar, but not identical, ones that Cohen offers at various points in the book.

28. Ibid., p. 23.

29. Ibid., pp. 20–21. The qualifications in my paraphrase ("suggests," "may," "perhaps") reflect Cohen's formulations. His claims and suggestions are put forth modestly and scrupulously, but they—and the insistence just mentioned—are nevertheless put forth.

30. Many of the distinctions Cohen draws would not, however, be intuitively obvious to a speaker of *American* English and, especially in the case of "accept that," seem to be the product of specifically British usages.

31. Habermas specifies cultural relativism as the issue in the hypothetical skeptic's claim that (U), the universalization principle,

"is only a hasty generalization of . . . Western culture" (*Moral Consciousness*, p. 76).

32. For examples, see Stephen Stich, *From Folk Psychology to Cognitive Science: The Case against Belief* (Cambridge, Mass.: MIT Press, 1983).

33. Cohen, *An Essay*, pp. 22–23, my emphasis.

34. See Chapter 4 for discussion of supplemental (or higher) lexicography. As noted there, dictionary definitions are always more or less obsolete and, for certain purposes (for example, rhetorical analysis or intellectual historiography), relatively thin or crude. It might be added here, however, that, for the same general reasons, even the most exquisite elaborations and rigorous refinements of the implications of—and distinctions between—terms worked out by analytic philosophers are likely to seem to some extent quaint and curious to those who encounter them in future generations.

35. Among the key relevantly questionable assumptions and definitions here are: (a) that there are internal connections among verbal expressions that are independent of learned patterns of usage, (b) that to question something is equivalent to asserting its negation as an absolute truth, and (c) that reasoned argument is equivalent to the raising of absolute and presumptively transcendentally justifiable truth-claims.

36. The skeptic here is like the wised-up child who, at the insistent "Knock! Knock!" of her would-be humiliator, just tightens her lips more firmly. See note 22.

37. The distinction between involved participation and detached observation is significant for Habermas, marking a key difference between humanistic "rationally reconstructive" sciences and empirical, naturalistic sciences.

38. See, for example, William E. Connolly, *The Ethos of Pluralization* (Minneapolis: University of Minnesota Press, 1995). Connolly treats the thought of Foucault and Nietzsche—not incidentally here (see Habermas's remarks on both quoted above)—as especially relevant.

39. In a more recent work replying to mainstream critics and philosophical rivals of discourse ethics (for example, Alisdair MacIntyre, John Rawls, and Bernard Williams), Habermas claims that the latter fall back on, or into, the very "transcendental modes of justification" they question and seek to replace (Habermas, *Jus-*

tification and Application). His observation of backsliding may be apt in many cases, but the question here is whether *any* posited alternative to transcendental moral theory *must* move into that mode, inescapably. The answer seems to be that it must do so if it is to qualify as (genuine) moral theory from Habermas's perspective. Accordingly, there are no alternatives, given that perspective.

40. The implications of these definitions for the conduct of quotidian intellectual life are suggested by Habermas's justification of his criticisms of Derrida's thought via secondhand reports of it: "Since Derrida *does not belong to those philosophers who like to argue*, it is expedient to take a closer look at his disciples in literary criticism within the Anglo-Saxon climate of argument to see whether this thesis [of his] really can be held" (*The Philosophical Discourses of Modernity*, trans. F. Lawrence [Cambridge, Mass.: MIT Press, 1987], p. 193, my emphasis).

41. These and other questions of in/commensurabilty are considered in Chapter 8.

7. Arguing with Reason

1. Peter Dews, *Logics of Disintegration: Post-Structuralist Thought and the Claims of Critical Theory* (London: Verso, 1987), p. xvi. For another example, see Carl Rapp, "The Crisis of Reason in Contemporary Thought: Some Reflections on the Arguments of Postmodernism," *Critical Review* 5 (1991): 261–290, especially pp. 289–290.

2. "I am not dramatizing the situation when I say that faced with the demand for a justification of the universal validity of the principle of universalization, cognitivists [i.e., rationalist moral theorists] are in trouble" (Jürgen Habermas, *Moral Consciousness and Communicative Action*, trans. Christian Lenhardt and Shierry Weber Nicholsen [Cambridge, Mass.: MIT Press, 1990], p. 79). Subsequent page references appear in parentheses in the text.

3. See Richard Rorty, *Philosophy and the Mirror of Nature* (Princeton, N.J.: Princeton University Press, 1979), pp. 306–311.

4. The failure in question is complicated (and obscured) by the fact that "unconditional" is equivalent to "transcending" in the idiom of rationalist philosophy, so that "the idea of . . . the unconditional" *must* have transcending power, by definition—in that idiom. This situation of necessity-by-definition is taken up below.

5. Habermas does not deny that logical problems are involved in classic transcendental justification, but he remains persuaded that something like it is, as he puts it, "a necessary condition for humane forms of collective life." In view of the gravity of that necessity as Habermas, in accord with the classic self-conception of rationalist philosophy, sees it, the strenuousness of his resistance to the post-modern critique is understandable. The question, however, is whether the self-conception of rationalist philosophy is itself necessary.

6. Habermas insists on this irrelevance in a more recent work, where, *contra* a number of naturalizing (or "empirical" or "objectifying") moral theorists, notably Bernard Williams, he rehearses the classic is/ought distinctions (see Jürgen Habermas, *Justification and Application: Remarks on Discourse Ethics,* trans. Ciaran P. Cronin [Cambridge, Mass: MIT Press, 1993], pp. 20–21). As I suggest in Chapter 4, note 23, efforts by contemporary analytic philosophers (and others) to naturalize ethics may indeed be seen as problematic, and certain formulations of the is/ought distinction could be invoked to articulate the difficulties. Here as elsewhere, however, the question is whether the exposure of such problems validates rationalist moral theory as the only possible alternative.

7. Habermas's speech acts are often difficult to characterize because they seem simultaneously to grant important points but to deny that any granting is involved.

8. Philosophers pursuing such projects (Habermas does not cite any by name here) include Patricia Churchland, Andy Clark, Daniel Dennett, and Owen Flanagan. The resistance to those pursuits on the part of more orthodox epistemologists and philosophers of science is considered in the next chapter.

9. Stressing the necessary modesty of (deontological) moral theory, Habermas writes in the final paragraph of the book: "What moral *theory* can do and should be trusted to do is to clarify the universal core of our moral intuitions and thereby to refute value skepticism [i.e., presumably, the idea that our moral intuitions may not have a universal core]. What it cannot do is make any kind of substantive contribution . . . [M]y modest opinion about what philosophy can and cannot accomplish may come as a disappointment. Be that as it may . . ." (*Moral Consciousness,* p. 211).

10. The bracketed hinges ("however") that would seem to be

logically and syntactically required at the points indicated here do not actually appear in Habermas's text, perhaps because they would signal turns he cannot justify executing too decisively.

11. For a somewhat different but acute and not incompatible analysis of these difficulties, see Raymond Geuss, *The Idea of a Critical Theory: Habermas & the Frankfurt School* (Cambridge: Cambridge University Press, 1981).

12. See, for example, Seyla Benhabib, "The Generalized and the Concrete Other," and Nancy Fraser, "How Critical is Critical Theory? The Case of Habermas and Gender," in *Feminism as Critique: On the Politics of Gender,* ed. Seyla Benhabib and Drucilla Cornell (Minneapolis: University of Minnesota Press, 1987). Habermas acknowledges Benhabib's concerns in a more recent book (see Habermas, *Justification and Application,* p. 154), but it is not clear to what extent his replies satisfy either her or others with comparable objections. See also Seyla Benhabib, *Situating the Self: Gender, Community and Postmodernism in Contemporary Ethics* (New York: Routledge, 1992), for Benhabib's conscientious effort to salvage Habermas's discourse ethics as a "dialogically reformulated universalist ethicist theory" (p. 28) despite what she acknowledges as its conceptual weaknesses and indicates, once again, as its political risks and limits from a feminist perspective.

13. Habermas sometimes comes quite close to acknowledging, as well as achieving, this sort of self-transformation/reconception. For example, conceding but defending the circularity of the relation between discourse ethics and the (not quite) empirical sciences said to corroborate it, he observes that the demand "for an *independent* corroboration of the normative theory" is itself "too strong." The best any theory, empirical or normative, can claim in competition with other such theories is adequate "fit," "coherence," and "relative reliab[ility]"; and, he remarks, if such criteria are adopted, then "philosophy and science must change their self-perceptions" (Habermas, *Moral Consciousness,* pp. 117–118). These are important concessions and, as positive formulations, compatible with many revisionist conceptions of validity and justification. They are not compatible, however, with the reaffirmations of the classic claims of rationalist philosophy and deontological moral theory found throughout the book and elsewhere in his recent writings.

14. The general pattern described here is most evident when the

sets of beliefs in question have explicit and significant implications for quotidian social and political practices, as is the case, for example, in religious systems, moralities, or political theories (themselves not always clearly separable, of course). Any set of beliefs, however, could be expected to exhibit comparable equivocations in response to comparable pressures for both rigor and accommodation.

15. In a vivid metaphor, Habermas describes the contemporary world as "a tangled mobile" in which a former and proper "interplay between the cognitive-instrumental, moral-practical, and aesthetic-expressive dimensions . . . has come to a standstill" (*Moral Consciousness,* p. 19). His subsequent defense of modern(ist) philosophy has affinities with the nostalgic *anti*-modernism of Alisdair MacIntyre (for whose work Habermas displays a specific though skittish respect) and of other politically as well as philosophically conservative theorists. One need not speak here, however, of "inconsistencies" or "self-contradictions." Rather, one may observe that, here as elsewhere, the lineages, clusterings, and antagonisms displayed in theoretical controversies may be exceptionally complex. Familiar philosophical classifications and distinctions, such as "left" and "right" Hegelianism, "moderate" and "extreme" relativism, "weak" and "strong" emotivism, and so on, do not capture this complexity. On the contrary, they tame it while perpetuating the dubious idea that the intellectual world is a static map (or "logical space") on which one can locate a set of finite, mutually exclusive, historically immutable positions with only internally differentiable versions and variants. In accord with the general conception of intellectual dynamics outlined in this book, our theoretical convictions and philosophical allegiances, like all our other beliefs, may be seen as shaped by and responsive to our more or less highly individuated personal/intellectual histories. No matter how similar people's intellectual positions may be in *some* respects and what common cause they may make under *some* conditions, their individual beliefs are still likely to have more or less different emotional and intellectual stakes for each of them, and those differences are likely to play themselves out differently under *other* conditions. Thus, in regard to some issues, Habermas's views will be closer to those of the conservative, religious-minded MacIntyre than to those of the more liberal, secular-minded Rorty, and, on other is-

sues, vice versa. Similarly, under some conditions, he might want to stress his affinities with Hegel and Horkheimer rather than with Plato and Kant, and, under other conditions, vice versa. It is for these reasons, too, that, contrary to facile charges of "complicity" or equally facile celebrations of "solidarity," people's specific political sympathies and stances cannot be directly derived or reliably predicted from their evident theoretical commitments (or, of course, vice versa).

16. Habermas distinguishes different forms and historical phases of hermeneutics. In the passage quoted here, the versions he appears to have in mind are Gadamerian and/or Rortian.

17. Comparably universalized intuitions are invoked elsewhere in *Moral Consciousness* to support transcendental moral theory generally. According to Habermas, it is *only* the experience and conviction of the universal validity of moral norms that controls moral behavior. "[M]oral norms in the strict sense," he writes, are experienced as valid "for all competent actors . . . This *alone* explains the guilt feeling that accompanies the wrongdoer's self-accusation," which is his realization that he has "violated something impersonal or at least suprapersonal . . . It is *only* their claim to general [i.e., presumably, universal] validity that gives an interest, a volition, or a norm the dignity of moral authority" (*Moral Consciousness*, pp. 48–49, my emphasis). The evidence for this arguable theory of human motivation seems to consist mainly or wholly of Habermas's own introspected experiences as confirmed by the testimony of other persons also deeply instructed in the conceptual idioms of classic moral philosophy. Thus he cites, in addition to Lawrence Kohlberg, the British philosopher P. F. Strawson, who agrees that nontranscendental accounts of the operations of moral norms are counter-intuitive because, as such, they "leave out something vital in our [*everyone's?*] conception of these practices" (P. F. Strawson, *Freedom and Resentment* [London: Methuen, 1974], p. 22, as cited by Habermas, *Moral Consciousness*, p. 49).

18. See Paul K. Feyerabend, *Against Method: Outline of an Anarchistic Theory of Knowledge* (London: NLB, 1975 ["anarchist" is changed in the book's preface to "dadaist"]), and *Farewell to Reason* (London: Verso, 1987).

19. I do not say "force" or "power" here, though either term would be appropriate in many senses, because the association of

each with violent coercion and political oppression is unshakable for many readers. For discussion of the Might/Right *topos* and a powerful (precisely) alternative conceptualization, see Bruno Latour, *The Pasteurization of France,* trans. Allan Sheridan and John Law (Cambridge, Mass.: Harvard University Press, 1988), Part II, "Irreductions."

20. The Might/Right account of exerting influence does, of course, recognize more subtle forms of coercion, such as sophistry, rhetoric, and the inculcation of ideology or false consciousness. As these ancient/modern terms themselves remind us, however, these subtler forms remain firmly imbedded in the dualistic account itself, routinely lined up against their familiar positive twins (rational persuasion, objective truth, due enlightenment, and so forth), and, thereby, participate in the larger system of claims, concepts, and distinctions at issue here.

21. For examples, see Chapter 2, note 16.

22. See the appendix to this chapter for a systematic listing of these and other interrelated definitions.

23. Thomas McCarthy, in his introduction to *Moral Consciousness,* uses a number of Habermas's philosophically technical, system-defined terms (for example, "practical" and "reason") as if they had their idiomatic meanings, simplifies Habermas's painstakingly qualified formulations, irons out his exquisitely poised equivocations, and makes claims that are more plausible or (so to speak) reasonable-sounding than those Habermas himself makes but also, by the same token, less self-consistent. McCarthy's soft-edged paraphrases tend to avoid the problems of rigor that I am stressing here, problems well understood, it seems, by Habermas himself— hence his notoriously angular and virtually *non*paraphrasable formulations.

24. Roy Bhaskar, *Scientific Realism and Human Emancipation* (London: Verso, 1986).

25. Norris, *What's Wrong with Postmodernism: Critical Theory and the Ends of Philosophy* (Baltimore: Johns Hopkins University Press, 1990), pp. 98, 79.

26. Dews, *Logics of Disintegration,* pp. xiii and xvi, my emphasis. For other examples of such double reversals (including versions of the phrases cited above), see Thomas A. McCarthy, *Ideals and Illusions: On Reconstruction and Deconstruction in Contemporary Crit-*

ical Theory (Cambridge, Mass.: MIT Press, 1991), pp. 6–7, and Steven Connor, *Theory and Cultural Value* (Oxford: Basil Blackwell, 1992), pp. 15–17.

27. The forfeiture of claims to transcendental validation could be seen, I think, as generally preferable to the risk of cognitive stultification. Indeed, because the rhetorical (justificatory, persuasive) force of such claims depends on the prevalence of convictions that are themselves only relatively stable (for example, the conviction that the justification of norms requires the presumption of universalizability), their actual advantage is dubious and certainly historically fragile. Thus, although Enlightenment-style universalist invocations may have been significant in the past (it is often argued, for example, that without them there could have been no French Revolution or anti-slavery movements), it does not follow that such invocations remain crucial to radical social change or that they will always be decisive or even significant. To be sure, one would still want to say only *generally* preferable here: there are certainly emergency situations (for example, when one or more lives is immediately at risk) in which *any* rhetorical advantage will be seen as crucially desirable, though disagreements may be expected over whether a particular situation qualifies as an emergency in this sense. Related tradeoffs and disagreements are involved in current debates over "strategic essentialism" (see Chapter 1, note 13): that is, the idea of a currently acute or chronic political need for appeals to otherwise rejected claims and categories (universal norms, essential natures, objective truths, natural rights, and so forth). Thus, questions can be raised over how acutely necessary or even how immediately effective such appeals are in ameliorating the particular situations that supposedly require them (communally sanctioned racism, homophobia, violence against women, and so forth). As indicated earlier, there may be alternative arguments or more effective courses of action that are ignored or overlooked by activists who depend heavily or exclusively (whether out of profound conviction or in the name of strategic necessity) on appeals of those kinds.

8. Microdynamics of Incommensurability

1. Philip Kitcher, *The Advancement of Science: Science without Legend, Objectivity without Illusions* (New York: Oxford Univer-

sity Press, 1993). Page references appear in parentheses in my text.

2. Allusions to Scylla and Charybdis are common in contemporary theoretical controversy, along with more general statements as to the desirability of steering a middle course between such alleged extremes as objectivism and relativism, realism and constructivism, old-fashioned rationalism and newfangled postmodern irrationalism, and so forth. The advertised *via media* usually turns out to be, as here, a (con)temporized version of received (for example, objectivist, realist, rationalist) wisdom.

3. See, for example, David Papineau, "How to Think about Science," *New York Times Book Review* (July 25, 1993): 14–15; and J. A. Kegley's review in *Choice* (November 1993): 471–472.

4. See, for example, John Ziman, "Progressive Knowledge," *Nature* 364 (1993): 295–296; and Steve Fuller, "Mortgaging the Farm to Save the (Sacred) Cow," *Studies in the History and Philosophy of Science* 25 (1994): 251–261.

5. See Bruno Latour, *The Pasteurization of France*, trans. Alan Sheridan and John Law (Cambridge, Mass.: Harvard University Press, 1988), and *We Have Never Been Modern*, trans. Catherine Porter (Cambridge, Mass.: Harvard University Press, 1993).

6. Kitcher seems unaware of critiques of the traditional referentialist model of language to which he appeals or of related alternative accounts (see Chapter 4). Given the mutual segregation of continental and Anglo-American philosophy, it is not surprising that neither Foucault nor Derrida appears in his lengthy bibliography. It is surprising, however, that neither Wittgenstein nor Rorty—or, aside from one minor brush-off, Hesse—does. For related discussion, see Michael A. Arbib and Mary B. Hesse, *The Construction of Reality* (Cambridge: Cambridge University Press, 1986), pp. 147–170.

7. As is commonly the case in these some-of-each compromises (including the genetic/environmental one itself), the assignment of weight to the forces in question is rather lopsided here. When, in his concluding chapter, Kitcher finally explains the contribution of "social forces" to the advancement of science, it turns out to be limited exclusively to the operations of the scientific community itself—which, as he sees it, is a "social system" that rewards the individual scientist for discovering significant truth and thus, like

the invisible hand of classical economics, works through individual self-advancement to advance the (cognitive) benefit of all (*Advancement*, pp. 303–389). For detailed critical discussion of the economic model on which his analysis here is based, see Philip Mirowski, "The Economic Consequences of Philip Kitcher," *Social Epistemology* 10 (1996): 153–169.

8. See, especially, Susan Oyama, *The Ontogeny of Information: Developmental Systems and Evolution* (Cambridge: Cambridge University Press, 1985). For related models of reciprocal determination, see Humberto R. Maturana and Francisco J. Varela, *Autopoiesis and Cognition: The Realization of the Living* (Boston: D. Reidel, 1980), and *The Tree of Knowledge: The Biological Roots of Human Understanding* (Boston: Shambhala, 1988); Russell Gray, "Metaphors and Methods: Behavioral Ecology, Panbiogeography and the Evolving Synthesis," in *Evolutionary Processes and Metaphors*, ed. Mae-Wan Ho and Sidney W. Fox (Chichester, England: John Wiley & Sons, 1988), pp. 209–242; and Esther Thelen and Linda B. Smith, *A Dynamic Systems Approach to the Development of Cognition and Action* (Cambridge, Mass.: MIT Press, 1994).

9. Bruno Latour and Steven Woolgar, *Laboratory Life: The Social Construction of Scientific Facts* (Princeton: Princeton University Press, 1986 [1979]), p. 180.

10. With a glance, it seems, at S. J. Gould and R. C. Lewontin's celebrated essay, "The Spandrels of San Marco and the Panglossian Paradigm: A Critique of the Adaptationist Programme," *Proceedings of the Royal Society of London* 205 (1978): 581–598, Kitcher explicitly rejects the telling of "just-so stories" in the history of science. Nevertheless, he cites, endorses, and is evidently influenced by Howard Margolis, *Paradigms and Barriers: How Habits of Mind Govern Scientific Beliefs* (Chicago: University of Chicago Press, 1993), which features a defiantly and explicitly Whiggish history of science. Margolis maintains that the symmetry postulate of the Edinburgh sociologists and historians of science—that is, their refusal to privilege present scientific knowledge methodologically as always already true—is a foolish overreaction to "an older history of science" that got "a bad reputation" because it said impolite things about the losers in scientific controversies. That was, Margolis observes, crude—but, he adds, "of course, being winners, the winning side must have had more of *something*" (*Paradigms*, p. 197, his emphasis). I take up Kitcher's version of that "something" below.

11. Misunderstandings and misrepresentations occur on both sides of these debates, of course, for revisionists as well as traditionalists interpret the arguments of their adversaries through their own assumptions. Symmetry-conscious constructivist epistemologists such as Latour and Woolgar would presumably acknowledge this in principle but, since one is always blind to one's own blind spots, would not be able to point out their own misunderstandings and misrepresentations; nor, given my own perspective on these issues, am I well situated to do so for them.

12. Steven Shapin and Simon Schaffer, *Leviathan and the Air-Pump: Hobbes, Boyle, and the Experimental Life* (Princeton: Princeton University Press, 1985). Kitcher believes that a "pessimistic" overestimation of the significance of theory-ladenness is a general feature of contemporary sociology of science. The claim that "we see just what our theoretical commitments would lead us to expect" is "a gross hyperextension of what philosophers and psychologists are able to show" (*Advancement*, 167, note 53; see also p. 141, note 18). His statement of that claim is itself something of a hyperextension, however, setting up a spurious contrast with the "eminently sensible conclusion," attributed by Kitcher to Kuhn, that "anomalies emerge in the course of normal science." The crucial issue, of course, is not the emergence of anomalies—something that no sociologist of science would, I think, deny—but how to describe their operation in intellectual history. Kitcher evidently sees them as epistemic arrows shot straight from reality, piercing our otherwise theory-clouded or theory-skewed observations and setting us, and our theories, straight. The alternative view—and, arguably, the one Kuhn himself favors—is that perceived anomalies may destabilize specific theories but, like all other perceptions, must themselves be interpreted via prior conceptualizations and prior practices more generally. For detailed discussion of Kuhn's views on this and related topics, see Paul Hoyningen-Huene, *Reconstructing Scientific Revolutions: Thomas S. Kuhn's Philosophy of Science*, trans. Alexander T. Levine (Chicago: University of Chicago Press, 1993), pp. 223–244. See Alan Lightman and Owen Gingerich, "When do Anomalies Begin?" *Science*, 255 (1991): 690–695, for a nice analysis of what they call the "retrorecognition" of anomalies, in other words, the tendency of practicing scientists to discount anomalous findings until *after* they have been given stable explanations in a new conceptual framework.

13. Theories are said to be "underdetermined" by evidence or observation of fact; conversely, observation of supposed fact is said to be overdetermined by, or "laden" with, prior theory.

14. It should be recalled here that knowledge and cognition, and, by implication, "theory" (and indeed "philosophy," as seen in Chapter 7), are conceived in this book as embodied processes, practices, and products, not as sets of propositions or representations nor as matters of disembodied or purely formal intellectual activity.

15. Kitcher defends this traditional goal of philosophy of science rather awkwardly and equivocally. On the one hand, he maintains that the abstractions and idealizations of "philosophical reflections about science," like the models of economic theorists vis-à-vis "the complicated and messy world of transactions of work, money, and goods," are necessary to "lay bare large and important features of the phenomena" and to "recogniz[e] the general features of the . . . enterprise." On the other hand, he cautions that, "to rebut . . . charges [of unrealistic irrelevancy]—*or* to concede them *and* to do better service to philosophy's legitimate normative project—we need to idealize the phenomena *but* to include in our treatment the features [for example, the complicated and messy ones?] that critics emphasize" (*Advancement*, 10, my emphases). These equivocations, which recall comparable ones examined in Chapter 7, seem to reflect a fundamental dilemma: that is, a reciprocality that calls for a tradeoff in practice which, however, is prohibited by some aspect of theory. Here the reciprocally related goods are abstractness or "idealization," required to be maximal if philosophy of science is to retain its definitive *generalizing* ambitions, and the historical specificity or "messiness" of scientific practice, adequate responsiveness to which is required if philosophy of science is to gain credibility for its equally definitive *normative* claims. For a somewhat dated but still instructive analysis and comparison of the respective projects of (Popperian) normative epistemology and "strong programme" sociology of knowledge, see John Law, "Is Epistemology Redundant: A Sociological View," *Philosophy of Social Science*, 5 (1975): 317–337.

16. See, for example, Bruno Latour, *Science in Action: How to Follow Scientists and Engineers through Society* (Cambridge, Mass.: Harvard University Press, 1987), *The Pasteurization of France*, and "On Technical Mediation—Philosophy, Sociology, Genealogy,"

Common Knowledge 3 (Fall 1994): 29–64; Michel Callon, "Society in the Making: The Study of Technology as a Tool for Sociological Analysis," in Wiebe E. Bijker, Thomas P. Hughes, and Trevor J. Pinch, eds., *The Social Construction of Technological Systems: New Directions in the Sociology and History of Technology* (Cambridge, Mass.: MIT Press, 1987), pp. 83–103; Andrew Pickering, "From Science as Knowledge to Science as Practice," in *Science as Practice and Culture*, ed. Andrew Pickering (Chicago: University of Chicago Press, 1992), pp. 1–26; Ian Hacking, "The Self-Vindication of the Laboratory Sciences," in Pickering, *Science as Practice and Culture*, pp. 29–64; and Wiebe Bijker and John Law, eds., *Constructing Networks and Systems* (Cambridge, Mass.: MIT Press, 1994). On the significance of the collaborative use of research instruments, see also Charles Goodwin, "Seeing in Depth" *Social Studies of Science* 25 (1995): 237–274.

17. Contrary to common misunderstandings, "around again," in both the classic idea of the hermeneutic circle and more recent analyses of the reciprocal determination of theory, action, and observation, describes not a continuous repetition of the same path but—if spatial images are sought—a set of continuously linked loops. See also Chapter 3, note 14.

18. This observation is not offered as—and, read appropriately, does not amount to—a (re)definition or, as the term is sometimes used in Anglo-American philosophy, "theory" of truth. On the relevant contemporary controversies, see Chapter 2, note 13, above, and Barbara Herrnstein Smith, *Contingencies of Value: Alternative Perspectives for Critical Theory* (Cambridge, Mass.: Harvard University Press, 1988), p. 218, note 10.

19. For an influential account of stabilization at this level of analysis, see Jean Piaget, *Biology and Knowledge: An Essay on the Relations between Organic Regulations and Cognitive Processes*, trans. Beatrix Walsh (Edinburgh: Edinburgh University Press, 1971 [1967]). Piaget's work, though significant for later developments in revisionist epistemology, is itself framed in more or less realist terms.

20. See Humberto R. Maturana and Francisco J. Varela, *Autopoiesis and Cognition* and *The Tree of Knowledge*. For more recent formulations, see also Maturana, "The Origin of Species by Means of Natural Drift, or Lineage Diversification through the Conser-

vation and Change of Ontogenic Phenotypes," unpub. trans. by Cristina Magro and Julie Tetel, published in Spanish as *Occasional Publications of the National Museum of Natural History*, Santiago, Chile, 43 (1992).

21. See Latour, *We Have Never Been Modern*, pp. 111–114.

22. These observations comment on current controversies within the sociology of science. For Latour's own views on the rigors and liabilities of reflexive/symmetrical consistency, see his "Politics of Explanation: An Alternative," in *Knowledge and Reflexivity: New Frontiers in the Sociology of Knowledge*, ed. Steve Woolgar (London: Sage, 1988), pp. 155–176. For other relevant views, see Malcolm Ashmore and Steve Woolgar, "The Next Step: an Introduction to the Reflexive Project," in *Knowledge and Reflexivity*, pp. 1–35.

23. See Chapter 3, notes 15 and 16.

24. Kitcher illustrates the point with the success of genetics, which he explains as follows: given the crucial role of "references" to "genes" in genetics' explanatory "schemata," the reason why it can explain and predict biological phenomena so well is "that there are genes" (*Advancement*, p. 157).

25. Kitcher acknowledges the general approach of John R. Anderson, citing his *Architecture of Cognition* (Cambridge, Mass.: Harvard University Press, 1983), and, regarding the representational nature of beliefs, the "sensible ecumenical position" of philosopher Alvin Goldman, *Epistemology and Cognition* (Cambridge, Mass.: Harvard University Press, 1986).

26. See also Kitcher, *Advancement*, p. 179, note 3.

27. The impropriety in question is commonly referred to as "the naturalistic fallacy." While the relevant traditional distinctions and definitions can themselves be seen as questionable, that is a somewhat different issue. On the latter, see the following note. For related discussion of efforts to naturalize normative ethics, see Chapter 4, note 23, and Chapter 7, note 6.

28. The dilemma and equivocations described here and below are recurrent and arguably inevitable in attempts to naturalize *normative* philosophical projects to some carefully controlled degree. We recall, in Chapter 7, the same dilemma and comparable equivocations in Habermas's effort to give rationalist moral theory a quasi-empirical boost from highly selective and distinctly pre-rationalized work in linguistics and developmental psychology. For

related discussion of efforts to naturalize normative aesthetics, see Barbara Herrnstein Smith, *Contingencies of Value: Alternative Perspectives for Critical Theory* (Cambridge, Mass.: Harvard University Press, 1988), pp. 55–72.

29. For extensive critique of just such storage-and-retrieval propositional/representational models, see Gerald E. Edelman, *Bright Air, Brilliant Fire: On the Matter of the Mind* (New York: Basic Books, 1992).

30. The example Kitcher singles out for rejection here is Paul M. Churchland, *A Neurocomputational Perspective: The Nature of Mind and the Structure of Science* (Cambridge, Mass.: MIT Press, 1989), but, given his reasons for the resistance (discussed below), he would presumably also reject the following: Gerald E. Edelman, *Neural Darwinism: The Theory of Neuronal Group Selection* (New York: Basic Books, 1987), and *The Remembered Present: A Biological Theory of Consciousness* (New York: Basic Books, 1989); Maturana and Varela, *The Tree of Knowledge;* William H. Calvin and George A. Ojemann, *Conversations with Neil's Brain: The Neural Nature of Thought and Language* (Reading, Mass.: Addison-Wesley, 1994); and Antonio Damasio, *Descartes' Error: Emotion, Reason, and the Human Brain* (Chicago: University of Chicago Press, 1994).

31. See Stephen P. Stich, *From Folk Psychology to Cognitive Science: The Case against Belief* (Cambridge, Mass.: MIT Press, 1983).

32. This (somewhat parodic) explanation of Kitcher's resistance to connectionist models should not be read as an endorsement either of those models themselves or of claims to the effect that they are proper scientific translations of mere folk descriptions of mental activity. Other reasons for resisting such models (and related claims) could be framed by, among others, constructivist antiepistemologists, and different objections to them have been raised by neurobiologists, psychologists, other philosophers, and rival cognitive scientists. On connectionist models per se, see David Rumelhart, James L. McClelland, and the PDP Research Group, *Parallel Distributed Processing: Explorations in the Microstructure of Cognition,* vol. 1 (Cambridge, Mass.: MIT Press, 1986). For other naturalistic models of mental activities, see note 30. For different (and mutually conflicting) views of the relation between traditional epistemology and contemporary neuroscience, see Patricia Church-

land, *Neurophilosophy: Toward a Unified Science of the Mind/Brain* (Cambridge, Mass.: MIT Press, 1986); William Ramsey et al., eds., *Philosophy and Connectionist Theory* (Hillsdale, N.J.: L. Erlbaum, 1991); Daniel C. Dennett, *Consciousness Explained* (Boston: Little, Brown & Co., 1991); Philip Quinlan, *Connectionism and Psychology: A Psychological Perspective on New Connectionist Research* (Chicago: University of Chicago Press, 1991); Owen Flanagan, *Consciousness Reconsidered* (Cambridge, Mass.: MIT Press, 1992); and Andy Clark, *Microcognition: Philosophy, Cognitive Science, and Parallel Distributed Processing* (Cambridge, Mass.: MIT Press, 1991), and *Associative Engines: Connectionism, Concepts, and Representational Change* (Cambridge, Mass.: MIT Press, 1993). For related discussion of artificial intelligence and epistemology, see Hubert L. Dreyfus and Stuart C. Dreyfus, *Mind over Machine: The Power of Human Intuition and Expertise in the Era of the Computer* (New York: Free Press, 1986), and Terry Winograd and Fernando Flores, *Understanding Computers and Cognition: A New Foundation for Design* (Norwood, N.J.: Ablex Publishing Corp., 1986). For an evocative fictional treatment of the issues, see Richard Powers, *Galatea 2.2* (New York: Farrar, Strauss & Giroux, 1995).

33. Kitcher's substitution of "psychological" connections for "logical" ones does not, of course, commit him to the more controversial substitution of *physiological* connections for *mental* ones. Similarly, while he distances himself from the simple equation of rationality with logic, he retains, as passages quoted here indicate, such classic rationalist notions as "formal rules," "principles," and "canons" of reasoning.

34. See Donald Davidson, "On the Very Idea of a Conceptual Scheme," *Inquiries into Truth and Interpretation* (Oxford: Clarendon Press, 1985), for an influential argument to the effect that, since any two putatively incommensurable conceptual schemes are at least partly intertranslatable, then the idea of conceptual incommensurability—and thus, significantly, "conceptual relativism"—must be rejected. Davidson does not consider the contingency of the condition of intertranslatability (and, by implication, of incommensurability) as discussed below.

35. See P. M. Churchland, *The Engine of Reason, the Seat of the Soul: A Philosophical Journey into the Brain* (Cambridge, Mass.: MIT Press, 1995).

36. See Clark, *Microcognition;* Flanagan, *Consciousness Reconsidered;* Calvin and Ojemann, *Conversations with Neil's Brain;* and Damasio, *Descartes' Error.*

37. See Philip Kitcher, *Abusing Science: The Case against Creationism* (Cambridge, Mass.: MIT Press, 1982).

38. Kitcher's term here is "Darwinists," not "Darwinians," perhaps to indicate that the defenders of evolutionary accounts are not always professional biologists.

39. Interestingly enough, one of Kitcher's most rhetorically compelling arguments in *Abusing Science* is, in effect, the epistemic asymmetry of creation scientists, who, he points out, appeal to different criteria for determining the scientificity of the Darwinian account and their own.

For an empirical study of the "interpretive resources" used by practicing scientists to explain their colleagues' agreeable and disagreeable views, see G. Nigel Gilbert and Michael Mulkay, "Accounting for Error: How Scientists Construct Their Social World When They Account for Correct and Incorrect Belief," *Sociology* 16 (1982): 165–183. Mulkay and Gilbert make a number of points relevant to the present discussion, noting, for example, that "whereas *correct* belief is portrayed [by the scientists interviewed] as exclusively a cognitive phenomenon, as arising unproblematically out of rational assessments of experimental evidence, *incorrect* belief is viewed as involving the intrusion of distorting social and psychological factors into the cognitive domain" (p. 181, emphasis mine). Their conclusion, however, namely that "asymmetrical accounting for error and for correct belief in science is a social device which is linked to a particular conception of scientific knowledge and rationality (181)," seems unduly restricted. The tendency to devise self-privileging/other-pathologizing explanations of other people's beliefs and practices is, as we have seen, quite common, and seems as much a cognitive device as a social one. While the tendency may be articulated (or literally rational-ized) among scientists through, among other things, appeals to traditional notions of specifically scientific rationality, non-scientists, including religious believers, are by no means at a loss for interpretive resources. Neither, it seems, are philosophers.

40. Latour, *Science in Action,* p. 192, his emphasis.

41. A comparable slide appears in the series, quoted above, that

goes from people's (merely regrettable?) "perceiving badly" and "inferring hastily" to their (intellectually reprehensible? morally culpable?) *"failing to act* to obtain inputs from nature that *would* guide them to improved cognitive states" (my emphases). Kitcher's equivocal allusions to our evidently passive "undergoing" of inappropriate cognitive propensities and evidently voluntary, and thus arguably culpable, "activating" of them (*Advancement,* p. 186) indicate the more general conceptual instabilities and rhetorical difficulties involved in such distinctions. Also relevant here are the efforts by L. Jonathan Cohen (*An Essay on Belief and Acceptance* [Oxford: Clarendon Press, 1992])—discussed in Chapter 6—to distinguish a cognitively passive state of "believing that *p*" from a rational, voluntary state of "accepting that *p.*"

42. On the relation between social class and epistemic authority, see Steven Shapin, *A Social History of Truth: Civility and Science in Seventeenth-Century England* (Chicago: University of Chicago Press, 1994).

43. To question the classic normative projects of epistemology is not to suggest that processes of epistemic evaluation cannot occur or that they are random or pointless. I am suggesting, rather, that traditional *rationalist* understandings of those processes are dubious and that attempts either to regulate the conduct of such processes or to validate their products in accord with such understandings are conceptually strained, pragmatically gratuitous or confining, and, under some conditions, arrogant. In accord with the general views of belief and cognition outlined in Chapter 3, epistemic evaluation (theory choice, belief assessment, scientific validation, and so forth) is conceived here as an ongoing part of the very process of *operating through* our beliefs (scientific theories, personal credos, philosophical assumptions, pragmatic hunches, and so forth), that is, applying, extending, and accordingly modifying them *in situ* or, so to speak, on the wing. This conception of specifically epistemic evaluation corresponds to the analysis of judicial, ethical, and political justification outlined in Chapter 1, and to the more general conception of value and evaluation I develop in *Contingencies of Value.* In the latter, see, for example, p. 42: "It follows . . . that evaluations are not discrete acts or episodes punctuating experience but indistinguishable from the very processes of acting and experiencing

themselves. In other words, for a responsive creature, to exist is to evaluate."

44. Difficult and important practical situations of this kind—dealing with published denials of the Nazi Holocaust is another example—are often cited as real-life refutations of epistemological "relativism." The implication is that at the "limits of tolerance" posed by such situations, the choice can only be between accepting the "equal validity" of the personally disagreeable and otherwise objectionable claims at issue or denouncing the people who make or believe them as manifest scoundrels or manifest fools. As just indicated, however, and discussed in Chapters 1 and 2, these are not the only alternatives; nor is it clear that the recommended be-yond-tolerance responses, that is, full-throated denunciations in the name of objective truth or absolute morality, would (in themselves) have (only) the presumably desired outcomes.

45. Philosophy of science appears, in some places, to be merging with its own subject-sciences, for example, philosophy of biology with theoretical biology; see Robert N. Brandon, *Adaptation and Environment* (Princeton: Princeton University Press, 1990), and *Conceptual Issues in Evolutionary Biology,* 2nd ed., ed. Elliott Sober (Cambridge, Mass.: MIT Press, 1994). In other places, it seems to have naturalized not only its lingo but also its projects and methods, either jumping ship altogether in anticipation of neurophysiological replacements of philosophical accounts of cognition (see Patricia Churchland, *Neurophilosophy*) or reconceiving its task as that of me-diating or "intertranslating" the discourses of traditional episte-mology and contemporary cognitive science; see Clark, *Microcog-nition* and *Associative Engines;* Dennett, *Consciousness Explained;* Flanagan, *The Science of the Mind* (Cambridge, Mass.: MIT Press, 1992) and *Consciousness Reconsidered.*

46. See Andrew Pickering, *The Mangle of Practice: Time, Agency, and Science* (Chicago: University of Chicago Press, 1995). See also Shapin's recent (and, from the present perspective, dubious) affir-mation of the "incorrigible presupposition" of a realist ontology by "virtually any form of praxis" (*Social History of Truth,* pp. 29ff., 122). In his formal acknowledgments there, Shapin alludes to "a series of friendly arguments with my colleague Philip Kitcher" (iii). Kitcher, in turn, notes in the formal acknowledgments of *The Advancement*

of Science that his "thinking about epistemology and the history and philosophy of science has been greatly helped by discussions with . . . [among others] Steven Shapin," who, he adds, is not "likely to agree with the conclusions of this book, but . . . can pride [himself] on having diverted me from even sillier things that I might have said" (p. viii).

Index

Albert, Hans, 90–91, 93, 188n8, 190n16
Allen, Barry, 159n13
Ambivalence: of cognitive processes, xvii–xviii, 50–51, 84–85, 120–123, 139; of linguistic differences, 71–72. *See also* Dilemmas; Equivocation
Analytic philosophy, 53, 64, 171n4, 193n34, 195n6. *See also* Conceptual analysis
Anderson, John R., 206n25
Andresen, Julie Tetel, 170n1
Anomalies, xv, 163n1, 203n12
Anti-foundationalism, 1, 90–93, 108–109, 114
Anti-Semitism, 162n26
"Anything goes," 62–65, 78–80
Apel, Karl-Otto, 89–93, 93–94, 179n25, 187n35, 188–189n9, 190nn15,16. *See also* Frankfurt School
Arbib, Michael A., 163n3, 166n14, 201n6
Aristotle, 81
Arkes, Hadley, 184n22
Ashmore, Malcolm, 164n4, 182n2, 202n22
Asymmetry, epistemic, xvi, xix, 7–8, 27, 83, 136–138, 147, 209n39. *See also* Self-privileging, epistemic
Austin, J. L., 53, 91, 171n2, 177n19, 187n1, 189n10, 192n24
Autopoiesis. *See* Circularity, in living systems; Maturana, Humberto; Varela, Francisco J.
Axiology, 1, 21–22

Baker, G. P., 172n4
Baker, Lynn A., 155n15
Barnes, Barry, 128
Barnes, Jonathan, 188n2
Barrett, Michèle, 159n15
Bartley, W. W., III, 167n16
Battersby, James L., 184n24
Baxtin, Mixail, 171n3
Begging the question. *See* Question-begging
Belief: conceptions of, 37–39, 40–43, 51; and historical dynamics, 39–44; and cognitive dynamics, 42–43, 44–48; conceptual analysis of, 97–100. *See also* Cognition; Conviction; Knowledge
Benhabib, Seyla, 196n12
Bennett, William, 9, 154n10
Bernstein, Richard J., 163n3, 186n34
Bhaskar, Roy, 120
Bijker, Wiebe, 205n16
Biology, 51. *See also* Darwinism; Evolutionary epistemology; Evolutionary theory; Cognition, and innate tendencies; Developmental systems theory; Language, and evolution
Bloom, Paul, 173n5
Bloor, David, 128, 157n1, 164n4, 168n18
Bostock, David, 182n3, 183nn10,11
Bourdieu, Pierre, 53, 165n7, 177n20
Brandon, Robert, 169n20, 211n45
Brooks, Rodney, 164–165n5
Brown, Wendy, 159n16
Buddhism, 84
Burke, Kenneth, 171n2
Burnyeat, Myles, 182n3, 183nn6,7,13

213

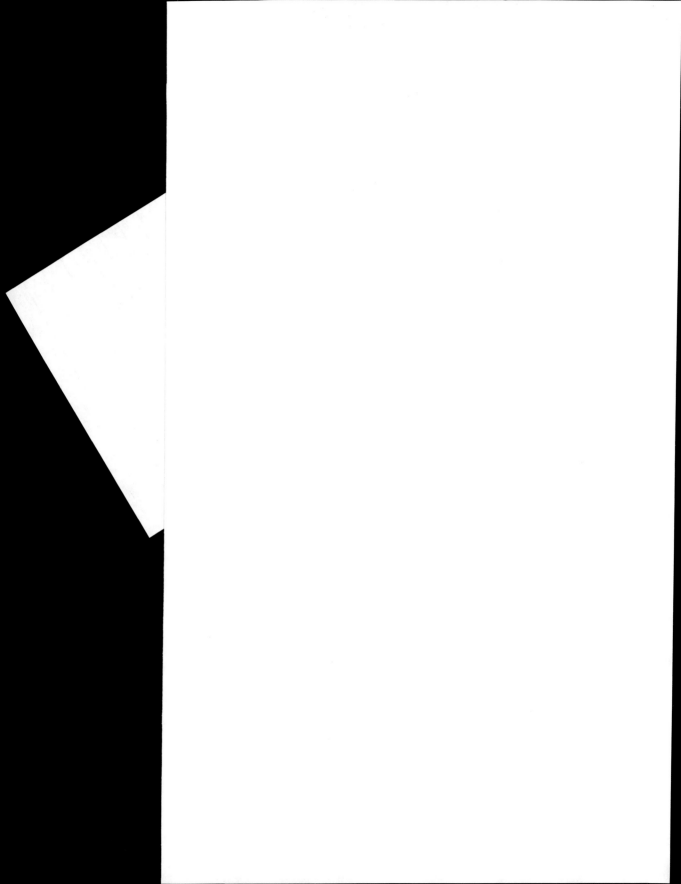

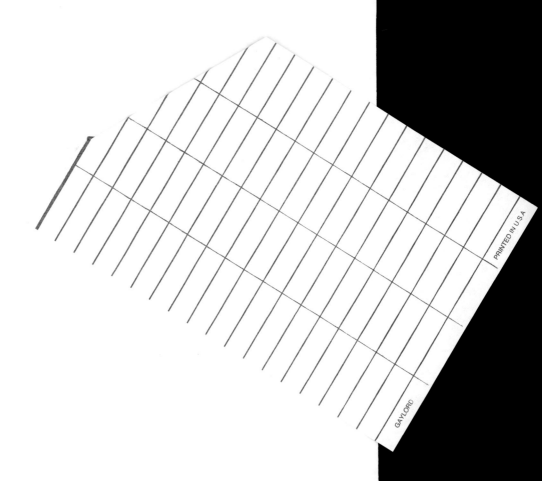